THE EARTH KEEPER'S HANDBOOK

ASSUMING LEADERSHIP IN A NEW WORLD

Loren Swift

BALBOA.PRESS

A DIVISION OF HAY HOUSE

Balboa Press books may be ordered through booksellers or by contacting:

Balboa Press
A Division of Hay House
1663 Liberty Drive
Bloomington, IN 47403
www.balboapress.com
1 (877) 407-4847

Print information available on the last page.

ISBN: 978-1-9822-3511-6 (sc)
ISBN: 978-1-9822-3512-3 (e)

Library of Congress Control Number: 2019915947

Balboa Press rev. date: 11/08/2019

CONTENTS

Preface...xv

Acknowledgments...xix

Introduction...xxi

PART 1: THE WAY IN

Chapter 1   The Inward Journey...1

    Ancestral Wisdom 1

    Acceptance as Path...3

    Self-Compassion 4

    Explore this Practice: The Compassionate Observer 4

    The Ego's Place 7

    Secrecy, Fear and Shame 9

    Hannah's Story 10

Chapter 2   The Story of Belonging 11

    Fractals, Beauty, and Compassion 11

    Naming Our Story 12

    Acceptance is Key to Peace of Mind 14

    Reality and Belief..16

    Explore this Practice: Inviting the Self-Critic to Tea 19

Chapter 3   The Science of Oneness...23

    Intentionality and the Zero Point Field 24

    The Heart and Universal Qualities of Life..26

    How It Works 28

    Brainstorming Resonant Qualities of Life 29

Coherence and the Spectrum of Love...30

Explore this Practice: Embodying Universal Qualities of Life in the Spectrum of Love...30

Tammy and Roger's Vacation...33

The Ripple Effect and Morphic Resonance.......................................34

Chapter 4 Coherence and the Coordinates of Presence.......................37

The Being of Doing..38

The Power and Pleasure of Coherency...38

The Holomovement...39

Science, Mysticism, and Presence...41

Vulnerability: The Birthplace of Joy...42

Explore this Practice: The Coordinates of Presence.........................43

Courage and Vulnerability...46

Chapter 5 Gratitude: The Gateway to Abundance.................................49

Gratitude is the Root of Happiness...50

Everything has Already Been Given..51

Gratitude and Abundance..52

Anatomy of a Prayer...52

Expressing Gratitude and Appreciation..54

Explore this Practice: Embodying and Expressing Gratitude.........56

To Receive Is As Important As to Give..57

Explore this Practice: Self-Gratitude...58

Gratitude in Nature..58

PART 2: THE WAY THROUGH

Chapter 6 The Hidden Heart of Judgment...63

Friend or Foe?..64

Beyond Us versus Them..64

Our Common Ground..65

The Hidden Gold..66

Explore this Practice: Getting to the Heart of Judgment................67

Discernment versus Judgment..73

The Assumption of Innocence...75

Chapter 7 The Healing Power of Empathy 77
   Mirror Neurons 77
   The Witness Effect 79
   A Global Mythology...80
   Self-Empathy 81
   Explore this Practice: Self-Empathy and Your Internal Coordinates.............82
   The Healing Effect of Empathy 83
   Explore this Practice: Empathetic Presence with Another 85
   Specifics of Empathetic Presence 88
   Is it Empathy or Sympathy?...89

Chapter 8 Celebration and Mourning 91
   Emotional Intelligence...91
   A Story of Grief and Celebration 92
   Explore this Practice: Surrender, Grief, and Praise...........94
   Earnest's Story 98
   Explore this Practice: Making Decisions Whole with Grief and Celebration... 100
   To Feel or Not to Feel 103
   Debbie's Story 104
   Grief and Wholeness.. 105
   Surrender, Acceptance, and Will..................................... 106
   Emotions and the Body 107

Chapter 9 Wisdom and the Wounded Child........................ 109
   Carol's Story 110
   Befriending the Inner Child... 111
   Conscious Meets the Unconscious 112
   Re-parenting the Inner Child... 113
   Explore this Practice: Re-parenting the Inner Child........ 114
   Hannah's Story, Part 2 119
   The Familiar and the Unknown.. 122

Chapter 10 Beyond the Blame Game 123
   The Blame Game... 124
   The Pain of Hurting Others... 125
   Explore this Practice: Beyond Blame with Self-Empathy 126

Making and Breaking Agreements with Integrity 128

Steve's Story 128

Explore this Practice: Turning Resentment into Acceptance 129

Chapter 11 The Heart of Communication 133

Connection and Understanding 133

Getting to the Heart of Communication 135

Components of Communication 136

The Empathy Dance 137

Explore this Practice: Empathetic Listening and Self-Expression ... 137

The Empathy Dance 138

Connecting beyond Judgment 140

Shift versus Compromise 141

Explore this Practice: Making an Internal Shift 143

Do-Overs 144

Explore this Practice: Do-Overs 145

PART 3: THE WAY TOGETHER

Chapter 12 Meeting in a Container of Care 151

Expanding Ripples of Influence 152

Explore this Practice: Weaving a Container of Care 153

Master Desire 156

The Uncertainty Principle 157

A Component Practice: Dancing in the Gap of Uncertainty 158

Making Clear Requests 159

Chapter 13 The Adventure of Resolving Conflict 163

Duking It Out 164

The Discomfort of Confrontation 164

Viewing Conflict as Adventure 165

Connection through Conflict 167

Andrew and Rita's Story 168

Explore this Practice: Conflict as Adventure 170

Getting beyond a Trigger 173

Explore this Practice: Choice Point—To Get beyond a Trigger......................174

Expressing Emotions in Disagreements and Conflict: No Blame.................176

Finding Our Common Ground: Mark and Shannon's Story...........................177

Chapter 14 Coming Home to Tribe...179

Giving the Best of Ourselves 180

Social Capital and the Gift Culture...181

Collaboration within Diversity 184

Cohesion and Reciprocity 185

Wisdom Circles: How and Why...188

Setting Up a Circle Meeting 189

Explore this Practice: Wisdom Circle for Decision Making.......................191

Gather perspectives...191

Name disagreements...193

Proposals for implementation 194

Make agreements...195

Chapter 15 Restoring Connection and Integrity in Community 197

Individuals Reflect Community 198

Restorative Circles 198

Remembering Community Power..199

The Circle Format: Horizontal Power Structure 200

Overview of Restorative Circle Meetings...200

The Restorative Circle Meeting 201

The Post-Circle...204

Chapter 16 Compassionate Action 205

Wise Reasoning 205

Heart of the Earth..207

Know Your Purpose 209

Explore this Practice: Gaining Clarity of Purpose......................................209

Collaboration Happens...212

Rights of Personhood for Nature 214

Twelve Principles of Collaboration..215

The Doorway of the Heart 216

PART 4: DIVINE INTIMACY

Chapter 17 Inspired Relationship.. 219

    Lightness of Being 219

    Descending into Divinity and the Cosmic Joke.. 220

    The Alchemy of Intimacy 221

    Active Surrender.. 221

    Intimacy: What Is It Really?.. 222

    Intimacy and Inspired Relationships.. 223

    Relationship as Spiritual Path 224

    Transformation in the Holographic Universe.. 225

    Explore this Practice: Converging Circles.. 227

    Explore this Practice: Working through a Painful Dynamic 229

    The Final Frontier 233

Chapter 18 Into the Eye of Love.. 235

    Freedom from Polarity... 235

    The Field Possibility... 236

    Explore this Practice: Expanded Embodiment—How to Be the
    Change You Want 236

    Evolution in Intimate Partnership 239

    Sacred Sexuality.. 239

    Explore this Practice: The Openhearted Observer.. 241

    Cumulative effect.. 244

Appendix A Universal Qualities of Life 245

Appendix B Components of Connected Communication and the Container of Care 247

Appendix C Restorative Circle Reference Guides.. 251

Appendix D Message from Hopi Elders.. 253

Appendix E Further Resources 255

About the Author 263

Dedicated to the benefit of all beings.
In honor, respect and devotion to Life, to She who brings life and who supports life.

To the Mother, Ixcheel; to mothering; and to the Heart of the Earth, Grandmother Ixmukane; and to all children and all beings who make the beauty of the world.

My religion is kindness.

—the fourteenth Dalai Lama, Tenzin Gyatso

PREFACE

My path has been one of overcoming obstacles to get to my heart. I'm a work in progress. But I have gleaned crucial bits that can streamline the process for others. It seems that myriads of factors---personal, cultural and historical---have colluded to pull us out of our hearts and bodies and centered us right in our left brains. This is the territory of separation, of hard lines and clear distinctions; of right and wrong. It creates distance from our hearts and keeps us isolated from the soft animal body of the Earth and one another. The left-brain approach relegates the notions of care and consideration to very low priorities. We are surrounded by the results of our lack of care for each other, which inevitably translates into lack of care for the Earth. Because we are naturally caring, compassionate beings, it takes a colossal emphasis on external distractions to keep us isolated from our own inner knowingness, as well as from each other. There has been great success by Western culture, including fundamental religions, over the last three- to five-thousand years in facilitating our ignorance and disempowerment.

Most recently, the Age of Reason, an intellectual and philosophical movement that dominated the ideological thinking of Europe in the 18th century, set the stage for a mechanistic view of the world. Marked by Newtonian physics, Cartesian philosophy and Darwinian science, the tone was set to separate mind from body and spirit from life. The inculcation of a mechanistic model left little room to experience ourselves as integral to life or as relevant agents of our lives. Whereas, the new science reveals that everything is connected and that we are inseparable from the inner workings of life itself. We live in the time of the marriage of science and mysticism.

Although I may not have known it the whole time, my path has been to close the gap between my head and heart and spirit. And to best learn how, I share what I discover with others. This book is the culmination to date of what I have learned, practiced and facilitated in others. I was compelled to write it, motivated by my trust in the process of evolution and the indominable human spirit. At our core, I know we are good. We are drawn to help others, to give the best of ourselves when asked. It is our external focus and false beliefs in separation, the illusion that we don't need each other, that keeps us held back.

What is at stake is our freedom. The embedded habit of consumerism and now, artificial intelligence (read: smart phones, smart cars, robot companions, computer chips under our skin and in our brains, designer babies), are vying for our souls. Whereas, we have the technology inside of us already. Within our hearts together with our brains we have the capabilities to connect to the field of possibility, to heal ourselves, to ignite our deep intuitive powers and to know our belonging in the universe. The daunting truth is that we are potent creators. We are capable of amazing feats in every realm. Just look around---our imagination and creative abilities are visible everywhere. All of this and more is available from the inside, by implementing our innate capabilities. But to engage our inherent powers, we must be free from beliefs that tells us we are small, alone and powerless. We need the freedom and inner authority to know what truly matters to us to become the leaders of our lives.

Our purpose is found inside ourselves and, at the same time, is part of a larger mission. Contrary to the Newtonian-Cartesian model of the universe, there is a great net we all inherently belong to. And there is a net we each create with intention, using our individual purpose to help weave the container that holds all of us. The new era we live in reveals that indeed, we are all in this together.

Because we are being asked to cross the threshold into a new world of our own making, we need to know how. We are being challenged to navigate a time of upheaval perhaps unprecedented in human history. I feel it in my nervous system, as do so many of us. It feels unsettling at times, and disorienting. Without the insight and tools to navigate the uncertainties, we tend to resort to denial, or to appease our angst we fall prey to numbing out with recreational use of drugs and alcohol. I have to come back to my body, my heart and the Heart of the Earth. It is crucial now that we remember who we are and come back to connection, to find our internal motivation to live aligned with our vision of truth and beauty and goodness. Real connections are the antidote to the increasing anxiety of separation. Connection feeds our innate longings and informs our ability to care.

I believe our success will take the leadership of many people inspired to unleash their passion into the world, to live their truth, to bring their unique talents, and give their best. True leadership comes from within, from knowing yourself well and living aligned with your deeper values. The need for change is drawing out of us the courage to live with passion and veracity, to seek real freedom, and the insight to work together. We are the visionaries and leaders for our time, innovators of methods that hold all of us with kindness.

Science shows us that evolution is inherently innovative. As visionary human beings, we are the face of evolution. We are the ones to catalyze the DNA sleeping in our nuclei and reach for the light in these shadowy times. We are being called to cooperate and to care in order to expedite many needed efforts, from protecting the environment to housing the homeless. This is our time.

I have found that the steps to liberation from our past also hold the unveiling of our future. This handbook is a template to move through personal and social encumbrances and into freedom—the freedom to be the leaders of our own lives and to create the future that holds our children and their children's children with thoughtfulness. Whatever method you choose or path you take, let it free and empower you to be the leader of your life and to unshackle your creativity and bring your unique purpose into the world. Your inspired life is what the world needs.

Your fulfillment is your gift, and it is also life's purpose. After all, that is what life does. It gives. It creates. It reaches for more. And when blocked, it doesn't give up. It transcends its own limitations.

ACKNOWLEDGMENTS

Every step of the way, I have been graced with friends, family, mentors, and teachers to guide and facilitate me through personal obstacles and into new horizons. This book is a testament to all of them. Each one gave me exactly what I needed. I am grateful for their insights, wisdom, and skillfulness. I mention only a few here.

From my paternal grandmother, Anne Davis Swift, I received curiosity to learn about the natural world of birds and flowers walking in the Northern California hillsides outside of Gilroy and picking blueberries in the bogs of Northern Vermont. From my maternal grandmother, Mary Loren Jeffrey Shannon, came direction in my early spiritual explorations and practices, from Zen Buddhism to esoteric Christianity, as well as transpersonal psychology. From my mother, Mary Loren (Molly) Shannon Donahower, I received the will to be myself and to create a life of passion and meaning. From my stepfather, Bill Donahower, I received trust, integrity, and self-confidence to accomplish what I put my mind to. From my father, Emerson Howland Swift, came the gumption to follow my heart. From my daughter, Iona Loren Swift, I've received love that breaks open my heart, kindness, and music. And from my husband, Scott Merritt, has come intimacy, tremendous gratitude, joy, and the adventure buddy I always longed to explore worlds with, both inner and outer. I feel immense admiration and gratitude for my longtime friend, Lisa Sarenduc, companion on the path through thick and thin.

I hold so much gratitude for the many mentors and spiritual teachers along the way—Norma Cordell, Nancy (Pema) Clark, Lama Lodru, Reshad Field, Murat Yagan, Marshall Rosenberg, Miki Kashtan, Robert Gonzales, Karina Schelde, and Miguel Angel Vergara, among others.

Gratitude to my long-time friend and talented copy-editor and graphics designer, Wendy Garrido, who swooped in near the finish to aid in refining many details. I have huge gratitude for my close friends, also mentors, who took the time to read the manuscript and offer feedback to support this project—Andy Suiter, Desiree Banzaf,

Sarah Kahn, Chris Horner, Donna Gianoulis, Diane Tetrault and Scott Merritt. The leap of faith to let the chapters be seen by others was as humbling an experience as I could have imagined. And a great big thank you to my editor, Geralyn Gendreau, who stayed with me from inception to finish, a nearly six-year time span. I learned volumes from her. Thanks, also, to Balboa Press for their guidance and input to complete and refine the manuscript and get it into print.

INTRODUCTION

This book details practical steps to shift the paradigm internally from conflict to cooperation and to make that same shift in relationships and in group endeavors. The purpose is to expedite our evolution so that we may more expediently attend to the work at hand. Our local efforts affect the global community. To that end, *The Earth Keeper's Handbook* implements practices that show us how to be the change we seek. The journey takes us from separation to connection and from powerlessness to becoming the leaders of our lives. The tale below is one of connection to self, to the Earth, and to assuming leadership in unassuming ways.

I met Don Jose in Belize in January 2019. A farmer-horseman with only two and a half years of formal schooling, he'd grown up in the jungle, his real teacher. He and his German-born Egyptian wife were the proprietors of an Airbnb on their farm just east of the Guatemalan border. Well-educated, she had a master's degree in human geography, the relationship of people to their environment. Don Jose left school at age seven and began hunting game in the jungle to help feed his family. He is Mestizo, a mixture of black African and Spanish, and Creole, a mix that includes Native American Arowak and Maya. He spoke Creole, Spanish, English, and a Mayan dialect. I have rarely met someone with as much clarity and human insight as he displayed. My husband and I soon discovered that Don Jose was also a philosopher-poet, spontaneously reciting his spoken word poems during the four days we spent in their hand-built Shangri-la.

His poetry was melodic and filled with thoughtful reverence for the natural world. He also spoke to the disturbing relationship he saw between humankind and nature. Don Jose was well aware of the destructive practices in all corners of the Earth due to lack of understanding the ways of nature. Other Maya we encountered on the trip were equally connected to the cycles of their local ecosystems and held the natural world as sacred. Miguel, a Guatemalan taxi driver we met, also of Mayan descent, was part of a group created to protect the jungles from further exploitation by logging and slash-and-burn farming techniques.

Don Jose seemed to understand so much of what I had spent a lifetime learning about. He was deeply connected to himself, to the jungle, to the animals he stewarded, and to the people around him. As with other locals we met, he shared his knowledge of the medicinal uses of certain plants, those that were edible, and what to avoid. As North Americans, most of us have very limited experience living directly from nature. The few times I have eaten wild-picked or locally caught food, I was filled with a surprising energetic quality I hadn't experienced. It was as if I was unaccountably in tune with the energies of the plant life around me. From that experience, I imagined that people who live solely from the land could have the seemingly uncanny ability to listen to the plants and intuitively hear what their abilities and gifts were. I saw them engaged in the living mystery, seamlessly connected to life chirping, creeping, and unfurling all around them, like Don Jose.

The ceaseless abundance of nature is reflected in the generosity of spirit of people who know their interdependence with the natural world. Harmonious relationships are wrought from understanding our place in the scheme of things. At times, peace descends from the sense that there is no separation between us or from nature. Without having to retrain themselves to go inward to learn about themselves from the inside out, the local people we met from Belize were happy and generous.

Pedro, a Mayan from the jungle of southern Belize, was a natural leader. He had become a river guide on the Moho River at the behest of a budding tour operation thirty years previous. Pedro knew the river and surrounding region well. Having fished and played in it since childhood, he was well suited to guide others on its sinewy spills through the verdant primeval jungles he called home. To spread the wealth that contact with North Americans brought, he made sure that all the families of his village also benefitted from the tour company's presence. It was a balancing act that Pedro handled with grace and humility. As an example, on a rotating basis, one family at a time would cook lunch for the tour group coming through to kayak the river. Twice we were invited into a village family's thatch-roofed, earthen-floored hut and fed from the bounty of their local plants and animals.

Pedro brought us into his thatch-roofed home, replete with an open-air cooking fire. His wealth was evidenced by the cement floor and shiny aluminum pots on the walls. He explained the community effort that goes into building and roofing a family's house, a two-day project that involves a good number of the villagers. The family receiving the help hosts a feast, roasting a pig or two to feed all who help upon completion of the new home. The community celebrates the accomplishment together, and all involved strengthen their bonds.

Pedro was not in a formal leadership role, but he ensured that his whole village was cared for by the influx of ecotourism. As the intermediary between the villagers and the tour company, he lived in integrity. He took on the role of leader not as a path to power but as a path to inclusion. He was of the mind that everyone's well-being mattered. He knew that his life was made richer when everyone in the village was happy and healthy.

Granted, I'm outing myself as a privileged North American ecotourist. It's a quandary. How are we to find our way through the morass of the dominant culture's effects on the planet? What is the way back to caring for one another and our home, the Earth? There is wisdom for us in the cycles of life. To return to connection with nature is to reconnect with the wisdom of earth-based societies. Indigenous cultures hold the knowledge and understanding of living within natural rhythms, the seasons, and ecosystems upon which we all depend.

We need more of Pedro's kind of leadership. We need to go inward, to make a clear connection with our inner knowing. It is through our inner landscape that we open to the subtler realms and walk the interface between the worlds. Self-connection taps us into the wealth of creative insight and beauty that we depend on for fulfillment. Our inner life has been sorely depleted by a long history of separation—not only from our food sources but also from our bodies, our hearts, and one another. The spirit world itself was usurped from the individual by would-be leaders of men, the authors of fundamental religious beliefs. Modern society's obsession with the superficial diversions of consumerism plays into the epidemic of separation, as does the well-established fear of being judged. The fear of punishment and the hope for reward hold us hostage to a formless external power, leaving many of us disconnected from our intuitive knowing and our innate wisdom.

I am heartened by the reminders that Pedro, Don Jose, and Miguel gave me—that there are people who still remember themselves and honor their place in the world. As leaders, they offer their gifts freely and care for those around them. This handbook is an offering too. It is a pathway to our sovereignty, to the inner freedom needed to lead the way forward from here. The practices in part one take us on the inward journey. They bring us to our internal wisdom with compassion. On the way, the judgmental chatter we may have internalized from the right-wrong paradigm is dismantled, with acceptance of *what is* with kindness. Each practice is designed to increase our freedom to think and feel for ourselves and to know what we need and what is no longer relevant to pursue. Part one culminates with gratitude, a practice that generates happiness.

Part two brings us into deeper self-awareness and highlights how to be the person we truly long to be, free of internal conflict. Personal liberation and insight increase our ability to resolve differences with others. The way through the conflicts brought on by polarized thinking is also how to live life from our hearts. Part two has specific practices for communicating transparently and yet with empathy, helping us to understand others. Once we experience being understood, we are more open to listening to others from their perspective. It is this kind of listening and hearing each other that feeds constructive dialogue. Together, our creative potential far exceeds that which we could have accessed alone.

The power of belonging to community is the focus of part three. In community, we share work and celebrate life together. Here we use the foundations laid in parts one and two to stretch ourselves to include a wider latitude of diversity. Once we are free to live life from the inside out, we can harness the wisdom inherent in our sovereignty. As leaders of our lives, together we can expedite innovative solutions to our collective woes. Climate disruption affects much of the world's population now, and we can only surmise that it will increase in frequency and intensity. Until everyone has a full belly and access to health care, as well as education, we all suffer. There are solutions available to these issues. It is a matter of shifting our priorities from separation to connection and from exclusion to inclusion. We are reorienting ourselves to natural laws, the new science and contemporary physics to usher in our new world gracefully.

From current scientific discoveries, we are shown the radical perspective that everything is connected. We have proof of the power of our beliefs to affect change. When we merge our thinking and feeling with our passion, we can change the world. This handbook contains pragmatic skills supported by scientific research to affect change, starting with internally updating our dominant paradigm. Your freedom from the past is your ticket to the future and your part in the shift from separation to connection. The intent of this handbook is to accelerate your evolution and open the way to be the sovereign leader of your life. As leaders, we live in service to life. With generosity of spirit, our purpose is to give our beauty to the world and to receive and celebrate the abundance that surrounds us.

PART ONE
The Way In

Don't ask yourself what the world needs; ask yourself what makes you come alive.
And then go do that. Because what the world needs is people who have come alive.

—Howard Thurman

CHAPTER ONE
The Inward Journey

Only from the heart can you touch the sky.
—Rumi

It may seem paradoxical that the fastest route to connection with others is to go inward. Nonetheless, it's true. It is through our inner landscape that we are offered a direct line to the whole complex web of life. The network of connection we inhabit reminds me of mycelium, the delicate white strands of fungi, commonly known as mushrooms, beneath the ground. "This fine web of cells courses through virtually all habitats ... unlocking nutrient sources stored in plants and other organisms."[1] The invisible matrix of interconnections between us is demonstrated in every ecosystem on earth. We are born of it, and from it we are continually fed and nourished. Separate from it, we would not exist. And yet, our greatest challenge is to know that we are integral with all that is. It is the illusion of separation that both proffers us the greatest individual glory and invites us to perpetrate the most heinous of acts. But connection redeems us, offering fulfillment and a whole universe of untapped resources.

Ancestral Wisdom

The more we learn about nature, Earth's myriad ecosystems, and the imperative of biodiversity, the clearer it becomes that human oversight regarding our interconnectedness is the root cause of our burgeoning woes. When we know our interconnectedness intimately, we walk on the earth with reverence. We hold one another with the understanding that you are another me. Earth-centered, native

---

[1] Paul Stamets, *Mycelium Running* (Berkeley: Ten Speed Press, 2005).

cultures have revered nature and our interdependence with all things for eons. Their worldviews hold all things as sacred and interwoven. In earth-based cultures, the elevation of individuals was due to their prowess within the context of serving their community, say as a skilled hunter, medicine-herbalist, or talented shaman. From our Western vantage point, we can only imagine what it may be like to live knowing no separation from the web of life. Yet this ancestral wisdom pulls at us to remember ourselves as part of the whole.

As radical as it may seem, science has now proven our ancestors correct. We live in a world of seamless connectivity. When we experience the potent connections that start with our inner world, we amend the soil for our own growth. In this chapter, our exploration focuses on self-connection, the crux of the inward journey. Metaphorically, it reminds me of a stone dropping into the mirrored surface of a pond. The deeper the stone descends, the wider the ripples of understanding spread. So it is with us. Deep self-connection affords us a wide range of insights via our expanded awareness. It gives us access to our hearts and minds, to intuitive awakening and creativity, to one another, and to spirit. Self-connection is also the basis from which we can skillfully navigate the world around us, from clear communication to conscious choice making.

Inevitably, as we descend through the layers of self-awareness, our assumptions about ourselves and the world will surface. It can feel like taking off outer garments and regarding them quizzically. To look objectively at our personal habits and tendencies can be disorienting, like walking through a hall of mirrors. It also can be amusing or frightening, or inconsequential. No matter how much meditation or introspection you may have done, there is more to garner from the inward journey. I invite you to try a new approach. This isn't about overcoming the obstacles to inner peace or slaying the demons of the monkey mind. It's about letting your self-awareness drop even further inside, allowing every passing thought, feeling, and notion to be seen and acknowledged along the way. To do so is the inception of deep states of acceptance and inclusion, necessary qualities for both inner peace and transcendent awareness. They also lay the foundation for connection and understanding with others. To look inward first is the way to mend disconnection from ourselves and each other. It is also the path to liberation.

Acceptance as Path

Acceptance as path opens the door to radical aliveness. It is an internal shift of perspective that allows room for whatever arises in us to simply be there. Acceptance promulgates a wide array of possibilities for living and working together. Simultaneously, it neutralizes the generally held assumption that there is an all-knowing, external judge of what is "right and wrong" or "good and bad" outside of us. Our own internalized judge perpetuates this insidious premise, bestowing the appropriate punishment or reward depending on what we "deserve." Such core beliefs hobble us with guilt and shame and undermine our self-esteem. They separate us from ourselves and divide us from each other. The reorientation to self-acceptance relieves us of the moralistic burden of judgment. With self-acceptance, real change is possible. Our return to self-connection, seeded by deep self-acceptance, is free of judgment. This freedom is the ground for personal sovereignty, for becoming the leaders of our own lives. It inoculates the shift germinating inside from fear of judgment to empowered action. Acceptance is like an enzyme that metabolizes the anxiety produced from the familiar, authoritarian meritocracy. With self-acceptance, we become free to share what is gritty and authentic of ourselves with others.

If going inward as a practice is new to you, and even if not, the beguiling ways of your innate self-protection mechanism, also known as the ego, will likely want to meddle in your adventure. No problem. This is to be expected. As we build up the nutrients of our internal resources and establish a new ground of being inside, whatever shows up is responded to with acceptance and compassion. This is about making room for all of it. Everything is included; everything is greeted with respect.

As we learned when we were very young, the best way to chase monsters away is to turn on the light. Simply by shining the light of our awareness on what clings below the surface often frees it to morph right then and there. Awareness with acceptance also empowers us with choice. We are free to face and even befriend that particular thought, fear, or feeling, whereas to keep it hidden in the dark only drains our precious internal resources while feeding its influence over us from the shadows. Self-awareness, as with information in general, is power.

Self-Compassion

Compassion is the great equalizer. It tames what is wild and comforts what is fearful. It illuminates what is hidden in the light of love. It is the light of love, as compassion, that we want to engender in ourselves, letting it nourish our souls and feed the core of our beings. In the armchair of compassion, like a wise and comforting grandmother cradling us to her bosom, we can let the pages of our resistance fall away. The pool of light surrounding us will migrate inside, until it shines forth from our own eyes.

As I well know, the lack of compassion for oneself results in a harsh internal world. Constant judgment and self-berating fill the spaces between our thoughts. In contrast, self-compassion, the active aspect of self-acceptance, allows us to move through the world with kindness and care for ourselves. It is the same consideration and kindness we naturally express to close friends and relatives. We are in the same boat with everyone else. We are human and fallible; we make mistakes, fall short, and upset ourselves and others. Ultimately, there is nowhere else to be but exactly where and how we are. It takes self-compassion to appreciate ourselves as we are, rather than to castigate ourselves for not being other than that, imagining there is another option. Change can come once acceptance has occurred and not before. When our inner witness is compassionate, acceptance is possible. Then the skids are greased for all manner of being and doing in the world, like a joyful child who knows she is loved. This kind of freedom, catalyzed by love, is resourceful. It begets creativity.

The exploration here is to awaken and establish your compassionate observer self. My hope is that it becomes effortless to respond to yourself with compassion, kindness, and understanding no matter what is happening or has occurred. Once embodied, the compassionate witness becomes your intimate friend and confidant. Our compassionate observer self is the purveyor of self-connection. They go hand in hand because kindness and compassion open us to self-acceptance, which in turn allows us the freedom to be honest and true to ourselves. Kindness and compassion provide the confidence we need to show up authentically for ourselves and with others.

Explore this Practice: The Compassionate Observer

There are three interwoven parts to this practice:

- Kindness meditation—general softening with curiosity and acceptance

- Bodily awareness—noticing sensations and emotions
- Mental states awareness---noticing thoughts and stories that keep a loop of experience going

Eventually, the three parts will be one fluid state of self-awareness. It is called a practice because, as a new skill set, it will take practice to learn it. Even though this practice is meditative and you start by sitting quietly, once familiar to you, the practice can be implemented at any time during the day.

My hope is that developing a consistent, compassionate presence will feel so warm and sweet that it will start to show up spontaneously inside without prompting. Compassion is a large part of who you are at your core. It naturally resonates with you and invites the best of you forward into the world. Compassion links your doing with your being, facilitating your sense of belonging and presence. From there, it kindles your passion and creativity, allowing you to really show up with love for life.

1. Kindness Meditation

Sit comfortably and quietly for five to ten minutes, or longer if you wish. Begin by taking three deep abdominal breaths. On each exhale, make an audible sigh with the sound *aaahhh* until the exhale is complete. Within your time frame, notice your breath passing in and out of your nostrils. Find a gentle, even rhythm. If it helps, count to seven on the inhale, one between inhale and exhale, and seven on the exhale. This helps focus the mind and bring awareness to your body. Continue to sit quietly watching your breath for the time you've allotted. When your mind wanders, simply bring it back.

As you sit and focus on your breath, you may also add the following: Visualize light filling you with loving-kindness as you inhale, and on the exhale release any tension or stress. Feel your body relax more deeply as your *breath as light* permeates your body with kindness and compassion and you release tension. Notice and allow whatever arises to simply be there. Explore relaxing with your breath while observing your internal world with compassion and kindness.

You may also visualize breathing love into your heart as you inhale and simply relax more with each exhale. Choose which focus works for you or create your own.

2. Bodily Awareness

Once you feel the lightness and expansion of kindness and compassion filling you while sitting and breathing during kindness meditation, sit comfortably for five to ten minutes more, or longer if you wish.

Gently scan your body as you breathe. Notice any tight or constricted places inside. Just notice; bring your attention there and simply breathe into that place without trying to change it. Bathe it in the loving-kindness of your breath. Notice any emotions that may arise as you breathe into tight areas. Just notice, keep breathing, and simply observe what arises with tender attention. There is nothing to do but breathe and observe, notice and keep softening into the loving-kindness of your breath. Allow emotions to flow into your awareness if they arise, noting where they are in your body; feel them, express them, and let them pass on through while observing them with compassion. As emotions pass through and release their energy, simply observe the process, being mindful to bring your attention back to your breath and your body when your mind wanders.

If you desire, take a few minutes to journal your experience of the feelings that arose, where you noticed them in your body, the thoughts and/or images that came, and how it felt once they passed through.

3. Mental Awareness

Once you've settled in and are present and connected to your body from the inside out after sitting and breathing during kindness meditation and bodily awareness, sit comfortably for five to ten minutes more, or longer if you wish.

Until we are well practiced at quieting the mind, thoughts keep coming. Each time you become aware of a thought, simply notice it and allow it to disperse like a cloud floating by. Return to your loving-kindness breath. Follow your breath down into your body and let it wash through you with the light of compassion. Continue to soften and accept what you observe.

You may notice a recurring thought. Look to discover if there is a feeling accompanying it. When a thought has an emotional component, the combination can keep us in a loop of experience. Simply observe this coupling of thought and feeling with tender attention. Without attachment, simply witness the thoughts without engaging in the content. As they relax their grip, let them drift away. Return to your breath, breathing in loving-kindness and relaxation, noticing and allowing whatever shows up to be there and to disperse with your breath, like a cloud in the summer sky.

Let the energetic effect of loving-kindness and compassion spread and fill you from the inside out. Dwell in this state for as long as you wish with a quiet, calm mind and body.

When you have completed your meditation, make a note of how you feel in your body, heart, and mind. If you wish, write your observations in your journal. If not, simply make a mental note of your experiences. Acknowledge yourself for having done what you planned to do—taking the time to explore and engage your compassionate observer. Celebrate the accomplishment of having done what you intended. If significant information arose or notable experiences occurred, journal or make notes to yourself for future reference.

Do this practice daily for a week to a month, or more if you choose, preferably at the same time of day. Notice what effect it has on your sense of yourself, your presence, and kindness with yourself in general. You may find strong resistance to softening and letting go of self-judgment or hard edges. Respond even to that with gentleness and compassion. Whatever arises, bring it to the armchair of compassion and hold yourself with acceptance and kindness.

The Ego's Place

When we turn our sight inward, there can be great discomfort at first. Our mind throws up a barrage of thoughts as a smoke screen to distract us and defend against the amorphous threat of the unknown. The nervous system is hardwired to keep us safe. Biologically, the unknown can ring as threatening, even if it is inside our own skin. That is the benefit of approaching ourselves with compassion. Compassion can alleviate our fears of looking inward and, thus, create trust by guiding us in with kindness and acceptance. The part of us that is set on keeping us safe is our ego. It acts like a big guard dog at times, growling at anything that could impinge on our internal status quo, our fenced yard of limited self-awareness.

The ego has gotten a lot of bad press in the last fifty years or so. We admire people who have "no ego" and are annoyed by people with "a big ego." But what is the ego, really? Ego is often used as a synonym for a person's degree of focus on him or herself at the exclusion of others. When we meet someone who is self-respecting and humble, we might think of him or her as having little or no ego. Such people don't make a big deal about themselves or drain our energy by needing attention. But in fact, I would say that they have a healthy ego or even a strong ego. From this perspective, *ego strength* is necessary. It serves our internal sense of safety and belonging in the world and brings trust in ourselves to navigate life's twists and turns.

In psychoanalytic terms, the ego is described as the part of the mind that mediates between the conscious and the unconscious and is responsible for reality testing and a sense of personal identity. When we look into it a bit further, we find that the ego is very necessary to our successful functioning in the world and for relating to others. The problem comes when our ego *isn't* strong enough. A healthy ego serves to keep us alive and integrated in the community we belong to. A weak ego doesn't have the capacity to care much about others. It is desperately focused on meeting its own needs, even at others' expense. It doesn't have much ability to empathize, that is, to see or understand the situation from another perspective. A weak ego has selfish motives. It is only able to serve itself, whereas a healthy ego lives in service to life.

We've all met people who have a very clear sense of who they are in the world—people who, even if they have an important role or are publicly visible, live with humility. They are very happy to give time to other people and to lend a hand when needed. A healthy, strong ego is willing to take a back seat. Someone with ego strength has the ability to discern ego-motivated selfishness from Self, the part of us that maintains an objective viewpoint and includes others equally.

When the ego's deficits are subsumed and the ego made whole, objectivity and consideration for others is possible. When a person knows and trusts who he or she is, that person is free to utilize his or her ego's strengths to serve the greater good, a naturally arising inclination. Until the ego is healthy and strong, a person can only see how he or she needs to be served by the world at large. Such people's internal weaknesses become a point of vulnerability not only to themselves, but also to their community. What is it, then, that feeds our internal resources? How do we develop self-confidence and high self-esteem and maintain a healthy ego? How do we come to know and trust ourselves? And how do we live in service to the life we truly want to live? Answer: Go within.

Some part of us knows it's worth the effort to quiet our mind and penetrate the fearful ego's smoke screen. The ego acting alone is only equipped to fend for itself, desiring to keep itself intact, which means to protect itself at all costs. Change of any kind is a threat to the ego's need to feel permanent. A healthy ego, on the other hand, is flexible, integrated into the whole of who we are, and able to recognize our interdependence with others. A strong ego willingly serves our whole being, including our higher motives, even if to do so invites fear of the unknown. A healthy ego chooses to approach fear with courage and supports the healthy self's inward journey.

Secrecy, Fear and Shame

As we traverse the variegated landscape of the inward journey, we naturally encounter obstacles to our freedom. We have internalized numerous less-than-kind messages from the surrounding mainstream culture. Shame has drilled its way into our psyches and tends to dominate our responses, with fears of being seen and known, holding our life hostage from spontaneously expressing its beauty. How can we find our way back to full aliveness? Is it possible to overcome fear and shame and to really live passionately? Unequivocally, yes! The path inevitably begins with going inward, with quieting the mind and unlearning the dominant culture's admonitions that would have us stay small, helpless, and frightened.

Nearly all of us live in shame's shadow to some degree and remain caged by its secrets to a certain extent. Sometimes shame is so well hidden that it invisibly orchestrates our thoughts and actions while evading detection. It is often tied into the moralistic conditioning that tells us we are bad if we make a mistake, flawed if we need help, or wrong even to think certain thoughts. We learned early on to keep our shamefulness under wraps and, by extension, to hold in our own vibrancy. For us to look inside and pass beyond our shame is to break through a barrier the weak ego works desperately to keep in place. The ego's misguided sense of self-protection ends up keeping us from what our Self truly craves—freedom, connection, and love. Sadly, "Shame undermines our ability to give and receive love."[2] If I hold a story that I am unlovable, then that shame will indeed keep me from experiencing the love and connection available to us all.

To strengthen our egos, we shine the light of love and acceptance on our secrets and dissolve our shame. Simply voicing our secrets and shame aloud to a trusted confidant takes away the angst of being known and the antipathy we might feel toward ourselves. To be seen and accepted gives breathing room to our souls. It offers us the chance to be free of our conditioning and releases us from the bonds of shame that hold us back. Our obscured parts need to be acknowledged if we are to know ourselves, to enjoy self-confidence, and to live resourcefully. We must be still enough

---

[2]   Jalaja Bonheim, *The Hunger for Ecstasy* (Emmaus, Pennsylvania: Rodale Press, 2001).

to drop in and be present with ourselves—with *what is*. This journey is about opening the curtains of our mind and looking freely into our hearts.

Hannah's Story

A client I'll call Hannah lived in profound yet hidden shame. She held an unconscious story that she was flawed and even stupid. Her father had raged at her frequently as a child, shaming her for being incompetent at just about anything she did. Given her background, she wanted to raise her children differently. She told herself that she would be the kind, supportive parent that she didn't have. It mattered so much to her that she took parenting classes and studied Nonviolent Communication. And yet, she repeatedly lost her patience to the point of yelling at her children. Her uncontrolled and unintended behavior reawakened her story of not being good enough. Now she was failing in her own eyes, which triggered her childhood shame. But her shame was masked, hidden even from herself, and insidiously undermined her ability to do better, no matter how hard she tried.

Shame can have a debilitating hold on us, camouflaged as it often is. With shame, perhaps more than anything, self-acceptance is needed to gain freedom. Hannah desperately needed to find self-acceptance, but until she let herself be seen with the shame lodged in her own upbringing, it was out of reach. Eventually, she grew to trust that she was safe to feel her childhood pain and grief in the context of our therapy sessions. As distressing as it was, she let herself feel and speak of her shame in my presence. Letting her shame surface allowed her to feel the emotions that were locked away with it, her anger and sadness at how she had been treated by her father. Eventually, she was able to choose a new way to be with herself free from shame and self-judgment. With growing self-acceptance, she found her way to kindness and budding compassion for herself, which then could flow to her children. Acceptance and kindness for ourselves are the foundation of true change. A ready compassionate observer is the initial step to remembering who we really are.

CHAPTER TWO
The Story of Belonging

*Your task is not to seek for love, but merely to seek and find all
the barriers within yourself that you have built against it.*
—Rumi

The mind is a powerful thing. It is probably the most potent agent of change at our disposal. It might also be considered the most baffling of things in the known universe. Is it part of the brain? Where does it actually reside? Is it biological or an aspect of pure consciousness? It's fascinating that we use our brain in order to understand the brain, as well as our minds. As a seeker, I studied and practiced Tibetan Buddhism for a number of years while living in Eugene, Oregon. In one talk, the lama pointed out to a group of us that the mind cannot actually be found within our biological makeup. We don't know where the mind is. Nor do we know how thoughts are formed. The same lama said that the mind is like a wild horse and must be tamed. It must be brought under control and trained so that, instead of running us, we guide it to serve our true purpose. Only then can we be free. We can use our mind intentionally to tap the true power of the mind. As with any wild or frightened thing, compassion is the universal language of understanding.

Fractals, Beauty, and Compassion

Look around and you will notice that everything is composed of patterns. All of life, each living system and every organism is a beautifully constructed, complex set of often simple yet repeating patterns. Some patterns resonate deeply with us. We seem to vibrate inside when we see them. Often referred to as sacred geometry, such forms indicate a shared experience of pattern recognition. In 1975, a French-born mathematician, Benoit Mandelbrot, coined the term *fractal*, from Latin, meaning fractured or broken. He then applied the relatively simple mathematical equations that he called fractals to repeating geometric patterns in nature.

The familiar patterning of the nautilus shell, snowflakes, and fern fronds are examples of fractals. I find such images both breathtaking and calming and somehow deeply comforting. The effect is startling at times and speaks of an invisible resonance I can't ignore. When I feel it, I call it beauty, but it is more than that. It is a subliminal experience of connection—the part of me as an individual organism that is a fractal of life itself, witnessing itself. To experience such a profound level of belonging in the universe is awe-inspiring. It opens my heart, inviting gratitude and compassion to flood in. This spontaneous effect informs me that compassion is a quality that lives at the heart of life itself.

To know that we are loved has everything to do with being at home in the universe and with being comfortable in our own skin. Because compassion is integral to the essence of life, it is a capacity we can cultivate and source from within ourselves. We simply need to discern and modify the stories that keep compassion for ourselves at arm's length.

Naming Our Story

To name a story we hold, to notice it objectively, opens us up to a unique opportunity for freedom. To see a personal pattern in our life has a similar effect. At the same time, it is often the stories themselves that keep us blind to seeing our patterns, the protective ego keeping them below our awareness. The more deeply connected to our survival a story or pattern of relating is, the harder it can be to see it objectively. Our patterns establish themselves to give us the best possible chance to stay intact, or as whole and viable as our life's circumstances permit. In this way, we are able to withstand the travails of insufficient nurturing of our developmental needs, should it occur as children, and also gain a sense of belonging.

In fact, we live with an imperative to find a way to belong. As a vulnerable human infant and child, our safety depends upon belonging. To belong to our family or tribe is synonymous with survival. We depend upon the protection and sustenance provided by our surrounding community. Throughout the eons, this fact has not changed. Belonging is the human need to be an accepted member of a group. Whether we experience this with family, friends, co-workers, a religion, or something else, we all have an inherent desire to belong and, more than that, to be an important part of something greater than ourselves. Our innate wisdom and creativity are utilized by the subconscious mind to develop stories and patterns of relating that give us the sense of belonging. To do so includes finding ways to matter—to be seen and known.

Sometimes we are recognized in our families and supported by those relationships to be the best "me" possible. But when the sense that we matter and are cared about is undermined by our circumstances, say with a critical, overbearing, or emotionally unavailable parent, then we live in fear of not belonging. One story people make up is, *I'm not good enough.* Or, *I am flawed,* and if anyone sees that about me, *I'll be banished* or *I'll be abandoned.* This can become a self-critical voice vigilantly attempting to secure our place in the family or peer group. Although intended to help with our safety and belonging, unfortunately the self-critic feeds the story of not being good enough with its chatter riddled with judgment and blame.

The self-critic wants us to be good enough to belong, perhaps the way a critical parent admonishes us to become an integral member of society by being successful. However, judgment and criticism only serve to increase our sense of separation, of being outcast and even uncomfortable with who we are. We don't feel better about ourselves with criticism and judgment. We shrink. We separate from our inner knowingness and from the sense of trust in our surrounding community and oftentimes from our own family.

Many of us have lived with a vociferous self-critic throughout our lives. We create our own narratives, such as, unless I am perfect, *I am unworthy of being loved*, in other words, of belonging or even mattering. What a heartbreaking story for a child, or anyone, to assume. Of course, it's impossible to be "perfect," but we conjure up all kinds of criteria to pit ourselves against in any case. Not surprising, we resort to judging, blaming and criticizing ourselves (and others) for not making the grade. No matter how well we may do something, it is never quite good enough. There is always another criticism hovering nearby, pulling us in like an endless revolving door from which there is no escape.

In my practice as a psychotherapist, I've heard many horrific stories from survivors of childhood abuse. Why, I wonder, is there so much unkindness? How is it that it seems normal for us to resort to hurting one another, to violence, to selfishly using power over others when what we really want is to know that we are loved? We simply want to belong and, in order to thrive, to be treated with kindness and respect. Why are we so disconnected from our hearts and from expressing kindness and care toward each other? Unfortunately, we end up internalizing the unkindness perpetuated upon us, the judgments and criticism, or worse, that we may have endured. As habitual as it may be, the self-critical voice can be transformed. The practice in this chapter explores the shift from our vocal self-critic to our compassionate observer.

To name the narrative—the assumption we're making that generates an unkind thought or behavior—is the start to dismantling our internal critic. With that objectivity, we can verbalize a new story---for example, the desire to live with kindness or to live with our heart open enough to make thoughtful responses even when faced with the self-critic. This is our compassionate witness's call to stretch beyond our habit to first judge ourselves or others and then to squeeze our heart closed, leaving room for only separation and disconnection.

The world of possibility narrows considerably when we succumb to the habit of judgment and criticism. In that territory, there isn't enough room for others inside our minds and hearts or even for ourselves at times. To open our minds and, thus, our hearts, the quality of acceptance is needed. A significant contributor to the humanistic psychology movement, Carl Rogers (1902–1987), developed what he termed "person-centered" psychotherapy in the 1960s. He found that for optimal personal growth, that is, to prepare the ground for self-actualization, we need the environment to provide three fundamental things. We need to be met with genuineness, meaning openness and self-disclosure; acceptance, meaning being seen with unconditional positive regard; and empathy, which is to be listened to and understood.[3] "The curious paradox is that when I accept myself just as I am, then I can change."[4] To belong with ourselves and transform the habit of self-judgment, we need to first come to acceptance of our various aspects, including our inner critic.

Acceptance is Key to Peace of Mind

My husband and I love backpacking in the wilderness. On one such trip high in the Sierra Nevada Mountains of Northern California, we stopped to chat with a lone woman hiker, presumably in her late sixties or early seventies. Toward the end of our conversation, my husband shared his distress at the influx of so many young Pacific

---

[3] Saul McLeod, "Carl Rogers," Simply Psychology, updated February 2014, retrieved from https://www.simplypsychology.org/carl-rogers.html

[4] Carl Rogers, *On Becoming a Person: A Therapist's View of Psychotherapy* (Boston: Mariner Books, 1961)

Crest Trail hikers who seemed to have little regard for the natural beauty surrounding them. He saw them as speeding through the pristine wilderness of the High Sierra that is so sacred to him, intent on racking up miles. He shared his dismay about this with her and his expectation that others treat nature with the same level of appreciation and respect that he does. The statuesque woman narrowed her eyes and said to him, "Acceptance is key to peace of mind." Before her words had fully landed, she abruptly turned and set off once again down the trail. Stunned, we continued our hike in the other direction, meditating silently on her potent dispatch. The further we hiked, the more of an apparition she seemed to become. The ring of her message continues to reverberate in us, emerging at pertinent moments.

Indeed, to expect or wish or even demand that things be different than they are is futile. It drains our internal resources and keeps us stuck in conflict, both with ourselves and, by extension, with others. And yet, the idea that one way is right (appreciation and respect for the beauty of nature, for example) and another way is wrong (prioritizing completion of a personal goal in a particular time frame) exacerbates separation, both inside of us and out. Curiously, acceptance of *what is* allows us to remain openhearted in the face of differing values. What remains mostly under the radar of awareness is that our personal values are what motivate our thoughts and actions. When we understand that it is our values, all of which have virtue, that inform our choices, then we are graced with the ability to see others as mattering, too.

Connection is wrought from understanding and understanding starts with acceptance. Accepting our differences is the beginning of dialogue. Without acceptance, we resort to judging. When we think something is *wrong,* we are consumed by judgment. In that moment, our hearts and minds shut down to *what is.* We negate it and attempt to rid ourselves of it, even if to do so means to deny its existence. We are caught in a trap of our own making. When we don't make room inside to accept *what is*, our hearts atrophy and interpersonal struggles abound. Whereas, when we see with the eyes of compassion and acceptance, we tap into resourcefulness. We remain openhearted and can approach differences with empathy and creatively address one another's needs.

A clear example of the attempt to deny something that does, in fact, exist is the dogmatic belief that the body, along with human sexuality, is sinful. Therefore, pious folk should behave as if sexual energy does not exist. Since sexuality is not only natural, but also a powerful force of nature, it does not slink quietly away and lie still in the corner. Our attempts to negate and ignore the fact of our sexuality only function to shame and distort what is natural. When we deny or suppress our sexual energy, the seeds of inner conflict are sown for many people. Wrapped in the stranglehold of good versus bad, it simmers below the surface warping the naturally ecstatic energy of our sexuality. When not honored and respected, it becomes perverted, causing trauma and abuse when it slithers out of its hole seething with desire.

The rampant sexual abuse of children by the clergy is a perfect example of this. Sexual expression, as with any focused energy, isn't in and of itself bad or wrong. It is how we choose to respond to the energy and the degree of awareness with which we wield its power that determine the results. The effects of "sacred energy exchange," or sex, can be sublimely transcendent. Or, if we deny its potent place in human life, sexual energy can be misused and the effects hellishly traumatic.[5] Acceptance of *what is,* is key to our health and wholeness in every realm.

Reality and Belief

Our adaptive stories are derived from our perceptions of and responses to what has happened to us. Sometimes they are the result of physically or emotionally traumatic experiences over which we had no control. Many of our beliefs and assumptions are informed by the surrounding culture of our families and society at large. In all cases, our internal narratives necessarily color what we see, hear, and experience, just as a particular filter on a camera lens creates a specific effect in the photo taken. This is a subtle, yet very influential factor that informs our take on reality.

If I believe that the world is out to get me, I will perceive everything through that lens, substantiating my belief with the "facts" I collect and using the filters that my beliefs provide. I can prove to myself and anyone who will listen that my interpretations are true and correct. Time after time, I will see and experience the events of my life through that filter, the perspective that confirms my beliefs, thus concretizing it as *real.* Likewise, if I believe that people are well-meaning, I will perceive the world through that lens, and the way I view external events will prove to me that *that* is so.

Given the power of our beliefs to construe how we perceive reality, we can *always* find evidence to support their accuracy. As Neville Goddard, a twentieth-century metaphysician, teacher, and author, writes, "Your assumptions determine not only what you see, but also what you do, for they govern all your conscious and subconscious

---

5   To explore this topic further, please see Jalaja Bonheim, *The Hunger for Ecstasy: Fulfilling the Soul's Need for Passion and Intimacy* (Emmaus, Pennsylvania: Rodale Press, 2001).

movements towards the fulfillment of themselves." This can be an unsettling concept to consider. In one way, it implies that we are utterly helpless to determine the direction our life takes. In another way, it implies personal responsibility at the subtlest of levels. Because of that, we must take great care not to blame ourselves for traumatic events that have happened to us. And yet, we can be heartened to know that we can overcome the negative effects of trauma on our psyches. The plasticity of our body-heart-mind is susceptible to change by applying kindness with focused intention. Personal empowerment is all about healing and transforming debilitating stories and creating wholesome ones of our own choosing. We can shift our experience by changing our beliefs and vice versa.

That your beliefs color your perceptions can only be proven to yourself by yourself through experimentation. To do so requires an objective perspective. The compassionate observer and self-acceptance go a long way to accomplishing a kind, yet objective view of ourselves. In his book *The Biology of Belief,* cell biologist Bruce Lipton explores how our beliefs and expectations about medical treatment impact the efficacy of the treatment. He writes, "When the mind, through positive suggestion, improves health, it is referred to as the placebo effect. Conversely, when the same mind is engaged in negative suggestions that can damage health, the negative effects are referred to as the *nocebo* effect."[6]

Our negative self-talk creates a nocebo effect in our normal day-to-day living. The ill effects run the gamut from holding us back professionally to compromising our immune systems.

A client I'll call Randy lived in the shadow of severe self-doubt and self-judgment for much of his adulthood. He came to understand intellectually that these were stories he had devised from deficits in his childhood. And yet, he believed so strongly in them that they held him back from seeking the joys and pleasures of life and from even taking good care of himself. His negative self-talk, his vocal self-critic, was alive and well, creating a palpable nocebo effect. As we explored how the negative stories he held were actually serving him, self-acceptance became more plausible. Sometimes our ego is so attached to our stories, good or bad, that we become victimized by our need for the comfort of their familiarity. In and of themselves, disempowering stories aren't helpful. But in the context of maintaining the status quo of our personality structure, they keep us safely contained in the known with no impetus to make changes. Our personal stories and habits afford us the sense of belonging because they

---

[6]   Bruce Lipton, *The Biology of Belief* (Carlsbad, Calif: Hay House, 2008).

are familiar and, therefore, feel comfortable. But often they undermine our prospects to better ourselves and fulfill our life's purpose.

Logically, we are wired for survival. Illogically, indoctrination into believing we are flawed and/or inconsequential becomes the skeleton onto which we hang our personal identity. The ego becomes attached to this identity and grips tightly to avoid the terror of falling into the unknown. In terms of the personality structure, what is unknown, or below our conscious awareness, is hidden from us because of the pain and/or fear held there. This story too, needs airing out in the light of day. Eventually, Randy was able to recognize how his story served his sense of belonging in the familiar world of his emotionally abusive upbringing. As victimized as his sense of self was, he gained enough self-acceptance to begin to free himself of the bonds of his shame-riddled stories. Over time, he gained the courage to show up for himself and to invite more promising options into his workaday world and social life. He took better care of himself physically, got some dental work done, and soon was dating again.

The exploration in this chapter deepens the quality of acceptance for ourselves. Acceptance fertilizes the soil in our ground of being and nurtures the seeds of love. It is the antidote to internal and external judgment and affords greater resourcefulness with our expenditures of energy. In other words, we are no longer bound to repeating our unconscious, subversive patterns of relating. With the practice of acceptance, our internal resources are freed from being tied up in an endless tug-of-war with ourselves. Freedom from the narrow track of right versus wrong uplifts us with sweetness. Now free of the criticism and blame from our self-critical voice, we are instilled with the comfort and confidence of true belonging—beyond the notions of right and wrong. As the thirteenth-century Persian mystic-poet, Rumi wrote, "Out beyond ideas of wrong-doing and right-doing there is a field. I'll meet you there. When the soul lies down in that grass the world is too full to talk about."

With acceptance, we find empowerment in belonging with ourselves and in knowing we are not separate from the rest of life. We are filled to overflowing by a true sense of contentment from the inside out. When we dismantle self-criticism the release of energy is palpable. Our freed energy then can be used to constructively navigate the spaces within us and the relationships between us. We can choose new options.

Fortunately, we are innately caring and compassionate beings. We know this because compassion allows us to relax. It is expansive and enlivening. By cultivating a compassionate witness, we drop into who we really are. As compassion furrows in, the critical, judgmental voices dissipate. Compassion heals and opens our hearts.

We all thirst for kindness and compassion. And by infusing ourselves with it, we are more apt to respond to others in kind as well. A world of new possibilities is born inside with this expanded shift in perspective. As the 1960s counterculture author, Tuli Kupferberg aptly reminds us, "When patterns are broken, new worlds emerge."

The following practice will help you to see and accept yourself as you are, which is an integral step to change. Our self-critic often has a well-worn track in our brains that may be daunting to face. The automatic impulse to resort to self-criticism and judgment make it seem normal or even natural, but I assure you, it is learned. What is most natural to us is to live in expansive, coherent states of being like compassion. To invite such states in can feel awkward or foreign to us at first. The resourcefulness of coherent states makes them fruitful to engender and compelling to return to, however.

Explore this Practice: Inviting the Self-Critic to Tea

Our compassionate observer is fundamental to our inquiry into the self-critic. With our compassionate witness, we invite any discarded, unaccepted, or unappealing parts of ourselves to tea. These are the parts of ourselves most susceptible to our self-critic, the inner voice that assumes our unaccepted parts don't belong. But there they are, so they exist for a reason. To explore this logic, we invite our self-critic to tea, metaphorically setting the tone for kindness and generosity of spirit toward ourselves. We want to make room inside to simply observe and to be with whatever is there, warts and all.

This practice has five parts. With each step, you will increase self-awareness and self-acceptance at the pace that is right for you.

1. *Sit in kindness meditation* (the first step to engaging your compassionate observer, chapter 1). Engage your compassionate observer and feel the warmth and expansion inside as you embody kindness. When ready, go to the next step.
2. *Notice with acceptance*: Approach yourself with a curious, welcoming attitude. In a relaxed manner, watch your thoughts as if you were gazing softly at leaves floating on the surface of a stream, for example, or clouds in the sky. In this way, you simply notice the critical and judgmental thoughts objectively, without engaging with them. "Ah, there it is, the self-critical voice." And it floats on by, disappearing downstream.

3. *Recognize with compassion*: By employing compassion, your willingness to be present with yourself is increased. "There's that harsh voice again. Okay, I recognize that habit," and breathe compassion into yourself. Feel the warmth and spaciousness of embodying compassion.

4. *Acknowledge yourself*: "Yep, I paid attention, recognized, and acknowledged my self-critical voice." Self-awareness is happening. You are growing your objectivity and distance from reactivity, while reducing the tendency to buy into the critic.

5. *If/when the critic-judge takes you in*: Invite him or her to tea.

A. Recognize and acknowledge

"I did engage with the critical voice, and this is what happened inside me when I did." Make a note of your internal experience when your critical voice took over and your compassionate objectivity left. Did you believe the message? Did your heart contract? Did you project blame onto someone for the criticism you felt? What happened inside, in your body? To name the factors, the thoughts and feelings that perpetuate self-criticism, will help to unravel the pattern and create space for more resourceful options. Accept what you discover and however the process unfolds as you go.

Return to your compassionate observer. Notice the relaxation and warmth inside when you come back to acceptance and compassion for yourself. Once you have regained objective self-awareness and acceptance, make time to have a relaxed chat with the self-critical/judgmental messenger. Either take a few minutes to do it in the moment or make a time to return to it soon.

B. Invite the Self-Critic/Judge to Tea.

Set a specific time and give yourself ten to thirty minutes for tea and conversation. After the first couple of teatimes, it will become easier to converse with your self-critic from an objective and compassionate stance.

You can set the imaginary stage to whatever degree feels good to you—table, chairs, teacups, and so on. Or simply sit comfortably and invite the self-critic/judge into your awareness. To tap into your inner judge or critic, remember the critical thought you engaged with above or bring another self-judgment to mind. Take a minute to welcome the critic with appreciation for showing up and ask him or her to please sit down with you. Maintain your compassionate internal state as you make room inside yourself to receive what the inner critic has to share with you.

In your mind, ask questions out of curiosity to know about the critic, just as you would an intriguing new acquaintance. Approach your self-critic from the understanding that this part of you came into being as an attempt to serve you and your life. Trust that, and let it guide your line of questioning. For example, you may ask questions like: How long have you been with me? What is your job? How are you helping me? What is your reason for coming into being? Whose voice are you? Simply listen with tender attention. Let compassion be your guide and acceptance your ground of being. Continue to engage your compassionate witness with your breath to remain objective, present, and openhearted. Make a note of the answers you get. One answer may lead logically to the next question. It is about the adventure of making new discoveries in an unfamiliar landscape. Remember gratitude for this part of you for showing up and revealing itself.

When you engage openly with your inner self, you have a direct line into your own internal wisdom. Allow the information to come to you in words, images, or as sensations inside. Listen compassionately and take note of whatever is offered. You will discover your own language and logic to the images and information that come to you. Allow yourself to open to and make sense of what arises, trusting the wisdom of it. Let the process be fluid and at times not necessarily rational. It is a symbolic language we tap into when we ask to be shown previously subconscious material. With a relaxed mind, allow the images and information to reveal their meaning to you. Whatever comes will be unique to you and your life. As you come to understand yourself more intimately, the logic of your internal symbolic language will become clearer. When you feel complete, thank your critic-judge for joining you and suggest you'd like to meet again to find out more regarding this part of your life. Leave your teatime on a note of gratitude and appreciation for the meeting.

Review the answers you got with an eye to discovering how this voice is really attempting to serve your life. With a particularly recalcitrant or nasty critical voice, definitely do set up another teatime meeting. With kindness, acknowledge how the voice has served or has tried to serve your life.

Once you've befriended this part of you, suggest to the critic/judge that there could be a way to go about living that is less draining and more resourceful. Eventually, the two seemingly disparate aspects of you will unite, and the energies will coalesce in support of your authentic Self. The self-critic will take a different role, such as simply to be an objective observer of what is going on in and around you. The critical commentator can instead become a gatherer of information to help navigate the world more eloquently. It can also morph into a protector, alerting you when something is off or not safe so that you can take appropriate action to care for yourself as needed. We will explore this transformation more fully in later chapters. Eventually, as you become adept at listening to and trusting your inner voice, it will become the voice of wisdom inside.

If you'd like to accelerate self-awareness and freedom from the self-critic, take a few minutes before bed to review your day. Remember where and when you had a critical or judgmental thought. Approach it like you would a young child who's had a rough day at school. This can help you to access your compassionate observer. When you become aware of the critic, come back to your breath, engage your compassionate observer, and acknowledge yourself for recognizing the self-critical voice. Notice if there is a difference in how your body feels when your self-critic is active versus when you activate your compassionate observer. Make a note of which state is more enjoyable for you. Remember, just because something is familiar does not mean it is necessarily beneficial or life serving.

As your practice continues, you may notice a critical thought right when it happens, or you may notice it minutes, hours, or even days later. Either way, acknowledge yourself for noticing your inner process. Bring in gratitude for your willingness to engage in the journey of self-discovery and to remember who you really are.

If writing is helpful to you, keep a journal and note your experiences with the practice each day. I find that writing things down helps me better understand my inner workings and gives me the chance to reflect on my growth over time. As you look inward more deeply, find how it is that *you* truly want to be living and serving your life.

As we gain more acceptance and compassion for our critical voices, we also overcome being victimized by them and are released from the struggle of combating them. This frees up energy to engage in the experiences we do want to cultivate. We can effectively create the experiences we want by simply knowing what that is—with greater self-awareness. Not surprisingly, this awareness is gained by going inward. Although we often think that our experiences are caused by outer circumstances, as we have seen, our perceptions rely on our internal states of being, including our beliefs about ourselves and our lives. Our attitude is the lens through which we observe ourselves and the world, and it fairly well determines our experiences, too. As we loosen the grip of habitual attitudes and narratives that no longer serve us, we have more internal resources to invite in what we do want. The next two chapters offer specific skills to create the experiences we desire and to write more wholesome narratives to live by.

CHAPTER THREE
The Science of Oneness

To see a World in a Grain of Sand
And a Heaven in a Wild Flower,
Hold Infinity in the palm of your hand
And Eternity in an hour.
—William Blake

The rational mind is hard-pressed to grasp the notion that solid matter is mostly scintillating light dancing in empty space. Mystics, such as William Blake, have written and spoken for millennia about their vision of the unity of all things. For mystics, this understanding comes from their direct experience. Such experiences have an ineffable quality. Words to describe it fall short of the full impact it has on them, such that their descriptions tend toward the poetic and lyrical. This makes sense, as in that moment of awakening, the mystic knows him or herself as inseparable from that same light-filled radiance. Mystics experience their oneness with all that is, a different reality than our usual state of being.

Modern-day psycho-nauts, such as Gregg Braden, Lynne McTaggart, Tom Kenyon, and Bruce Lipton, among others, explore the intersection between science and mysticism. Quantum physics is proving true concepts that were previously relegated to mystical realms alone.

In his book *The Divine Matrix*, Gregg Braden speaks of our ongoing conversation with the universe. "In this dialogue, our deepest beliefs become the blueprint for everything that we experience."[7] With scientific research in hand, he suggests that our very assumptions and beliefs determine how the external world shows up in our

---

[7]   Gregg Braden, *The Divine Matrix* (Carlsbad, Calif: Hay House, Inc., 2007).

lives. It isn't coincidental—it is a perfect reflection of who we are. The determination that we are not separate from what appears to be external reality takes an unexpected turn when he goes on to propose that, "our conversation with the world is constant and never ending. Because it doesn't stop, it's impossible for us to ever be passive observers on the sidelines of life ... if we're conscious, by definition we're creating."[8]

We can use science and the rational mind to help us grapple with the idea of our interconnectedness with the universe, our *oneness*. Quantum physics is leading the way to confirming much of what mystics have described over eons—that we are not separate from external reality. The big takeaway is that we can consciously apply our will, as intention, to ourselves and our circumstances to directly affect our experiences. When we do so, the power of our own creativity becomes apparent. This "new" way of seeing reality is key to comprehending our connectedness with one another and the world around us. To perceive our interconnectedness naturally infuses us with the sense of belonging in the world. Care and consideration for one another follow when we know that we belong. It is belonging that inspires us to work together and, thereby, to more expediently remedy the varied crises looming before us.

We all can have a direct experience of our interconnectedness and creative potential through the explorations offered below. A new more user-friendly reality is available to us when we comprehend how science explains the dovetailing of matter, energy, and consciousness.

Intentionality and the Zero Point Field

When we have a clear understanding of our personal values, meaning the *qualities of life* that motivate us to believe what we do and take the actions we take, then we can generate them intentionally. The reason for doing so is to implement conscious choice about what we experience. To consciously apply your will, as intention, has a demonstrable effect on what you experience. This idea is founded in the fact that we are not separate from the vast expanse of the universe itself. Cutting edge physicists call it the *zero point field*, or simply, the field. The field is a sea of energy from which quantum particles both emerge and submerge in a continuous energy exchange. It is this perpetual exchange of energies that holds the universe in dynamic equilibrium, or the relative stability that we enjoy within the flux of life. From the midst of her extensive research, Lynne McTaggart explains:

---

8   Braden.

"The existence of the Zero Point Field implied that all matter in the universe was interconnected by waves, which are spread out through time and space and can carry on to infinity, tying one part of the universe to every other part. The idea of The Field might just offer a scientific explanation for many metaphysical notions, such as the Chinese belief in the life force, or qi, described in ancient texts as something akin to an energy field. It even echoed the Old Testament's account of God's first dictum: 'Let there be light', out of which matter was created." (HarperCollins, 2008, p 24).[9]

We live immersed in and are integral with a unified field that is mediated by waves of information. When quantum physicists include the existence of the zero point field in their calculations, they find that, in fact, *everything* is comprised of energy in the form of waves. Matter, as we think of it, does not exist. It is the condensed spheres of vibrating light held in the relative stability afforded by the zero point field that creates the illusion of solid matter.[10]

Understanding these recent scientific discoveries is liberating. It offers solid ground for utilizing our potential and aids in transcending archaic beliefs no longer relevant. If you are willing, please stay with me a bit further on this fascinating investigation into the field of possibility.

Waves have the distinguished ability to encode and carry information, as well as having what amounts to an infinite capacity to store information. Therefore, "If all subatomic matter in the world is interacting constantly with this ambient ground-state energy field, the subatomic waves of the field are constantly imprinting a record of the shape of everything. As the harbinger and imprinter of all wavelengths and all frequencies, the Zero Point Field is a kind of shadow of the universe for all time, a mirror image and record of everything that ever was."[11]

This viewpoint could explain the mystical experience of "universal oneness." It affirms that, due to the zero point field waves, we are actually connected with all matter throughout the immensity of the whole universe, on into infinity. However, this so-called matter is actually waves of information. When encoded waves bump into each other, *interference* occurs. In this process, the waves share information, and thus, all the information in the universe accumulates in the waves of the zero point field.

---

[9]   Lynne McTaggart, *The Field* (New York: HarperCollins, 2008), 24.

[10] McTaggart

[11] McTaggart.

Loren Swift

McTaggart writes, "The Zero Point Field had imprinted everything that ever happened in the world through wave interference encoding."[12] Encoded waves of information vibrate and eventually congeal in patterns of energy fields, into what we call matter.

Physicists surmise that the zero point field may also function as a "non-biochemical memory of the universe."[13] The zero point field appears to act like complex networks of connected information in an eternal *now*. As we are inseparable from it, the implication is that we could tap into this grand web of accumulated information. It suggests as well that we could influence the wave fluctuations around us by intentionally applying our consciousness to our life. Intuitively and through personal experience, I have found this to be true. This explains how conscious intentions, as well as unconscious expectations—all encoded waves of information—can affect our internal states of being, as well as our external reality. Everything is connected and continually exchanging information in the form of waves.

The implications of this all-pervasive sea of encoded waves can be taken a step further. I suggest that the field holds and expresses universal consciousness itself. As part of the unified field, we are always tapped into and exchanging information on myriads of fronts, with or without our awareness of doing so. Our human consciousness is part and parcel to universal consciousness. We simply need to apply our will, or conscious intention, to create our preferred results. Now let's drop out of our heads and into our hearts and put the science of oneness to practical use.

The Heart and Universal Qualities of Life

As you experiment with the exploration below, you will have the opportunity to experience your interdependence with the universe. The focus takes you deeper inside and taps into your heart as the intermediary between your personal consciousness and the all-pervasive universal consciousness. The benefits of the inward journey are more accessible when we align ourselves with the intelligence of the heart, as researchers have discovered. "New research shows the human heart is much more than an efficient pump that sustains life. Our research suggests the heart also is an access point to a source of wisdom and intelligence that we can call upon to live our lives with more balance, greater creativity and enhanced intuitive capacities. All

---

12   McTaggart.
13   McTaggart.

26

of these are important for increasing personal effectiveness, improving health and relationships and achieving greater fulfillment."[14]

We are coevolving a fundamental paradigmatic shift from the dualism of right-wrong thinking to awareness of ourselves within a unified field of existence. This is accomplished by descending into ourselves and connecting with our heart's natural tendency toward coherence. We can access the state of coherency by intentionally embodying a specific quality of life that resonates meaningfully with us. The exploration below details how to do this. As explained, each quality is a particular attribute of life that we resonate with and can generate at will. This proffers the experience of connection, not only with ourselves, but also with the surrounding field that encompasses us. Through intentional embodiment of a given quality of life, we can have the experience of interconnection with the field and with people in the field. In an embodied, coherent state we can discern the distinctions between us, but we no longer experience them as separating us from each other. We know ourselves as integral to the great web of life, along with everyone else.

In this exploration, we focus on the experience we desire and use that to usher in a coherent state of being. We name it as a particular quality of life. Universal qualities of life are the underpinnings, oftentimes subconscious, of what motivates us to do, to think, and to choose as we do. They indicate the qualities of being human that we are drawn to and want to express. We commonly refer to them as our values. In the Nonviolent Communication (NVC) lexicon, values are referred to as *universal human needs*. The concept of universally shared human needs is very practical. It is a tool for naming the commonalities within our diversity. It is a tangible way to understand one another better and is instrumental to resolving conflict. Universal human needs facilitate connection by highlighting our shared humanity. When we see others as human, like us, it is well-nigh impossible to do violence to them. Instead, we tend to care about them because we know they are another me.

I use the term *universal qualities of life* in place of the NVC term, universal human needs. Many people react to the idea of having a need or of needing something from others, relating it to being needy. And the thought of meeting a need tends to take our attention outside of ourselves, whereas I encourage us to reverse our habitual focus by bringing our attention inside. The power inherent in self-connection and

---

[14] "Science of the Heart (e-book)," HeartMath Institute, (2016). https://store.heartmath.com/item/esoh/heartmath-science-of-the-heart

self-awareness is very internal. What we long for gets much clearer and more accessible when we can name the qualities of life that motivate and matter to us.

How It Works

For example, let's say I want to go to the beach, swim in the ocean, and lie in the sun. That idea was engendered by a desired experience—a "need," or quality of life wanting expression in me. The motivating factor could be one of many specific qualities or a blend of them. I could be wanting relaxation, exercise, fun, connection in nature, or simply freedom from other responsibilities. To know what is behind my original desire can be helpful for a number of reasons. When I know and can name the *experience* I'm after, then the forms or strategies by which I can achieve it become more plentiful. It is when we hold onto just one possible way to fulfill a desire that we run into scarcity. This inadvertent sense of scarcity begets conflict. It can take us right into the polarized me-versus-you logic and the notion that only one of us can get what we want. The horizons of possibility expand exponentially when we distinguish between the underlying experience we seek as a specific quality of life from the particular form or *strategy* we expect can give us that experience.

In this moment, my idea of going to the beach is based on my desire to experience relaxation and connection with myself in nature. But I live in the mountains, a four-hour drive away from the ocean. It isn't a reasonable use of my time and energy to take a day to drive to the beach, sit for an hour, and drive home. It's not a relaxing or rejuvenating idea. But there are lakes and rivers near where I live. I could drive for half an hour, find a secluded spot on the river in the sun, and quite easily get the relaxation and connection in nature I'm seeking. Or I may live in a city center and don't have ready access to nature or seclusion. In that case, I could walk to a park and sit quietly by myself. Or I could put headphones on, close the door, and listen to sounds of nature, using my imagination to take me to the beach or into the woods. With a little creativity, I can accomplish the desired result by numerous strategies.

Any life-serving experience we desire can be named by a universal quality of life, once we identify it as such. These qualities are universally applicable because, by stepping back, we can see that anyone might want such an experience. It is not yours or mine alone in its desirability—it is common to most everyone. The particular *way* in which we choose to fulfill it, however, is specific to time, place, and person. The way we accomplish it is the strategy for fulfilling that experience and expressing the quality of life we're after. This significant distinction provides great freedom of choice and myriads of possible options for achieving the experiences we want. We shift from scarcity to abundance when the options for gratifying our desires are so readily multiplied.

> **Naming the Universal Qualities of Life**
>
> A simple way to find out what you most long to experience is to get out paper and pen and write down whatever comes to mind when you answer this question: If everything in your life was exactly as you would most love it to be, what words would describe that state of being? Sit quietly for a few minutes and jot down whatever comes to you. For now, set aside your concerns about how you can achieve the experiences you want. Strategies can come later. To answer the question, catapult yourself past the strategy, or how it will happen, to the end result and name your state of being when you experience it. For now, it's about naming the experience itself that you want.

Brainstorming Resonant Qualities of Life

The first step in this exploration is to know what experiences really matter to you. You name them with specific qualities of life that represent the experiences you value. A simple way to find out what you most value and long to experience is to get out paper and pen and write down whatever comes to mind in answer to this question: *If everything in your life was exactly as you would most love it to be, what words would describe that state of being?*

Sit quietly for a few minutes and jot down whatever comes to mind. For the purpose of this exercise, set aside your concerns about *how* you can achieve the experiences you want. Strategies can come later. For now, your task is to name *the experience itself* that you want, rather than the form the experience will take. In my example above, it came down to my wanting relaxation and connection. To answer the question, catapult yourself past the strategy, or how it will happen, to the end result and name your state of being when you experience it.

Once you've written down what comes to your mind, go to Appendix A, "Universal Qualities of Life" Look the list over and see if there are other qualities you'd like to add to your list. I recommend writing your personal list of ten to twenty qualities of life that resonate most strongly with you and keep it in your pocket. With your list handy you can glance at it to help see what quality of life is motivating you to think or do or want what you seek in any situation. Once you know what qualities of life matter most to you, you become more empowered to achieve your desired goals and are freer to enjoy life along the way. In part two of the handbook, we will apply this knowledge further. We will expand the embodiment skill to our interactions with others and to authentic yet caring communication skills.

Coherence and the Spectrum of Love

As I picture it, love is the grand, overarching quality of life that encompasses all the rest. Light can be used as a metaphor to help explain it. If we equate love to daylight, for example, then refracted light, like a rainbow, represents the spectrum of love. The rainbow is the palette of qualities of life nestled within the pure white light that is love. We bring forth the colors of love when we embody a particular quality of life in a given moment. We shine with that particular energetic that is a specific quality or aspect of love. At the same time, we have engendered a coherent state of being. Coherence is a cohesive energetic pattern that interpenetrates us and the world around us. As we embody coherent states of being, we are categorically choosing our experience in that moment. At the same time, we are weaving the energetics of that state into the field around us.

The following practice explains how to embody the universal qualities of life you want to experience. We create psycho-emotional coherence within ourselves when we embody a quality of life from the spectrum of love. This skill greatly supports your presence while serving personal empowerment, clarity, and compassion through deep self-connection. I learned the following embodiment practice from NVC trainer, PhD psychologist, mentor, and author Robert Gonzales. With deep respect and gratitude, I pass it on to you. For more information on the work of Robert Gonzales and the Center for Living Compassion, please visit www.living-compassion.org.

Explore this Practice: Embodying Universal Qualities of Life in the Spectrum of Love

Purpose

To offer you the choice to live the qualities you most cherish and wish to experience; to access coherent states of being regardless of outer circumstances; to constructively affect interactions and experiences; and to remember and to reconnect with your natural state, to be vibrantly alive, and to feel the expansive beauty of the creative life principle flowing through you.

How

This practice catalyzes the living energy of a specific quality of life in and around you. With conscious intent, you engage your will and choose to embody a specific aspect of the creative life force. This force flows through all human beings and can be tapped into at any time. Give yourself fifteen to twenty minutes for the practice. Soon, you will be able to embody a quality of life at will in the moment.

1. *Sit quietly in kindness meditation for five to ten minutes* or simply sit still and follow your breath until you are relaxed and present with yourself.
2. *From the place of quiet relaxation*: Notice what lies ahead for you in the day (if it's evening, then later on or tomorrow). What comes to mind first or stands out the most? Perhaps you have a meeting with your boss midmorning or a date after work. When you imagine that part of your day, what happens? Notice what you feel inside your body. Is it an emotion, like excitement, anxiety, overwhelm, or sadness? Is it a physical sensation, like tightness in your chest or jaw or butterflies in your stomach? Or relaxation in your shoulders or belly? Observe your inner state of being with tender attention.
3. *Next ask yourself, what is the experience I want to have during that part of my day?* Your emotion is information that points to the quality of life you desire. Go into your body's feeling state and notice what experience you are most longing for. If you come up with a strategy, a form of action, name the felt experience that action is intended to give you. That is the quality of life mattering to you in this instance.

   If the state isn't clear to you, look at your list of the ten to twenty qualities of life that resonate most strongly with you. Choose the quality that most closely represents the experience you want to have during the part of your day you are now considering. You will know you've landed on the quality that fits when you feel a bodily shift—you relax a little more; you feel a bit lighter inside; you sigh, exhale, or settle down more into your seat. Trust your perceptions and experience.
4. *Now, focus on the quality itself.* Allow yourself to be filled with the living energy of that quality. Breathe in the energy, the warmth, the relaxation and expansion

of the quality into your whole being, from chest to belly to pelvis, legs, and feet to back, spine, neck, and head and back to your heart. Stay with the experience for a few minutes, breathing in the quality and allowing its energy to deepen and expand within you. Notice what happens in your body-heart-mind as you dwell in the energy of the quality.

5. *If you are challenged to sense the quality in this way, call up a memory when you did experience this quality of life.* As you remember that particular experience, name the quality of life itself you enjoyed then. Take as much time as you need to call up the memory and fully feel into the experience of it. Focus on it and breathe it into your body here and now. As you feel that happening, let go of the memory and continue to allow the energy of the quality itself to fill you and breathe its life force into you as if of its own accord. Dwell in the experience of the embodied quality as it infuses your being.

6. *Notice your body. What sensations are you aware of inside? Write your experience in your journal, if useful.* Notice what happens in your body-heart-mind during and after the embodiment practice.

With practice, your conscious choice to embody a specific quality of life empowers you to tap into the field of possibility and create the experience you want. You can inhabit and spread your most cherished states of being at will. For example, you can increase harmony, respect, competence, understanding, and so on by applying your will purposefully to embodying the quality you desire.

Practice the embodiment exercise daily as a morning meditation or anytime you want to meet your day or a specific part of your day with the fullness and presence of body-heart-mind that embodying a specific quality provides. In essence, you are creating the state you desire to experience and thus, consciously cocreating how your life will unfold by inputting it into the field of possibility. Subsequent practices in the handbook utilize the embodiment practice too. It is fundamental to an expedient shift of your consciousness and to more fully being the person you want to be.

If you have difficulty fully embodying a quality of life, spend another week or more cultivating your compassionate observer. Take time to invite your inner critic to tea, also. Collect more information about what's going on inside. Sometimes we have an inner saboteur that keeps us in a stunted state. The saboteur might unconsciously be undermining your attempts to step directly into more fulfilling states. If it seems relevant, ask that part that seems to be holding you back, "What and how are you serving me?" Let your compassionate witness listen with kindness and understanding.

Work with the information you get. Explore the consequences of letting yourself stretch into more aliveness.

Rather than fighting against what we don't want, we embrace and embody what we do want to bring into our lives. This simple shift in focus allows us to thrive forward into the life we most long to live.

Tammy and Roger's Vacation

Tammy and Roger came to me to explore a painful long-standing dynamic between them. They were feeling hurt and resentful upon their return from a vacation in Europe. Married for nearly twenty-five years, they had entrenched communication patterns that naturally showed up during the stressors of traveling. We looked into a specific incident that held an old pattern and was a thorn in the side of their relationship. They had arrived at the Barcelona airport not long before the incident happened.

They decided to walk to their hotel as it was relatively close to the airport. They were both tired and hungry but wanted to save money. Tammy was behind Roger by five or ten yards when they came to a main thoroughfare that had train tracks running down the center. In a hurry to get to the hotel, Roger dashed across the street before the light could change, leaving Tammy at the curb on the other side of the train tracks. Bewildered with her predicament, she felt hurt that he hadn't waited to make sure she could get safely across the wide boulevard. She was especially upset that she'd had to schlep her suitcase over the train tracks unaided.

At the beginning of the session, we had brainstormed the qualities of life that matter most to them in their life and their relationship. Care, consideration, and kindness were high on the list.

I guided them through the process described above to fully embody care, the quality that resonated most strongly for them in this situation. Once they felt the quality of care flowing through them, I asked Roger to imagine himself on the sidewalk before he started to cross the street. I asked him to tell Tammy what he would like to do, as if it were happening now. I could see his face relax and his energy soften. He looked at her and said, "Let's go across this street together. I want to make sure you get across safely." He then apologized for failing to consider her needs when they were on the way to the hotel. She noticeably relaxed, exhaled a deep sigh, teared up, and gave him a sweet smile.

Next, we looked at her part in this dance between them, which was about her being better able to embody self-care and the willingness to ask clearly for support when she needed it. Their more conscious awareness of the universal qualities of life that matter to them has supported them to show up more engaged with those states and to be more honest and forthright with one another. There is greater trust in their shared values for the relationship as a result of the practice. Tammy and Roger's example shows the power we all have to make an internal shift from disconnection to connection by embodying the universal qualities of life we most value.

The Ripple Effect and Morphic Resonance

A scientific premise called *morphic resonance* corroborates that our power of intention can have long-term effects. Biologist Rupert Sheldrake understands morphic resonance as patterned energy that repeats itself through time and space. As such, it acts as the memory inherent in nature.[15] "I am suggesting that heredity depends not only on DNA, which enables organisms to build the right chemical building blocks—the proteins—but also on morphic resonance. Heredity thus has two aspects—one a genetic heredity, which accounts for the inheritance of proteins through DNA's control of protein synthesis. The second is a form of heredity based on morphic fields and morphic resonance, which is nongenetic and is inherited directly from past members of the species. This latter form of heredity deals with the organization of form and behavior."[16]

Morphic resonance fits with the zero point field concept in which everything is part of universal memory held in waves. According to Sheldrake, morphogenetic fields are invisible, nonlocal patterns that interpenetrate the physical and nonphysical worlds. In this model, every living organism shares a morphogenetic field with the others of its species, no matter where they reside on the planet. Because of that, information and abilities are readily transmitted between members of the species nonlocally. As such, it is the "memory of form," whether physical or mental, and it strengthens over time.

Morphic resonance is also revealed through what we call *cumulative effect*. Cumulative effect is when an activity becomes easier over time with practice, like driving a car, playing ball, or swimming, for example. The fact that Olympic athletes continue

---

[15]   Rupert Sheldrake, *A New Science of Life* (South Paris, ME: Park Street Press, 1995).

[16]   Rupert Sheldrake, "Part I—Mind, Memory, and Archetype: Morphic Resonance and the Collective Unconscious," *Psychological Perspectives* 18, no. 1 (Spring 1987): 19–25.

Morphogenetic Fields Influence Patterns

"There is mounting evidence that as more and more people learn or do something it becomes easier for others to learn or do it. In one experiment, British biologist Rupert Sheldrake took three short, similar Japanese rhymes—one a meaningless jumble of disconnected Japanese words, the second a newly-composed verse and the third a traditional rhyme known by millions of Japanese. Neither Sheldrake nor the English schoolchildren he got to memorize these verses knew which was which, nor did they know any Japanese. The most easily-learned rhyme turned out to be the one well-known to Japanese. This and other experiments led Sheldrake to postulate that there is a field of habitual patterns that links all people, which influences and is influenced by the habits of all people. This field contains (among other things) the pattern of that Japanese rhyme. The more people have a habit pattern—whether of knowledge, perception or behavior—the stronger it is in the field, and the more easily it replicates in a new person. In fact, it seems such fields exist for other entities too—for birds, plants, even crystals. Sheldrake named these phenomena *morphogenetic fields*—fields which influence the pattern or form of things." (The Co-Intelligence Institute, www.co-intelligence.org)

to increase their abilities and shorten times in events over those of their predecessors' points to the existence of morphogenetics.

We create a similar effect within ourselves and with others when we embody coherent states of being regularly. Over time, persistently embodied states create a resonant field within and around us. The more of us who embody coherent states of being consistently, the easier it will be for others to tap into and exist in those states too.

In any given situation, when you choose to embody a universal quality in the spectrum of love, you create a resonant field that permeates the space within and around you. You put the energetics of your consciousness into the field of possibility. It's as if you become a tuning fork vibrating to a specific tone that is a coherent pattern. With the tuning fork, we recognize coherence through sound waves. With states of being, we sense it on subtler planes, often unconsciously. The fabric of continual energy exchange that is the zero point field, the energized backdrop of everything, supplies the energy needed to form coherent patterns and morphic resonance.

In effect, you "grease the wheels" for connection and understanding by aligning your energy with the living energy of the experience you desire. Your intention to be love (as compassion, respect, kindness, consideration, and so on) actually pulls love (as the quality you've embodied) into being. You set the tone for the interaction and the experience you're after. The invisible energetics effectively ripple out and invite others to vibrate at the same frequency. When you are in a coherent state, it becomes much easier for others to vibrate coherently too. For example, I have noticed the sweet, expansive, and playful energy that Tibetan lamas exude. I feel uplifted and harmonious simply sitting in their presence.

The coherent wave pattern we invite into being while embodying a quality of life interacts with the surrounding field. The field responds by expressing the energetics of that quality through and around us. This can have a profound effect on your interactions by inviting insights, creativity, and even energetic alignment with others. It also has a positive effect globally, increasing global harmony and coherence, as we are intricately connected with the Earth's magnetic energies, as well.

The embodiment practice invites deep self-connection. With greater self-connection, kindness and compassion are more available to inform our choices. Consequently, we take to heart how our actions will affect other people. Accountability for how we affect others becomes integral to our decisions at every turn—in our personal and business relationships and in how we develop our social institutions.

CHAPTER FOUR
Coherence and the Coordinates of Presence

*Vulnerability sounds like truth and feels like courage. Truth and
courage aren't always comfortable, but they're never weakness.*
—Brené Brown

I remember exalting in the pale green waves and warm sunshine at the beach in summer. I felt the greatest exhilaration catching a wave on my surf mat. I would kick hard and paddle fast until I caught the crest of the wave just as it began to spill over and then plummet down the shining arc of water, only to be lifted and carried to shore by the billowing, foamy froth under me. I felt joyful exhaustion lying in the warm sand, lulled by the rhythmic sound of waves breaking in the distance and breathing the salty air. Caressed by the sun, I felt the alive beauty of being at one with my surroundings pulse through me.

When you look back over your life, what stands out as most wonderful to you? Do you remember a time when the world seemed to stand still, and you felt full and content? What were you doing? What was happening? Let that same feeling flood through you right now. Breathe it in and let it flow into every cell of your body. Rest in that experience for a few moments. Let the quality of being you felt then fill and energize you again now.

The Being of Doing

The most precious and memorable moments seem to be those in which our bodies, hearts, and minds are equally engaged. We have access to the full spectrum of ourselves when we're lined up with our whole being. Notably, we also have access to the heart of life itself when we are centered and awake on all fronts. When our *doing* is infused with our *being*, then there is no separation. We are fully present in ourselves and engaged with life. In those moments, time seems to pause, and we know we belong right here, right now. We can access this presence anytime by embodying a quality of life from the spectrum of love. We can chart our way there with the *coordinates of presence*—a map to self-connection and cohesive states of being.

To be *present* is a very resourceful state. There are no nagging or critical voices, no doubts or second-guessing ourselves, no disgruntlement. When our doing is imbued with our being, we can operate at high capacity. Our creativity is maximized. Our access to coherent states is seamless. We have the ability to utilize every skill at our disposal, to wield our personal power with the clearest of intentions.

You might ask, "But if I stay in the present moment, how will I plan ahead and get anything *done?*" That's just it. Without the distractions of mind chatter and the discombobulation of chaotic states like stress and fear, we can focus better—and stay focused. There is seemingly much more time and energy available with our presence intact. It is all about our relative state of coherence. Let's explore further the nature of coherence itself.

The Power and Pleasure of Coherency

The ability to focus our energy and to streamline our efforts is elevated significantly when we are in a coherent state. *Coherence*, a term used in physics, occurs when two or more waves are in sync with one another. This means that they vibrate at the same frequency, have the same waveform, and are in phase (meaning they peak and trough at the same time). Said simply, coherence is the state of cohering, or of sticking together. "Lasers, for example, emit almost perfectly coherent light; all the photons emitted by a laser have the same frequency and are in phase."[17] In other words, when all the forces at play are lined up with each other, their potency increases exponentially.

---

[17] *Dictionary.com*, s.v. "coherence," accessed January 16, 2019, http://www.dictionary.com/browse/coherency.

A laser beam is created simply by lining up photons of light coherently. There are endless possibilities with such a refined tool, from precision cutting of steel to splicing DNA to microscopic eye surgery and so much more. Lasers are a familiar and practical example of an extremely potent use of aligned and focused energy. As with the constructive application of laser technology, we too can focus our energy to accomplish our goals in a purposeful way. We can intentionally create coherent states of being and then apply ourselves to productive activity. We can design our approach to life specific to the experiences and outcomes we seek. Daily tasks feel more enjoyable when we're centered and present. Rather than being at the mercy of external events, the "shoulds" and "have tos" that take us out of self-connection, we are in a clear, empowered state.

Coherence is naturally occurring, patterned energy that we resonate with. Coherent waves of vibration connect us to the life force both in and around us, inciting creativity and the sense of belonging here in our bodies and on the planet. Coherent emotional states like gratitude and compassion activate our health and well-being. As you experienced with qualities of life in the spectrum of love, you can choose to vibrate in resonance with these states. Even the suggestion to remember a wonderful moment in your life invokes the particular state you experienced at a different time and place. It is our consciousness then, the attitude we carry, that determines our state of being, not necessarily the time and place of the actual event itself. This recognition points to the fluidity of time and space and highlights the profound impact our consciousness has on how we experience the world in and around us.

The Holomovement

As thinking, evolving beings, we face an imminent leap in our views of reality with the findings of cutting-edge sciences. Einstein's theory of relativity links time and space together as a continuum called the space-time continuum, meaning they are inextricably interconnected. It takes a certain amount of time to go from California to Hawaii, for example. That time is less for a beam of light than for a cruise ship, but nevertheless the space, or distance, covered takes time to cross. Life as we know it exists in time and space simultaneously, and because time and space function as a continuum, they affect one another.

Beautifully explained in Michael Talbot's book *The Holographic Universe*, the continuum idea, as expanded on by physicist David Bohm, suggests that everything in the universe is connected and part of a greater continuum. He views the universe as a hologram, a multidimensional structure in which everything is seamlessly connected. "Dividing reality up into parts and then naming those parts is always arbitrary, a product of convention, because subatomic particles, and everything else in the universe, are no more separate from one another than different patterns in an ornate carpet."[18] This is a very different framework than the one depicted by the Newtonian-Cartesian mechanistic model we are used to. And it has very significant ramifications for what is possible and what our part is in all of it. Because everything is connected, we affect and are affected by everything, wittingly or not.

A holograph is a three-dimensional picture in which every piece of the image contains the complete picture. Every part contains and reflects the whole within it. (An example of the holographic nature of life applied scientifically is asexual reproduction, or cloning. Every cell in an organism has the necessary DNA to replicate the whole organism, given the right conditions.) In Bohm's version, the holographic universe moves, evolves, and is in constant flux. He dubs it a *holomovement* to indicate the dynamic nature of the continually creating universe. According to quantum physics and the holomovement model, we are part and parcel to everything, and therefore, our very presence affects outcomes.

The holomovement is given credence by the quantum theory of nonlocality, meaning effects at a distance. A photon split and separated by miles still acts as if it is the same, singular particle. In this experiment, both parts of the electron reacted equally and simultaneously to stimulus applied to just one of them. In some unquantifiable way, they remain connected. Scientists deduce from the experiment that matter at the quantum level, even when separated by space, is still connected. This effect is referred to as *entanglement.*

As Gregg Braden explains in his brilliant documentary series, *Missing Links,*[19] before the big bang, all matter in the universe was condensed to the size of a pea. After the big bang, matter spread out in all directions and keeps spreading. And yet, no matter how far and wide the original matter of the universe spreads, it remains energetically connected. Physicist John Wheeler, a contemporary of Einstein's, believes that, "we are not simply bystanders on a cosmic stage; we are shapers and creators living in a participatory universe."[20] In this paradigm, everything we do has relevance.

---

[18] Michael Talbot, *The Holographic Universe* (New York: HarperCollins, 1991).

[19] "Missing Links" with Gregg Braden (Gaia TV, 2016) www.gaia.com.

[20] Discover: Science for The Curious, *Does the Universe Exist If We're Not Looking?* (June, 2002); accessed August 11, 2019. http://discovermagazine.com/2002/jun/featuniverse#.UvxOUrTVdnA

We belong to everything and, thus, affect the world by what we do and the energies we generate. When we see life and the world as one inseparable whole, our approach to problem solving changes dramatically. We begin to look at the long-range effects of our actions.

Most of us realize that we are affected by people and situations. That we also directly affect our circumstances and those around us may be a less familiar notion. However, every salesperson, motivational speaker, and charismatic leader uses the potential to influence people intentionally. In fact, we all affect one another, whether we know it or not. We *can't not* affect situations in which we are participants. The attitude we bring to any circumstance has a significant effect on our perceptions and experience, as we have seen with the embodiment practice. It points to the fact that our consciousness—our feeling state, beliefs, and expectations about a specific situation—affect the outcome, meaning how it plays out. We are integral to the holomovement. There is no separation.

Science, Mysticism, and Presence

We are the beneficiaries of the marriage of science and mysticism—a joining worthy of our celebration. It's outgrowth, characteristics like coherent states and entanglement, are harbingers of a new era. Both mysticism and now science subscribe to the interconnectedness of all things as the basis of reality. Our *presence* allows us to tap into that reality. True presence comes when we drop down into ourselves. From there, we can open and expand our awareness and affect our experiences. We can create real change. The inward journey is the path to full presence on the physical plane, as well as to our transmutation of it and transcendence beyond it. It is the route that connects us directly to source. Going inward to connect to source can be ecstatic as well as humbling. Either way, we are empowered.

Presence signifies that we are self-aware and openhearted, while at the same time solidly tethered here at home, in our bodies on planet Earth. The strength of our bond to our inner landscape and the physical plane determine how far we can expand beyond our own personal and collective stories. The inward journey also holds the map to our higher self, thus facilitating our capacity to transcend the small self. Freedom from the past connotes our transmigration into the present and to presence. Such change is possible when we have a solid connection with ourselves and when we're grounded in our physical form.

We can increase our self-connection with awareness of our internal coordinates, the *coordinates of presence*. This simply means to go inward and to notice and name what you find there in terms of your physical sensations, the emotions you're feeling and the quality of life seeking expression in you. When we know our coordinates, we are grounded in our body-heart-mind. We are aware from the inside out and, therefore, have access to our strengths and abilities because we are connected with the wholeness of ourselves.

To be grounded and self-connected via our internal coordinates is another way to say that we are in alignment with ourselves. Like a tree, the deeper our roots grow, the higher and broader we can reach while maintaining stability. Our internal coordinates of presence give us this equilibrium, like having ballast that comes along with us wherever we go.

Vulnerability: The Birthplace of Joy

To grow and expand beyond our current state can feel risky, however. With the sense of risk, courage is needed, and courage is more readily available when we are rooted in self-connection. With self-connection, we stand steady and centered while also remaining flexible. This is called resilience. Resilience fosters trust in ourselves to dance with *what is*, even when the next step is unknown.

In fact, to take the risk to go beyond the known and familiar requires our willingness to *not know* the outcome and to *not be* in control. We know this feeling as vulnerability. To feel vulnerable is a typically unappealing state for most people. Most of us do whatever it takes to *not feel* vulnerable. And yet, as social scientist Brené Brown points out, "Vulnerability is the birthplace of joy, love, connection, and creativity."[21] To step into vulnerability, as it turns out, is one of the greatest signs of inner strength. Even so, it is taboo for many of us to express our softer sides. It can be a stretch to live unguarded and transparent. The rewards are truly grand, however, and bring us most of what we truly want from life—connection, love, meaning—all that really matters in the end. The qualities of life that are most precious and fulfilling rely on our tenderness. They speak to our deeply embedded preference to not go it alone but to belong, and our inborn need to be seen and known by others. The coordinates

---

[21] Brené Brown, "The Power of Vulnerability," filmed June 2019 in Houston, TX, TEDx video https://speakola.com/ideas/brene-brown-vulnerability-ted-2011.

of presence give us a simple way to share ourselves openly with others so that we may be known.

The next step on our journey is to learn the specific method for self-connection called the coordinates of presence. It includes knowing your feelings, both physical and emotional, and involves naming qualities from the spectrum of love. This level of self-connection gives us the flexibility we need to meet daily challenges with equanimity. When you can readily come back to your center, you gain resilience and the ability to show up as you'd like to. To then embody a coherent state catalyzes connection with our higher self, as well as with those around us.

This method is a practical application of the new physics to your life. It could be considered your secret code to universal resourcefulness. The practice catalyzes alignment with yourself and taps you into the beneficial energetics of a coherent state. Coherency is the vibration of connection. When in a coherent state we pulse in resonance with the field of possibility. Embodied coherence is how our intentionality becomes creativity. The practice engages deep self-connection and opens your awareness to the whole of the situation almost holographically. You may find that time seems to slow down when you're in a coherent state or that you can sense what's happening for another person or what could happen depending upon your chosen response. This is deep intuition, accessible when we tap into the field through a coherent state. This is an invaluable practice to learn. Its versatility will become more apparent as we continue through the handbook.

Explore this Practice: The Coordinates of Presence

Overview

Your internal coordinates are your physical sensations, emotional state, and the universal quality of life that is either being experienced or longing to be expressed. They map where you are inside yourself at a given moment in time and space and offer a direct avenue to the ground of your own being. This information functions as your internal ballast, keeping you rooted in the present moment through self-connection. Self-awareness empowers you to make conscious choices from the state of presence. With practice, this state allows you to access your strengths, intentionality, and empathy and to communicate your feelings and needs clearly—all fundamental to successful relationships and most endeavors.

The steps to this practice are like nesting baskets; each step takes you to the next layer of awareness. As the steps become more fluid, you will be able to come into self-connection and coherency on the fly. For practice, use situations that have already happened. Later you will be able to do this in real time.

To start

Sit quietly and follow your breath. Focus your attention inside with your inhale and relax on the exhale. Think of a recent situation or conversation you had that sticks in your mind. Choose one that did not turn out as you would have liked or left you feeling unsettled in some way. You may use the first situation that comes to mind or find another that you want to work with. Take a minute to choose one. Use your journal to write down your findings as you go, if you wish.

1. *Breathe and take your focus inside.* Sit quietly and follow your breath for a few minutes. Focus your awareness inside. In your mind, put yourself in the situation you chose to practice with, as if it were happening now. Let your memory bring the experience you had then into this moment. Feel it as if it were happening now.

2. *Notice and name your physical sensations.* For example, you may feel uncomfortable sensations of tightness or constriction in your gut, legs, or jaw. With your attention inside your body, name what you become aware of—the physical sensations inside. Stay with your breath, focusing your attention inside, while remembering the scenario you chose until you sense your bodily sensations.

3. *As you focus your attention on your bodily sensations, notice the emotion that shows up along with your physical sensations.* Keep breathing and drop further into the experience that left you unsettled as you're remembering it. For example, if you feel tight or constricted in your chest, shoulders, or jaw, it might reveal anxiety, anger, or frustration. If you feel tightness in your belly, chest, or heart center, you may be feeling sadness, regret, or disappointment. Name the emotion(s) you are feeling.

   Your emotion is a facet of your current state of being. It expresses the fulfillment or lack of fulfillment of the experience—the quality of life—you desired in that moment (the situation from your memory, as if it is happening now). For example, if you feel sad or mad, something you wished to experience was unfulfilled. In situations where you feel warm, relaxed, and expansive, it might reveal happiness, contentment, or gratitude. In such cases, what you wished to experience was fulfilled. In this process, you may notice your emotion even before you become aware of your physical sensations. In that case, simply reverse the order of exploring both emotional and physical awareness.

4. *What is the experience you are wanting to have? Name it.* Your sensations and emotions point to your desired experience. It can be named by a universal quality of life in the spectrum of love. For example, if you are feeling frustrated, perhaps you wanted to be heard and understood and were not. In a situation in which you are feeling content, perhaps you wanted understanding and connection with a family member, and it happened. In a situation in which you are feeling sad or disappointed, perhaps you made a presentation at work that wasn't received as you'd wanted it to be. You didn't get the sense of competence and recognition you'd hoped for. Name the universal quality of life, the experience you are longing for that went unfulfilled in this situation.

5. *Embody the quality of life you desire to experience.* Once you have charted your internal coordinates, increase self-connection and personal empowerment by including the embodiment practice from chapter 3, "Embodying Universal Qualities of Life in the Spectrum of Love." Breathe the living energy of your chosen quality of life into yourself and let it fill you from the inside out. If helpful, recall a time when you did experience that state, name the quality being expressed, then embody it and release the memory. Take as much time as you need and want in the embodied state.

Once embodied, your awareness will shift from contraction to expansion. Your emotions will also shift from uncomfortable to pleasant. In the embodied state of coherence, you will have access to a broader awareness of yourself in a wider, perhaps even transcendent, context. From your embodied state, view the situation you worked with. Let yourself "see" the steps that would bring that state into being in your remembered scenario.

Notice that, from this perspective, you might also "get" how your choices affect the other people involved. An embodied, coherent state can tap us into deep intuition. Intuition in this sense is simply connecting with the holomovement in an intentional way and allowing ourselves to receive information about the situation from a broader perspective. Because getting information in this way is non-linear, we experience it as "intuitive."

**Your Internal Coordinates of
Presence for Self-Connection**

1. *Look inside.* Breathe. Notice physical sensations. Breathe into tight places.
2. *Ask.* What am I feeling? Listen for your body's reply. Name your physical sensations and emotions as you become aware of them.
3. *Discover the universal quality of life up and mattering to you in the moment.* It is connected to your feelings. The emotion tells you whether the quality of life you desire is being experienced (fulfilled) or not being experienced (unfulfilled) as you would like. Name the universal quality of life your feelings point to.
4. *Embody the quality of life you want to experience.* Slow your breath, focus on your heart while feeling filled-up with the quality you wish to experience. Use your sense of holographic awareness, or expanded presence, to gain clarity about how you want to proceed.

Practice finding your internal coordinates in as many situations as possible throughout the day. The more familiar you become with finding your coordinates, the easier it will be to stay grounded, centered, and present. Practice gathering your coordinates at every opportunity to become facile with self-connection, which brings the flexibility and resilience needed to meet almost any situation. This is a way to vibrate in alignment with yourself—the starting point for presence in everything and anything that comes next. As your self-connection increases, your self-trust, clarity, and empowerment will too. As we move further into the handbook, this practice will help facilitate clear, authentic communication with yourself and others.

Courage and Vulnerability

The greatest benefits of the inward journey come by way of our vulnerability, in other words, by sharing ourselves transparently. I sometimes translate the term vulnerability to *transparency* or openhearted honesty. The idea of being vulnerable can be challenging. For some people, vulnerability implies being at the mercy of external forces. In most cases, we think of vulnerability as sharing or revealing something about ourselves when we are uncertain about how we will be received, fearing rejection or even retaliation. But when we step into courage and openly share something tender about ourselves and trust that we can navigate the consequences, we are no longer at the effect of outside forces. In that case, vulnerability can more accurately be defined as authenticity. In an empowered state, to be vulnerable is to be *transparently authentic.* In any case, we are empowered, knowing that it is our choice when it comes to revealing our inner states to others.

In my early days of practicing Nonviolent Communication, I squirmed inside at the prospect of leading with my true feelings in personal conversations. I had spent my life up until then guarding my heart. The vulnerability of revealing myself to others was a stretch beyond my comfort zone. That's when it occurred to me that my personal comfort isn't the only criterion for deciding how to show up. To prioritize connection, I would necessarily need the courage to be open and honest, to be willing to be seen and known. I discovered that I was received with respect and care when I shared myself transparently. With self-connection and self-compassion in place, we have the resilience and resourcefulness to communicate authentically and transparently with others, and to do so with kindness.

Due to our core need to belong, we may well feel vulnerable in sharing ourselves transparently with others, fearing we may not be received as we'd like. The degree to which we are self-accepting is directly proportional to our willingness to share ourselves honestly. Self-acceptance is the foundation of self-confidence after all. With self-confidence comes the courage to be transparent and authentic, to go for the promise of heartfelt connection. It is that promise and the deeper fulfillment it offers us that trumps remaining in our comfort zone. When we show up transparently, or authentic and open, then whoever we're with is much more likely to respond in kind. Our vulnerability invites connection and, with it, the sense of sharing in this human experience together.

CHAPTER FIVE

Gratitude: The Gateway to Abundance

*Gratitude is founded on the deep knowing that our very
existence relies on the gifts of other beings.*
—Robin Kimmer

gratitude; grat·i·tude (gradə,t(y)o͞od) *noun* . . . a feeling of thankful appreciation for favors or benefits received; warm appreciative response to kindness; thankfulness.[22]

I am so curious about gratitude. I notice an immediate and undeniable shift inside when I'm grateful. It doesn't seem to matter what the object of my gratitude is; the effect is the same. I feel expansive, openhearted, content, and present. It's extraordinary. When I remember, I can propel myself out of a bad mood or even a negative judgment by choosing to feel grateful and foregoing my focus on what's upsetting me.

Gratitude turns out to be a highly resourceful state. Our ability to enjoy life increases substantially when we feel grateful. In this sense, gratitude is a viable agent of happiness. To be in gratitude opens us up to feeling peaceful and content and yet vibrantly alive. In fact, gratitude may be our most trustworthy interface with the rest of the cosmos. When we feel grateful, there is no separation. We absolutely know that we matter and belong here because we have recognized and received what has been given. Gratitude is the face of awe, humility, and generosity of spirit all rolled into one. It is receiving life's bounty and reciprocating with heartfelt appreciation. And as Robin

---

[22] *Webster's New World Dictionary, College Edition.* (Cleveland and New York: The World Publishing Company) 1960.

Kimmer notes, "The evolutionary advantage for cultures of gratitude is compelling. This human emotion has adaptive value because it engenders practical outcomes for sustainability."[23] I believe this effect occurs because when we gratefully receive what has been given, we are truly fulfilled. In this way, gratitude dispels greed.

Gratitude is the Root of Happiness

To feel gratitude or appreciation is similar in effect to living in *yes* mode. This means to notice and acknowledge what is working, to see the glass half full, and to appreciate the simplest things in daily life. Gratitude can be felt and expressed for big significant things, such as newborns, job promotions, and graduations, as well as regular things, such as a delicious meal or a beautiful sunset. A sense of wonder arises when we stop to truly savor the beauty and abundance around us. According to the website, happify.com, "The benefits of practicing gratitude are nearly endless. People who regularly practice gratitude—by taking time to notice and reflect upon the things they're thankful for—experience more positive emotions, feel more alive, sleep better, express more compassion and kindness, and even have stronger immune systems."

Research by UC Davis psychologist Robert Emmons, author of *Thanks! How the New Science of Gratitude Can Make You Happier*, shows that simply keeping a gratitude journal—regularly writing brief reflections on moments for which we're thankful—can measurably increase well-being and life satisfaction. To be grateful catalyzes happiness with ourselves and appreciation for what we have. We effectively abolish lack and live with equanimity when we live in gratitude. The heart opens like a flower warmed in the sun when we receive what has been given as an unbidden gift.

In short, gratitude is a clear sign of personal health and well-being. When we embody gratitude on a daily basis, we create a foundation of agreeability inside as we navigate the ups and downs of our lives. As Brother David Steindl-Rast explains, "It is not happiness that makes us grateful. It is gratefulness that makes us happy. Every moment is a gift. There is no certainty that you will have another moment, with all the opportunity that it contains."[24] The coherent state of gratitude is fulfilling and energizes us to live with an open heart and generosity of spirit.

---

23   Robin Kimmer, "Returning the Gift." *Minding Nature*: Spring 2014, Vol 7, #2.

24   HH the Dalia Lama and Desmond Tutu with Douglas Abrams, *The Book of Joy* (New York: Random House, 2016).

Everything has Already Been Given

Indigenous peoples have ceremonies and rituals in praise for all that is constantly being given—for life itself. One of modern Western culture's biggest losses is that we take so much for granted. Consumerism teaches us to expect so much more than we need, and as a result, we often feel the angst of lack. Yet we have been given life itself and the Earth to support our life; in that sense, everything has already been given. However, it is only when we recognize and appreciate what has been given that we can fully receive it. Gratitude is the intermediary by which we can receive what we need from Earth's bounty, as well as from one another. As such, it is the medium by which we know satisfaction and fullness. It also helps us to open our hearts, and thus, to see through difficulties with more equanimity.

In their *Book of Joy*, His Holiness the Dalia Lama and Desmond Tutu point to the words of Brother David Steindl-Rast, who reminds us, "The gift within every moment is the opportunity it offers us. Most often it is the opportunity to enjoy it, but sometimes a difficult gift is given to us and that can be an opportunity to rise to the challenge."[25] His words speak to the fullness of life when we accept *what is.* With acceptance, we can truly drop into recognizing the gifts within difficult moments. Certainly, there is something we can receive from such challenges. The opportunity is there to grow into more flexibility and openheartedness and, thus, to glean even more from life and to expand into greater resilience. The more grateful we are, the fuller we become and, consequently, the more we have to give.

The practice of gratitude guides us directly to happiness and contentment. But when we feel down or depressed, it can be hard to find gratitude for even the smallest things. Another intrinsic human need is to give to others—to contribute to another's well-being or to a cause. To give of ourselves is fulfilling. It completes the circle of life and lets us know that we matter, bringing us a sense of meaning and purpose. For example, to volunteer can increase your health and well-being by fulfilling the deep human need to be useful and, thus, to matter. When you're feeling down, look into helping someone in need. Do it simply because it feels good. Let the benefits to others be secondary to your own enjoyment of giving your time and energy to someone in need or a cause that you care about.

---

[25] Dalia Lama and Tutu with Abrams.

Gratitude and Abundance

When we are lost in our personal trials and tribulations, we can neglect the big picture, the beauty inside and around us. But when we look up from our problems and take a deep breath, the gift of life becomes accessible. The life force energy, by whatever name you call it, keeps filling us up and making itself available to us. When I stop and remember it this way, I feel so much gratitude. I feel honored to have this opportunity use my life purposefully, to live passionately, to be creative, or simply to have fun with close friends. Goodness and abundance overflow into our own and others' lives with the simple practice of remembrance.

Author and Sufi elder Murat Yagan gave his students a practice to increase abundance. It is simply this: *Be grateful for what you have and be open to receiving more.* It is fascinating that gratitude, in fact, is what encourages us to remain open and to be receptive to abundance.[26]

Gratitude offers grounding and brings us directly into the present moment. For that reason, I consider embodying gratitude to be one of the most potent practices available. It brings expansion and joy into our hearts. The practice of gratitude will always serve the highest good. It brings opportunities to offer the gifts we have to give and to receive abundantly as well.

Anatomy of a Prayer

Energy does not distinguish between "good and bad." Energy simply *is*. Energy in the form of waves *is* our life force, *is* consciousness, *is* love, and *is not* separate from us. We are creator-magicians, in large part blindly wielding the life force unbeknownst to ourselves. Our thoughts and emotions are constantly creating our experiences, simply because there is only one fabric of life. And we are cut from that singular cloth—the ornate carpet of the universal life force. We *are* it.

Because we are it, life force energy follows our thoughts, the focused energy of our consciousness. Therefore, how we employ our thoughts has much to do with how our experiences unfold. For example, if I spend time ruminating on what I *don't want* to have happen, more than likely, that is exactly what *will* happen. This is because energy follows thought and *does not distinguish* between a "good" thought and a "bad" one

---

[26] Murat Yagan, *The Teachings of Kebzeh—Essentials of Sufism from the Caucasus Mountains* (Vernon, BC: Kebzeh Publications, 1995).

or "don't want" from "do want." Our body-heart-mind responds to ideas, thoughts, and images with *feelings*. It is the strength of our feelings about those thoughts and images that engages creativity. Emotions, then, are the conduit for manifestation. Creativity, as the life force, doesn't discern whether we like or dislike those images and our feelings regarding them. The energetic impressions of our emotions, positive or negative, catalyze the creative impulse to go into action and manifest whatever our expectations are, whether we are aware of them or not. Knowing this, it becomes all the more pertinent to set conscious intentions.

For example, if I am afraid that I won't get the job promotion I want, then I am, in effect, writing that story and imprinting it in my nervous system, as well as in the field of possibility. The strength of my feelings imprints the thought-energetic into the field. Our emotions, as feeling states, are the fuel for manifesting our thoughts, beliefs, and expectations. When we couple a feeling state with a thought, it expedites those instructions to the cosmic production team. Twentieth century author and philosopher Neville Goddard writes, "Whatever the mind of man can conceive and feel as true, the subconscious can and must objectify. Your feelings create the pattern from which your world is fashioned, and a change of feeling is a change of pattern."[27]

To manifest what we do want, it is necessary to focus on precisely what that is— and *to feel the reality of that experience as if it is already true.* Once the feeling of the experience we want is embodied, we naturally let go of the fear that it won't happen. Because we have already created the internal experience of it having happened, that reality is encoded in our body-heart-mind, as well as the surrounding field. Since there is no separation between our creativity and the cosmic production team, the imprint is relayed via the field and set in motion with seamless precision. Neville Goddard speaks to this phenomenon: "Dare to believe in the reality of your assumption and watch the world play its part relative to its fulfillment."

The eternal now comes into play here. As Einstein said, "The distinction between the past, present and future is only a stubbornly persistent illusion." What we do in the present moment is inextricably linked to the rest of time. To embody the experience we want now is like planting a seed in the field of possibility. It will emerge or, as physicist David Bohm calls it, unfold into the manifest world, when the time is ripe.

The life force is poised to flood through us at the least provocation; creativity is at our fingertips. Once we envision and embody the felt experience of our intention as fully as possible, we can then let it go and let the holomovement (see chapter 4) work

---

[27] Neville Goddard, *Resurrection* (Los Angeles: DeVorss & Co., 1965).

its magic. As physicist John Wheeler, a contemporary of Einstein, suggested, "reality grows out of the act of observation, and thus consciousness itself; it is 'participatory.'"[28] Conscious intention with embodiment is a refined tool and a potent skill that reflects our active participation in creation. Our success with it depends upon complete alignment with ourselves on the subtlest planes. If we harbor even a wisp of resistance or doubt, a clear message of intent will not be sent. Our "prayer" will not be answered.

This may explain why prayer works when it works. People who pray to someone or something beyond themselves oftentimes have complete faith in whatever or whomever that entity is. They trust with their whole body-heart-mind that the beneficent being in whom they have entrusted their prayer is at hand to help them. Without a specter of a doubt in their belief and with the full force of their emotion, their supplication engages the field of which we all are creative participants. Ask—with the full force of your being—and you shall receive. This is why every faith, no matter its origin or kind, comes through for the believer. It is the believer him or herself that makes a belief true. This fact in no way diminishes the truth, beauty, and sacredness of any belief system. All beliefs are true and sacred for the believer, the one to whom it truly matters.

Gratitude shines brightly in those with faith. We can attribute life's bounty to any aspect of our existence, but the common thread that runs through prayer is the recognition that we are dependent upon a great and mysterious *something*. When we acknowledge it as sacred, humility begets our gratitude. In this same way, the embodiment practice offers us the opportunity to manifest our intentions. Gratitude is a powerful way to work with embodiment and to experience life as we most want it to be. Another beautiful aspect of gratitude is to express it to others.

Expressing Gratitude and Appreciation

To express gratitude is a gift in itself. Gratitude and appreciation go a long way to support relationships of all kinds to thrive. It feels good to express appreciation and gratitude. They are cohesive states and increase our feelings of happiness. We experience openheartedness when we are grateful and express it.

We can invite openheartedness between us by sharing our appreciation for how someone affected us, telling the person how what he or she did made our life more

---

28   Scientific American, April 14, 2008. https://www.scientificamerican.com/article/pioneering-physicist-john-wheeler-dies/

wonderful. In that way, we are willing participants in life, openly affecting and being affected by others. At first, it can feel awkward to share ourselves with openhearted honesty. We can feel vulnerable to actually tell someone that we were affected in a yummy way by what they did. That is part of the gift. I give you my true feelings, the experience as it lives in me right now about how you enriched my life. To do so, I look within, feel what's alive inside, and speak openheartedly. Our internal coordinates are perfectly suited to be that gift to someone.

It is very simple to share ourselves transparently using our feelings and the qualities of life serving us as our reference points. For example, if my husband cleans the stove and puts the dirty dishes in the dishwasher while I'm at work, I appreciate it. I may simply tell him, "Thanks so much for cleaning up the kitchen this afternoon. I really appreciate it." In this situation, saying this much may be plenty. He gets that it helped me, that it made my day easier. Or I could add more specifics and include my internal coordinates—my feelings and qualities of life being served. For example, "Wow, honey, when I walked in the door and saw how clean the kitchen was, I felt happy and relieved. I feel so much lighter knowing it will be easier to get dinner going now. Thank you so much!" This is a gift of gratitude and appreciation that cannot be missed. It lets him know exactly how what he did served me. Speaking my gratitude lands as a gift to him.

If my daughter makes a point to come over on Mother's Day, make brunch, and go for a walk with me, I appreciate it. I could say to her, "You're sweet to come over and make brunch. Thank you." It's nice to hear, but it's still an assessment of her by me ("you're sweet"), not a gift to her of how what she did benefitted me. Whereas, if I said something like, "I really appreciate the efforts you made to make Mother's Day so fun. The quiche was delicious. I loved it. And I really enjoyed our walk, chatting and catching up. I'm really grateful for you in my life!" This gets the point across in no uncertain terms. I give more of myself to her so that my gratitude lands as a thank you gift. This way, she knows exactly how I received what she gave to me. My expression of gratitude completes the circle.

Let's look at how to go about giving the gift of appreciation and gratitude.

Explore this Practice: Embodying and Expressing Gratitude

1. Embodying gratitude meditation

Look inwardly or around you to notice something you appreciate or that you are grateful for. Choose something specific, and as you focus on it, let yourself embody the feeling of gratitude. Breathe it in. Let it fill you up. Take a few minutes to rest in the state of gratitude and allow it to permeate your whole being. If tears come up, allow them to flow freely and continue to be infused with the feeling of gratitude. Tears are often a sign of dropping in, of surrendering into the beauty of the moment, or of letting go of holding a constriction around your heart. Welcome the tears as a sign of opening to your feelings and expanding your heart. When you are complete, take a moment of thankfulness that you gave yourself this gift. If you'd like, do this meditation daily.

2. Expressing gratitude to others

The more you choose gratitude, the more aware you will become of what you are grateful for. To offer appreciation or to express gratitude to others has the effect of opening our hearts and increasing connection and gives us an overall sense of well-being. As in the examples above, use your internal experience of your feelings and the qualities of life being served when you express your gratitude. This will let the other person know just what you received from them and how it affected you. To know you received their gift is your gift to them.

- *Name what happened that you are grateful for.* For example: I appreciate that you emptied the wastebaskets and took out the trash and recycling today.
- *Name what you feel about it and what qualities of life were served when it happened.* For example: I feel more relaxed knowing it's done; it's one less thing to think about now, so it will be easier to focus on getting ready to leave for the trip tomorrow.
- *Make eye contact to see if the person you're expressing gratitude to heard and received it or make a request to hear how it landed for him or her.* For example: Will you please tell me how that is to hear? By making eye contact while verbalizing your appreciation, you can usually sense if the person heard and received it or not. If you cannot tell, then make a request to find out.

To Receive Is As Important As to Give

There is no doubt that we want to give to others. We get a sense of meaning and purpose, as well as connection and belonging, when we give of ourselves, when we contribute to others' well-being. Conversely, it is just as important to be able to receive what is being offered to us. A gift has little to no meaning if it is not received. We cannot experience abundance if we do not receive what is offered and what has already been given. The circle of giving is made complete by receiving. When we don't really take in or acknowledge what we have received, we are not able to open to receive more. We are left feeling empty, rather than full.

To make clear requests for what we want or need also depends upon our ability to receive. For example, if one person in a relationship is, in general, a "giver" and the other a "receiver," there will be an imbalance in the relationship. Eventually, the dynamic could unravel into resentment and disconnection. Both people must be able to give *and* to receive for balance and harmony in the relationship. Both people must include themselves *and* the other with equal care and consideration for the relationship to thrive. To receive, our hearts must be open. Curiously, to receive we also must be able to let go of control. We have to trust ourselves to open and receive what is being offered.

In much of North American culture, self-sufficiency is highly valued. We consistently hear apologies to one another for needing or asking for something. There is an unspoken code that we should not "put anyone out." The fact that we are completely interdependent in nearly every way somehow escapes our awareness! Therefore, to make clear requests can take some practice. It may be foreign and feel vulnerable to do so. And yet, to ask and to receive increases connection and feeds the understanding that we're not alone.

The ability to receive begins with self-connection, with knowing ourselves well. This begets trust and self-confidence. When we know and trust ourselves, we know what we need to thrive and are more inclined to ask for it. A certain amount of courage is required to be able to make clear requests. An open heart comes into play too, to receive what we need or want when it arrives and, if what we've asked for doesn't show up, to accept no. Many people don't ask for what they want because they are afraid to hear a no. However, your chances for getting what you need and want are exponentially higher if you ask for it.

If you hear no to your request, remember that it is a yes to something else important to that person right then. When we have self-acceptance, a no won't send us spinning into the debilitating underworld of shame and unworthiness. With an objective perspective, it's clear that the no is about the other person and his or her priorities, not about you. Acceptance allows us to find the yes for them in their no to us, to keep our hearts open, and to more adequately discern how to respond in the moment. With acceptance, more options are available. Until we accept ourselves just as we are, it can be a challenge to receive what we need, to take actions to attend to our needs, or to make requests of others to meet our needs. To accept and appreciate ourselves and to feel gratitude for what we have is the foundation for opening ourselves to make clear requests and to receive even more.

Explore this Practice: Self-Gratitude

Think of one thing about yourself that you are grateful for. Take a few minutes to feel and to embody gratitude for this part of yourself. For example, I sometimes simply hold gratitude for my heart beating inside my chest or for my lungs and breath bringing life to all my cells and for all my organs doing their job with great intelligence and precision, without my conscious awareness.

Think of what you like and appreciate about any area of your life. Even take time to appreciate your idiosyncrasies. For example, you may like to keep your desk very clean and tidy. Clean, clear spaces may matter to you. Take time to feel appreciation about yourself for this quality you like to serve and that serves you. Or you may enjoy leaving things in a heap on the floor of your bedroom because it gives you a sense of freedom and ease. Take time to appreciate your love of freedom and ease and how these qualities serve you.

There are many ways to drop into the state of gratitude and appreciation. The point is to do it on a daily basis for both large and small things, for others and for yourself. As you live with more and more gratitude, you will live in greater abundance because you will be more aware of receiving. And through having the openheartedness to receive, you will give others the opportunity to give to you!

Gratitude in Nature

The natural world with all its wildness is dear to my heart. There are few words that can describe the soul-nourishing experience of being in the expanse of the wilderness. The famous naturalist, John Muir, knew well that, "In every walk with nature one receives far more that he seeks." People from all walks of life seem to resonate deeply with the beauty of the natural world. When we spend time in nature, we receive an intimacy with ourselves that soothes the soul and calms the mind. It drops us into connection with all-that-is in a profoundly simple, yet inspired way. Beauty itself feeds and nourishes us, bringing coherence into our oftentimes chaotic lives.

To simply breathe the sweet air can invigorate us walking in the woods, taking in the sea or sitting by a mountain lake. Immersion in nature connects us experientially to where we come from and what we are made of, simplifying our thoughts and quieting our minds. We are the elements of the Earth. We are composed of water, earth, air and fire—the spark of life. As Vietnamese Buddhist monk, Thich Nhat Hanh tells us, "The Earth is not just the environment we live in. We are the Earth and we are always carrying her with us."[29] With this understanding, our relationship with the Earth can change.

When we let ourselves remember and be touched by the beauty of nature, we are drawn into gratitude. Gratitude for the natural world inspires connection with ourselves and with it, care for the environment. The Earth truly is our mother, as many indigenous cultures refer to her. She gives us life and continuously supports life. Thich Nhat Hanh says it another way: "If you look deeply and feel this connection to the Earth, you will also begin to feel admiration, love and respect. When you realize the Earth is so much more than simply the environment, you will be moved to protect her as you would yourself. There is no difference between you and her. In that kind of communion, you no longer feel alienated."[30]

When we appreciate nature, we open to receive Earth's unflinching bounty and revel in her beauty. It taps us into gratitude for life. As John Muir tells us, "The clearest way into the Universe is through a forest wilderness." Connection with the Earth facilitates awareness of beauty as sacred. It reminds us of who we are down deep and what truly matters. To drop into ourselves and down to earth frees us to expand into realms beyond what we've known. It brings us face to face with the wild, where creativity dwells. We are left knowing the sacredness of life in all its miraculous forms and ourselves as an integral part of it all. As Henry David Thoreau (1817-1862) reminds us, "In Wildness is the preservation of the world."

---

[29]   Thich Nhat Hanh, *Love Letter to the Earth,* p 8. (Berkeley: Parallax Press, 2013).
[30]   Hanh, p. 14.

PART TWO

The Way Through

Our duty, as men and women, is to proceed as if limits to our ability did not exist. We are collaborators in creation.

—Pierre Teilhard de Chardin

CHAPTER SIX

The Hidden Heart of Judgment

We shall require a substantially new manner of thinking if mankind is to survive.
—Albert Einstein

Although he was an avowed pacifist, Albert Einstein's brilliance inadvertently led to the development of the atomic bomb. His famous equation, E=mc2, proves that matter is a form of highly concentrated energy (E). When the mass (m) of any object is multiplied by the speed of light (c)—186,000 miles per second and understood to be a universal constant—and then squared, the untold power held inside the atom is made evident. Einstein did not immediately realize the imminent danger inherent in his discovery that matter is another form of energy. When his colleagues told him of the possibility of a nuclear chain reaction, he was shocked. Recognizing that Hitler could develop a bomb and at his colleagues' prompting, however, he encouraged President Franklin Delano Roosevelt to fund research to develop the atomic bomb first. But he was aghast and humiliated to be associated with the destructive power unleashed by the atomic bombs dropped on Japan in 1945. His supplications to the US government to abolish war and ban the production of atomic weapons were to no avail. For Einstein, Gandhi was the political genius worth emulating.

Friend or Foe?

Since the existence of nuclear weapons, the combative stance of "us versus them" has posed an ominous threat to the planet. For their survival, our ancestors were obliged to recognize strangers as threatening and necessarily ward off potential marauders. Equally important has been our ability to live and work together for the common good. Differing tribes also gathered for celebrations, to trade goods, and to intermarry. Social evolution is expedited by cross-pollination and learning from one another. The two dichotomous ways of relating to others determine the strong connections between us on the one hand and feed our tendency to see others as enemies on the other.

We reinforce our sense of belonging when we identify with our beliefs, ancestry, or country—in other words, with those who are like us. It also strengthens our sense of belonging when we distinguish ourselves from other groups. This trait shows up vividly in nationalism, as well as in people's intense emotional attachment to a particular sports team's success. In that sense, we need an "enemy," someone who is categorically different, in order to experience the strength of the bonds within our particular group. The high degree of belonging we feel when we're united against the opposition brings a biological sense of safety, as well as purpose. But as Einstein was so well aware, we no longer have the luxury to imagine that our safety lies in seeing others as enemies. The polarity inherent in our ancestral wiring pinpoints the gravity of the circumstances we now face. To have a caveman's brain hovering over the technological ability to destroy ourselves in the guise of "other" is our conundrum. We are in a pickle.

Beyond Us versus Them

In a world so obviously interconnected and interdependent, doesn't it seem superfluous to take sides? We can be connected with people in any country in the world with the touch of a finger on a tiny screen. Global news networks bring us myriads of difficulties in the lives of other people both near and far. Their suffering, but for the grace of God, could as easily be ours. Our oasis, planet Earth, has never been so small, and everyone on it has never been so close. Truly, it is time to learn how to get along. The way through our global crises depends on it.

We have gleaned how to make peace within ourselves thus far on the inward journey. Now we start the slow turning outward again—but this time, with a whole new way of seeing and being in the world. Rather than cocked like a hair-trigger to take offense at the least provocation, we are primed to hear and see the humanity in others. The way through disconnection and conflict is to focus on our common ground. We consciously choose to implement connection over separation. Miki Kashtan relates, "In a separated world, I can attend to my needs or to your needs, not to both. In a chosen interdependent world, I can embrace both."[31] Now our explorations focus on the psycho-spiritual stretch that embraces both of us and includes our differences.

From this point forward, as leaders of our lives, we necessarily must choose to illuminate our similarities while, at the same time, celebrate our diversity. Our mandate is to prioritize our responses to apparent differences, verbalized as judgments, by naming our commonalities rather than highlighting points of contention. This is when the skills of self-connection and the desire to live from our true values take center stage. This is our coming-out party.

Our Common Ground

Membership in a group can give us a sense of meaning and purpose, as well as belonging. Our Achilles heel, the weakness we have all inherited, is castigating others not of our group, as if their differences are somehow threatening. It's easy to judge people when we feel threatened. Our differences need not be threatening, however. When we make the distinction between people's deeds and the motivation behind their deeds, we have a key to nonviolence.

The universal qualities of life inform our thoughts and actions and name our common ground. They shed light on our shared traits and connect us to the rest of humankind. There can be no enemy when we understand one another's humanity, the qualities that we all share and that incite our daily life decisions. Fortunately, they are hiding in plain sight. We can find them at the core of every judgment. When we comprehend the common values that feed our beliefs and motivate our actions, a new level of appreciation for our shared humanity rushes in. Judgment disperses. Acceptance and inclusivity naturally emerge to define a whole new template for interacting. Universal qualities of life become our method for assessing how to respond, replacing the right-wrong metric that feeds moralistic judgment.

---

[31]   Kashtan, *The Little Book of Courageous Living.* (Oakland: Fearless Heart Publications, 2013).

The simple yet powerful practice of finding the living quality of life at the heart of a judgment dissolves enemy images and transforms the punishment-reward paradigm. A side effect of this practice is clarity and compassion. It empowers us to cut through the tangled threads of our default thinking patterns and learned tendencies. In the moment that we move through a judgment and into understanding, we lay the foundation for a new way of being together. We are purposefully choosing connection over separation. It is that simple, while at the same time, not necessarily easy. This small yet significant action changes the dominant paradigm. In the next practice, we will explore our judgments to find the heart of life beating there, longing to be seen and understood.

The Hidden Gold

The practices in part one, "The Compassionate Observer," "Inviting the Self-Critic to Tea," "Embodying Universal Qualities of Life in the Spectrum of Love," and "The Coordinates of Presence," together lay the foundation for transforming judgments into their life-serving components. For most of us, judgments arise spontaneously and consistently throughout the day. When we notice them, we might even double-dip by judging ourselves for being judgmental. We end up in a vicious cycle we can only escape by accepting *what is* with kindness and compassion. The freedom we seek from our internalized critic comes by transforming our own judgments.

As with all true change, we must first recognize and accept our inner state as it is. Having accepted what's so, we can look deeper to get a better sense of what the judgment is really about. We tend to be judgmental about things that matter to us the most. When what we value isn't honored or what we need is placed out of reach, we tend to feel hurt or angry and readily shut down our hearts. We are inclined to demand what we want and ignore the effect demand energy has on other people and the environment. In some instances, people may even become aggressive. Demand and aggression are familiar tactics of the dominant system. They are misguided strategies for attempting to get needs met. The other side of aggression is submission, the scenario in which someone wins, and someone loses.

We don't often see a whole lot of room for dialogue or discussion in conflicts and disagreements. We don't have many models for working things out so that everyone involved, including the Earth, is taken into consideration. But we lose any sense of adventure or enjoyment in life when we turn friends and family into adversaries or the Earth herself into a grab bag. To turn the habit of separation around, we simply connect with the qualities we value and put them into practice. This frees us from the stranglehold that the scarcity model lords over us and our psyches.

If we view the habit of closing down our hearts as a form of violence to ourselves and any words that ensue from that as violence to others, then how to live peaceably becomes a significant endeavor. Marshall Rosenberg calls violence, "A tragic expression of unmet needs." The unmet need is couched in the judgment that arises from our contracted heart. For most of us, contraction is our learned response to disagreement or painful interactions. The practice of finding the gold at the heart of a judgment unveils our common ground—the quality of life (in Marshall Rosenberg's NVC lingo, the need) within the judgment. That is the gold we are seeking.

By investigating our judgments, we can connect with our own values, the qualities of life that motivate our actions. This opens the door to understanding and connection with others. Once we become facile at getting to the heart of a judgment, the path to equanimity becomes smoothed and worn. We humanize ourselves, as well as others, in our own eyes. I have deep gratitude for my mentor, Robert Gonzales, for sharing this practice and for the benefits it has brought numerous people.[32]

Explore this Practice: Getting to the Heart of Judgment

Intention

To see through judgment to the heart of the human being there, to transform judgments into their life-serving components in order to live more vibrantly, and to support mutual understanding.

Overview

In many ways, we have internalized habits that pit us against one another. For example, we learn to judge those who are different and to demand what we want. These tendencies blind us to our common state of being human, bringing alienation and disconnection into the mix. If we want instead to get along, we need to engender understanding and connection. Transforming judgments supports our desire to get along by recognizing the "me" in the "you."

---

[32]   Robert Gonzales, The Center for Living Compassion, www.living-compasion.org.

Although there is nothing intrinsically wrong with having a judgment, if we close down to another person, then we are living in a defended stance. To engage our full vibrancy, we need to be open to *what is*. Born and raised in the right-wrong mind-set, judgmental thinking comes readily to us, often with a "should" or "shouldn't" attached. "Should" and "shouldn't" are red flags indicating that the moralistic paradigm is in play. Another flag is "deserve language." Watch for thoughts like, *He deserved what he got*. Deserve language, like judgment, rationalizes closing our hearts to someone. It takes us out of our feelings and, thus, away from our humanity. In doing so, we lose access to our inquisitiveness, as well as our resourcefulness.

Once you learn this practice, it can be done anytime, anywhere, in any situation. Initially, set a time to do it as a practice and give yourself enough time to reflect as you go through it step by step. Practice it intentionally as needed. I suggest doing it daily for a week to a month or more and then weekly until it has been integrated as a natural response to life around you. However, choose when and how frequently to do the practice to best serve you.

To begin

Sit quietly and review your day. Focus on an incident in which you judged someone. As you bring it to mind, how do you feel? Do you notice any constriction, either in your thoughts or in your body? We often feel constriction in the physical body first, followed by an emotion, and then a thought that holds the judgment. But the three points of the cycle can come and go in any order. You may notice your judgmental or blaming thought first and then the emotion, followed by the constriction in your body. Or you may feel the emotion first and then sense the constriction in your body and then notice the thought. The important part is to notice, to stop, and to reflect.

In this initial stage, you are calling up a memory to understand the impact judgments have on you. The goal is to be aware the moment a judgment happens. At first, you will probably realize it after the fact. In time, you will catch yourself immediately and intentionally do this practice in the moment. Eventually, it will take just a few moments to come to acceptance and transform the judgment into its component parts and return to self-connection. At that point, it is natural to engage empathy, the subject of the following chapter.

Getting to the heart of a judgment

1. *Choose a judgment* you had recently about yourself or someone else. A judgment often has "should" or "shouldn't," in the wording. Write down the judgment.

   Example: A judgment—She should get a job and start saving money for college.

2. *Describe the situation in neutral language.* In other words, state the situation without the judgment. This is tricky to do at first because our habitual thinking immediately reacts unconsciously by evaluating, which can be a form of judging. When we judge, our focus is outward. The intention here is to go inward, to objectively understand the origins of our judgmental thought.

   Example: Statement of facts in neutral language—Emma is a senior in high school with her sights on college. Her family does not have the financial resources to pay for her college tuition and expenses. If she gets a job while still living at home, I think she could save some money.

3. *Enjoy the "jackal show"* (a term coined by Marshall Rosenberg meaning the critical, blaming, judgmental thinking that plays itself out in our minds). This means to let all the blaming, judgmental, and critical thoughts out to be witnessed. Write them down as they show up. "Shoulds," "shouldn'ts," and deserve language are often part of the jackal show.

   Example: The jackal show—She really should make some money so she can go to college. What is she thinking? She should have figured that out a long time ago and already been saving. Well, if she doesn't work and save money she doesn't deserve to go to college. She should have worked harder to get good grades; she could have gotten a scholarship if she'd spent more time on her homework and less time partying. It's going to be hard on her to have to work to put herself through college. Well, she deserves it because she didn't plan ahead.

   This kind of thinking may sound familiar. Sometimes we can be embarrassed or feel shame about letting these thoughts out. This is another way we've internalized the moralistic paradigm—we judge ourselves as wrong/bad to have judgments or negative thoughts about others. Judgment and blame are not intrinsically bad. But their effects on us include separation and mistrust and the action of divide and conquer—all of which is obviously not useful for creating connection. Because our judgments and jackal thoughts are there, we need to acknowledge them. To name them disempowers them. This is the path to freedom from our judgments and greater choice overall in our responses.

4. *Look for the heart inside the judgment.*

     a.   Translate the jackal show stories into your underlying concerns using your feelings and the qualities of life stimulating your reaction.

Drop out of your head and into your body to translate your jackal statements into your true concerns. Use your compassionate observer self for help and guidance. Include what matters to you, your values as qualities of life, and your feelings about the situation.

Example: *Translated jackal show*—I feel scared that she won't get to live out her dreams. I'm worried she won't have enough money for college. I'm upset that she won't get any scholarships. I wish she didn't have to struggle so hard and that it would be easier for her to get the education she wants. I'm sad for her and wish I could help her out. I'm disappointed that I can't.

     b.   Make two columns, one for "feelings" and the other for "universal qualities of life."

List the emotions (feelings) and the universal qualities of life (values or needs) you find in your translated jackal statements—your true, underlying concerns. This relaxes the contraction as judgment and opens your heart.

Listing the qualities of life within the judgment and the feelings connected to them will bring clarity regarding what's at the heart of your judgment. As you translate the judgment into your concerns, your investigation will show why it matters to you so much. Once you list the qualities of life and emotions from your jackal statements, more jackal show may come up. If it appears, write down more jackal stories. Proceed with translating them into concerns and write down the feelings and qualities of life within those stories too.

Example: Feelings—Scared. Worried. Upset. Concern. Sad. Longing (wish). Disappointed.

Example: Universal qualities of life—Hope (to live out her dreams). Financial resources (enough money). Financial support (scholarships, job). Ease. Education, Learning. Help. Support. Care. Consideration.

Once you've come this far in transforming your judgment, stop, breathe, and check in with yourself. Has the contraction in your body relaxed? Do you sense empathy for yourself, understanding why this matters so much to you? Do you feel open and receptive to the other person? You may conclude the process here or continue with the embodiment practice. If you want to communicate with the person you have judged, it can be quite useful to do the embodiment practice first.

To apply embodiment at this point will increase connection and understanding with yourself and potentially with the other person. It will open your heart and mind to the bigger picture. This is a good review and a practical application of embodiment to interactions and conversations.

5. *Choose the quality(ies) of life that stands out most to you and embody it.*

Example: I chose from; *care* for her and her plight; her need for *ease* and *financial support*; *hope* to live out her dreams; *education, learning; help, support.*

Discern which quality to embody. Review your list of qualities. What lives at the core of your experience with this situation? Find the quality that engages you the most with the person in the situation. One or more of them will stand out for you. (It is possible to embody more than one quality at a time.)

Example: In this case, I sense mine as *care* and *hope.* As I sit breathing in the quality of care and embody it, I find my body relaxes and opens; I feel warmth running through me, and my chest expands. I feel peaceful and energized inside. I feel how much I do care about her and want (hope for) the best for her. My heart opens, and my mind follows with creative ideas.

6. *Request—make a doable request of yourself.* Choose what you want to do. Decide exactly how and when that will happen.

From the place of embodiment (relaxed, expansive) of the quality you chose, bring the original situation or judgment back to mind. Picture yourself in the situation you're using for practice—in my example, that is, Emma wanting to go to college and not having gotten a job to save money to make it happen. From your state of embodiment, what is your spontaneous, internal response?

Example: As I embody the quality of care and remember the situation about Emma wanting to go to college, I feel a well of care and concern rise up for her. I would really like to be able to support her in some way. *I have absolutely no judgment about her situation.* I see it clearly and want the best for her. I wonder what I can do to help.

Respond naturally from the place of embodying what truly matters to you in the situation. Let ideas flow.

Example: As I sit in the state of care, I sense Emma's struggles and imagine talking with her to find out how she is with her situation. I'll ask her if she needs support in figuring out how to make college happen for her. I want to make myself available to her for empathy, understanding, and to look at options. I decide to phone or message her today to find out if she'd like to talk and brainstorm together about ways to support her going to college. I don't have the answer, but I am willing to engage and offer my support to her.

It is both humbling and empowering to recognize the underlying catalyst that brings us to judge others—the life-serving qualities that we value and want to express. But judgment's effect on us is to close off to life as it unfolds within and around us. When we gain clarity about the true concerns at the core of our judgments, awareness opens the door to new possibilities. It helps us to navigate the ins and outs of our edges with others. In the process, we overcome separation and remember what makes us truly human, our need for each other. We can explore our differences with curiosity and compassion for us both. To include apparent disparities rather than to shut down in the face of them urges us into our own evolution. It engages our internal resources and boldness to step into a new arena.

Even though we may long for it, expansion and openheartedness can be a little scary if foreign to our everyday experience. Thus, we take a deliberate, step-by-step approach as we gently open the wings of the heart. In time and with growing awareness, we find more equanimity and can respond kindly rather than react harshly

Getting to the Heart of Judgment

The gist of getting to the heart of judgment is to connect with the quality of life that is alive for you in the situation or person you are judging. This practice reduces internal conflict and constrictions while inviting wise and considered responses to daily challenges. We look to see what is in our heart that provokes us to make a judgment. Why do we care enough to be bothered by this? There is a life-serving motivator inside, the quality of life desiring to be known and attended to. Our body and mind react in judgment with feelings and thoughts, helping to point the way to the valuable nugget at the heart of a judgment.

1. Write down your judgment, just as you hear it in your head.
2. Enjoy the "jackal show." Let the familiar critical, blaming, judgmental thoughts about it come up and out. Write them down.
3. Now write down the situation *objectively* in one or two sentences. Disengage from your judgments, stand back, and look at the situation as if from the outside, using your compassionate observer self. What occurred? What was actually said and done in the circumstance?
4. Translate the jackal show into your concerns about the situation. This will help you with naming the feelings and qualities of life hidden in the jackal stories.
5. Note your emotions associated with the jackal show thoughts. What feelings do you have in response to the jackal thoughts? Write them down.
6. Notice what qualities of life the feelings are pointing to. What really matters to you in this situation? What do you wish was (or wasn't) happening here? Write them down.
7. Fully embody the energetics of the quality of life that matters most to you.
8. Once fully engaged with the living energy of the quality of life, look back on the original situation to see what request of yourself arises. What would you like to do from the place of deep self-connection, of embodiment of the quality that matters most to you in the situation?'

in difficult moments. This skill is infused by our desire to live from a more inclusive and resourceful set of values.

Discernment versus Judgment

Before we go further, let's clarify the difference between judgment and discernment. To *judge* in this context is to think less of someone who says or does something we cannot condone or that we think is *wrong.* To judge, we hold an *external frame of reference*, a belief that determines what the person "should" or "should not" be doing. For many of us, this mental habit thrums in the background like a metronome beating out the rhythm of our life in terms of good-or-bad and right-or-wrong thinking. We open and close our hearts blindly, reacting to the dominant, moralistic system we have internalized. At times we can feel so strongly that we completely shut down our hearts and minds and think of someone as undeserving of any consideration at all. Barely aware of what we are doing, we label and objectify them as they morph into the "enemy."

At the far end of judgment, we can turn a living, breathing, feeling human being into something less than human. When we do so, we are no longer required to "do unto others as we would have them do unto us." We have essentially turned the "other"

> For example, make a request of yourself to take an action. If so, what action? Do you want to request that someone engage with you? If so, how? A phone call? A conversation in person? When will you take the action? Be specific with yourself about what you will do and when and how it will happen.
>
> The more you practice going to the heart of any judgment to find the nugget there (as a quality of life), the more choice you will have to live openheartedly. You will have the foundation to further develop your inner authority. It is our inner authority that grows our personal sovereignty to live beyond the right-wrong paradigm and to expand into greater personal freedom and wholeness. The paradigm shifts right here, every time we transform a judgment into its life-serving components.

into something non-human. But to call another person "an animal" or "savage" is to suffer the loss of our own humanity. Such labeling breeds heinous acts of torture and violence that otherwise would be unthinkable. As perpetrators of violence, we become the monster. At its furthest reaches, judgment can have tragically detrimental consequences, as history shows us well.

However, when we use *discernment* rather than judgment, our hearts remain open. We investigate what is happening in terms of human needs—those core qualities that are the values that guide us. Discernment is an *internal frame of reference* that lets us know whether what's occurring serves life or not. For example, if I am deciding whether to take time to myself for self-care or go to an evening meeting, I use discernment to help me make that choice. I discern what qualities of life I most desire to serve in this instance. When I want to let my daughter know how I am affected when she doesn't keep an agreement with me, I use discernment about what I say and how I say it. I don't close my heart to her, but I let her know how her actions affected me. We use discernment all day long in our normal decision-making processes.

When we apply it intentionally, discernment allows us to recognize our own and others' motivations—that is, to look beyond words and actions for understanding. When we make discernments rather than judgments, we are far more likely to recognize our own idiosyncrasies in someone we sense is off track. In fact, to recognize when we are judging someone gives us the opportunity to check in with ourselves. What we judge in others often represents something we are hesitant to notice and accept in ourselves. When we look into it, we can see that the issue may have been sidelined in us, left in the shadows, and disowned. Again, acceptance allows us to expand through the edge of our limited understanding and reconnect with our core self. We might even find the objectivity to chuckle at ourselves and smile at our own fallibilities.

The Assumption of Innocence

It takes a certain generosity of spirit to implement the assumption of innocence, an internal stance I learned from NVC mentor and author, Miki Kashtan. When we are steeped in the right-wrong paradigm, we can readily view another's behavior as offensive, unjust, or even malevolent. Without knowing who someone is or why the person is doing what he or she is doing, we oftentimes assume intentional malice. It can be hard to see past the transgression we feel. Most of us are familiar with road rage. I have a pet peeve when drivers cut in front of me or don't use their turn signals. Inside this annoyance is my desire for safety—I want to be safe while driving. But when my daughter was bitten by a rattlesnake, I drove as fast as I safely could to get her to the hospital, passing and cutting in front of car after car along the way. No doubt, I upset any number of other drivers on our country highway.

After that experience, the next time someone cut me off, I paused to consider that he or she might very well have good reason. But the fact remains that I have no idea what their reason is! And there is no need for me to know. I really only need to understand that other drivers are responding to a need they have and to accept that. To relieve my own angst, I give them the benefit of the doubt. To give someone the benefit of the doubt is to *assume their innocence* rather than their idiocy, deviance, or mal intent. I want to be discerning when driving and recognize that, from other drivers' perspectives, whatever they are doing probably makes perfect sense, whether I understand their motivations or not.

Whatever the judging mind makes up only serves to constrict us. It diminishes our capacity to be who we would most like to be. To avoid getting defensive when we react to what someone says, thinking he or she is judging us, try assuming the person's innocence. We don't need to understand the "why" of it. We have access to feeling calm and less agitation when we accept *what is*. We can think more clearly and choose more consciously how to respond when we let go of expecting or wishing things to be different than they are.

CHAPTER SEVEN

The Healing Power of Empathy

Courage is contagious. Every time we choose courage, we make
everyone around us a little better and the world a little braver.
—Brené Brown

The impetus to care about and offer our presence to others is the essence of empathy. When given, empathy is received like rain on parched soil. Many of us are starved for it, but really have no idea what is missing from our relationships. Our facility with empathy may be rusty from lack of use, and yet it stands as our legacy and our hope. If we accept that we are all in this together, then empathy is fundamental to the next chapter of life as it unfolds on planet Earth. Empathy, like the strong, tender hands of a midwife, is instrumental to a healthy, gentle landing in our new world. The winding road to mutual understanding is cobbled with the connections that empathy affords.

Mirror Neurons

Without empathy, a lack of care and concern takes its place, resulting in a kind of isolation bordering on social deprivation. Ongoing disconnection in our relationships can start to pull at us, draining our energy and inciting misunderstandings that can lead to conflict. Empathy is the antidote to disconnection. It is the ability to share someone else's feelings, an invaluable trait that has served human evolution. Although it is found in other species, mammals in particular, humans are proficient at it. In large part, it is a forgotten aspect of our heritage, one that we are now obliged to rekindle and put into practice.

Scientific research shows that it is the *mirror neurons* in our brains that give us the ability to have empathy toward others. Brain research scientist V. S. Ramachandran says it this way: "The mirror neurons, it would seem, dissolve the barrier between self and others. I call them 'empathy neurons' or 'Dalai Lama neurons.' Dissolving the 'self vs. other' barrier is the basis of many ethical systems, especially eastern philosophical and mystical traditions."[33]

Empathy is truly a survival skill and one of the keys to our success as a species. It's hard to imagine a tribe or community wherein the members could not comprehend one another—could not stand in a family or community member's shoes, feel for a neighbor, or relate to a relative's suffering. And yet, in the international arena as well as social media, that is exactly where we are deficit. Even inside our own families we may come up short on empathy for the people closest to us.

According to P. J. Manning, "We learn to be in the shoes of another person through real-life observation or storytelling."[34] *Real-life* is the key element here. An advantage of social media's pandemic presence is that it brings like-minded people into contact who otherwise wouldn't be connected. One disadvantage is that the strength of our identification with a particular group on social media can also contribute to demonizing of the out-group. The polarized us-versus-them stance functions to increase the sense of belonging on the one hand. On the other hand, it obscures our ability to see those people not of our group as worthy of our concern. It is easier to label and demonize a group than an individual. History has shown us this horrifying tendency in situations such as the genocide of Native Americans in North America, of Jews in Germany, of the Tutsis in Rwanda, among others perhaps less extensive but no less bone-chilling.

When we hear about groups of people who we don't know and are different, or whose suffering is brought into our lives via the screen in our hands, we are left overwhelmed and under resourced to care. We can end up with *compassion fatigue* from hearing and seeing the daily barrage of emotionally draining stories. Although we may be empathetically drained by technology, we can replenish our empathy coffers quite simply.

---

[33] V. S. Ramachandran, "Mirror Neurons and Imitation Learning as the Driving Force behind the Great Leap Forward in Human Evolution," *Edge*, May 31, 2000, retrieved from https://www.edge.org/conversation/mirror-neurons-and-imitation-learning-as-the-driving-force-behind-the-great-leap-forward-in-human-evolution.

[34] P. J. Manning, "Is Technology Destroying Empathy?" (op-ed), livescience.com, June 30, 2015.

Empathy can be created when we focus on the things we have in common, the things we share.[35] When we share time and physical space with others, we are more likely to share personal stories and sense others' likeness to ourselves. Our need for connection is fed when we spend time together with other people. This is instrumental to our sense of belonging. And, no matter who someone is, we can invoke his or her humanity in our eyes knowing that he or she, too, has come through hardships and struggle, wants the best for his or her children, and works to make ends meet.

The Witness Effect

Empathy facilitates us to experience the *witness effect.* Both people are nourished by such an exchange. To witness another is to be present with compassionate objectivity and to receive the person just as he or she is. When we are witnessed, we feel more complete simply by being understood. This exchange has helped to weave connections and forge alliances throughout time. Successful relationships of all kinds thrive on empathy. It's a quintessentially human quality, this capacity to care about others, even those we don't necessarily like. It has been this way for our species for tens of thousands of years. "The emergence of a sophisticated mirror neuron system set the stage for the emergence in early hominids of a number of uniquely human abilities such as proto-language (facilitated by mapping phonemes onto lip and tongue movements), empathy, 'theory of other minds', and the ability to 'adopt another's point of view'."[36]

The ability to adopt another's point of view is tantamount to getting along. It means that we can see something from another perspective, whether or not we agree with it. This skill in particular is crucial for us to revive now. Somewhere along the line we have forgotten that it is understanding one another—within the context of our differences—that foments trust and belonging. Agreement isn't necessary in order to relate, but understanding is. Sometimes we resist really listening, erroneously thinking that if we understand someone, then we must agree with him or her. Not so. But when we work things through so that both parties come to understand and respect one another, we build trust and connection.

---

[35] Manning.

[36] V. S. Ramachandran, "Mirror Neurons and Imitation Learning as the Driving Force behind the Great Leap Forward in Human Evolution," *Edge*, May 31, 2000, retrieved from https://www.edge.org/conversation/mirror-neurons-and-imitation-learning-as-the-driving-force-behind-the-great-leap-forward-in-human-evolution.

Many of the opportunities people previously had for connecting have vanished in our current systems of socialization. We may rarely see or even talk with our neighbors, let alone help them with a barn raising. In the age of the World Wide Web, it is possible to live in a virtual reality, a kind of self-induced isolation. Social media has sped up time, shortened distances, and minimized our capacity for listening to others. Steeped in the world of social media, we can think we are connecting, but neurologically we remain disconnected from one another. There is prevalent social anxiety in young people in North America simply due to the fact that they may rarely interact with their peers in person. Person to person connections are made in the immediacy of physical presence and verbal exchanges. When we fully engage our mirror neurons in real time with our physical presence, the instinct to care about others arises. We need to listen and understand one another to work things out. Trust is strengthened when we work together to find solutions that include everyone involved, even when agreement isn't apparent. This is how lasting relationships are made and fortified.

A Global Mythology

To make room inside for self and other at the same time, with our differences, is our evolutionary leap forward, just as developing mirror neurons was in early hominids. The sign flashing before us now says that there truly is no "other." There is no one out there who is not of our village. Everyone on the planet is part of our group. We share a beautiful home in the sparkling expanse of the cosmic panorama. The Dalai Lama says, "This recognition that we are all connected—whether Tibetan Buddhists or Hui Muslims—is the birth of empathy and compassion."[37] A fresh page in our collective story is written every time one of us chooses understanding over shunning. As the leaders of our time, we are the authors of this new story, the creators of a mythology that speaks to our interconnectedness.

In his interview with Bill Moyers in 1988, famous mythologist Joseph Campbell said that we are in desperate need of "a global mythology."[38] He recognized the significance of the stories, as mythologies, that we live by. According to Campbell, "Myths are

---

[37]   Dalai Lama and Tutu with Abrams, *Book of Joy*.

[38]   Joseph Campbell, "Joseph Campbell and the Power of Myth," interview by Bill Moyers, *The Power of Myth*, PBS, June 1998, https://billmoyers.com/series/joseph-campbell-and-the-power-of-myth-1988/.

clues to the spiritual potentialities of the human life."[39] They inform our oftentimes unspoken assumptions about life and give us guidance for all manner of activities. He also was keenly aware of the perilous situation we live in with the technology of destruction just a button-push away.

A globally envisioned, shared story may determine our successful transition through our current sets of crises, both sociopolitical and environmental. Our forthcoming global mythology is necessarily grounded in the fact of our interdependence and the knowledge that we are all in this together—thus, the relevance to our understanding the science of oneness (see chapter 3). Insight into the scientific perspective that touts our interconnectedness is a good start. It gives us more confidence in the skills that encourage widening the aperture of our hearts. A sense of relief, like a sought-after homecoming, settles inside when we reawaken skills such as empathy. As leaders in a small world, we look to our similarities, rather than close off in the face of our differences.

Empathetic presence, to witness and to be witnessed, can be called the key to mutual understanding. The more facile we become with this skill, the more fluid and accepting we are of ourselves and others not like us. This sort of mental flexibility helps us to navigate life's wild ride with its unexpected twists and turns. As long as we're on board, we might as well make it fun. Creativity is activated when we're playful. According to Carl Jung, "The creation of something new is not accomplished by the intellect but by the play instinct acting from inner necessity. The creative mind plays with the objects it loves." The way forward then, is very much about discovering what we love. Love is the petri dish for creativity. It begins, of course, with loving ourselves.

Self-Empathy

One simple way to care for ourselves is self-empathy. Empathy and self-empathy can be learned and enhanced with a specific template for listening and responding. As with all the practices, empathy begins with self-awareness. The practice of focusing inside first, in any circumstance, brings self-connection and promotes our access to clarity and presence, both with ourselves and with others. This invites us to implement kindness in our actions.

---

[39]   Campbell.

As discussed at the beginning of this chapter, the hunger to be known by another is a basic human need that affords us a sense of connection, safety, and belonging. It lets us know that *I matter*. These needs are essential, superseded only by water, food, and shelter, according to Maslow's often-cited hierarchy of needs. Before getting to empathy with another person, let's employ empathy with ourselves. To be present and empathetic with another, we also need to be present and empathetic with ourselves. As with the previous practices, we begin with self-connection, knowing our personal internal coordinates, which are essential components to self-empathy.

The template to practice empathy, either with ourselves or with another person is simply to notice and name the quality of life that is "up" or stimulated and the emotions that arise in response to it. To make this awareness a regular focus of your attention will bring a quiet, calm, grounded presence to all that you do. Practice self-connection via your personal coordinates, as described below, before and during holding empathetic presence with another.

Explore this Practice: Self-Empathy and Your Internal Coordinates

Overview

Self-empathy is the practice of respectfully remembering what really matters to you, to accept yourself with kindness and compassion and, thus, to humanize yourself to yourself. It is openhearted self-connection and could be referred to as being honest and vulnerable with yourself. You can use the information gathered from your internal coordinates to empathize with yourself. Self-empathy is also a streamlined way to transform a judgment or come back to center if knocked off kilter by something unexpected. You can glean information about your state of being in any moment with this simple practice and be in empathetic presence with yourself at any time.

1. *Breathe and take your attention inside.* Notice physical sensations. Feel them and breathe into the sensations to increase your internal awareness.
2. *Notice your emotions.* Let your tender attention be the banks of the river; let the feelings flow through freely. Feel and experience your emotions. Name them, and if it's useful for you, write down in your journal what you are aware of inside, your physical sensations and emotions.

3. *Notice what universal quality of life is up and alive for you.* What quality of life are your feelings pointing to? Name it and experience the longing for that quality of life. Embody it.

4. *Accept and acknowledge yourself and your experience just as you are.* You are human, having a human experience of feelings and longings. When you tap into how much that quality of life matters to you in the moment, you may surrender into tears of longing and/or of gratitude for your experience. Or you may simply enjoy the experience of connecting with and understanding yourself this way. Take a few minutes to fully embody the quality of life or the longing for it.

5. *When you fully acknowledge and accept your experience as it is, you are in a state of self-empathy.* Notice your body-mind relax and your heart open as you accept and allow yourself to simply be in the state that you are. To fully accept, acknowledge, and understand your experience via your personal coordinates is self-empathy. Notice your body-mind relax and your heart open as you experience, name, and accept your state of being just as you are.

The Healing Effect of Empathy

We all crave to be seen and known. It fills and nourishes us and gives a sense of wholeness. When we receive the generosity of spirit of having been witnessed, we overflow with our own desire to give back. In that catalytic sequence, we learn to trust that our inner world will be understood and held with care. It may take courage to let ourselves show up transparently, as this is the essence of vulnerability. A wealth of riches is the result, however. Our hearts are revived by the presence of those we open up to. We are given a new life full of freedom to be who we truly are and to share our unique purpose with others.

When we are understood and received just as we are, a profound healing effect can occur. The beneficial effect goes both ways—it is a mutual gift. As renowned transpersonal psychologist Carl Jung shares, "The meeting of two personalities is like the contact of two chemical substances: if there is any reaction, both are transformed." Empathy streams in when we hear or see someone else's suffering and our heart naturally responds with compassion. This holds true with those we may have written off as unworthy of our attention and esteem or those we have judged so harshly as to make them less than fully human in our eyes or even with those who have hurt us.

When we truly see another, when we empathize with his or her human frailties and foibles, the hardened heart melts. Judgment vanishes in the expanse of the open heart.

This happened to me unexpectedly while I was assisting at an NVC workshop facilitated by Miki Kashtan, cofounder of Bay Area Nonviolent Communication (baynvc.org). The focus of the workshop was social change and collaborative decision making. I was very absorbed in the discussion; everything Miki had to say on the topic fascinated me. And yet, as an assistant at the workshop, I had agreed to make myself available should any of the participants need support.

There was one participant in the room, a slight nondescript man who I felt uncomfortable around. For no apparent reason, I found myself wanting to avoid him. Two hours into the workshop, Miki saw that this quiet man needed help and asked me to be his support person. I cringed inwardly, momentarily looking to finagle my way out of it. I did not want to miss even a second of what was happening in the room, much less spend one-on-one time with this particular man. I noticed my resistance and judgments, let go of them as best I could in the moment, and chose to honor my agreement to assist participants. So out I went with him, still feeling reluctant to leave the room.

I listened to the man, who I'll call David, as he told me his story. He spoke of being shunned as a child, of being ostracized from neighborhood baseball games after school, of being shy and uncoordinated, and of continuing to feel like an outsider when, as an adult, he joined a social change organization that didn't seem to really want or need his help. Drawn in by the tenderness with which he spoke, I was touched by his vulnerability and became curious to know more. David shared how helpless he felt, how much he wanted to be free of the past, and how frustrated he was that he couldn't seem to heal the hurts that plagued him. His story of not belonging had triggered his need for support right then. I sat. I listened. I felt my heart soften. In that moment, I saw this man who I'd so wanted to avoid just as he was—a human being with needs and feelings I could easily relate to.

We sat in the garden talking outside the workshop room. I listened empathetically as he stumbled onto insight after insight, gaining acceptance and compassion for himself at new levels. He soon realized that his story, "I am different," fed his assumption that he didn't belong. He had internalized his experience of being ostracized as a child and carried this with him wherever he went, thus bringing about the very condition he feared most—being left out. His desperate need to be included, coupled with his fear of being excluded, had built up a wall of distrust between him and others. During our conversation, it became clear to him that he was the one putting up the wall that kept him separate. This understanding helped him to relax noticeably and to feel sadness about how he had lived his life up to now. As he gained clarity, his confidence grew. Having been understood, he felt transformed, and a rush of new possibilities began to take shape in him. I noticed more openness in his demeanor as he shifted his awareness to others, rather than focusing on his fear of not being included. He spent the rest of the weekend connecting with people in the workshop, rather than standing apart and feeling like an outsider.

His newfound self-awareness also impacted me. It was as if he'd shone a spotlight on my initial reaction to him. It seems I had unknowingly reacted to his belief that he was different and didn't belong as if it were being broadcast right to me. Thus, I'd wanted to avoid him. That would certainly account for my inexplicable yet strong reaction to this unassuming man. Our shared experience and mutual "aha moment" forged a bond between us. Over the course of the next two days, we talked several more times, sat together at lunch, and made a point to check in with each other. What I gave him—an ear, attention, presence, and understanding—was as much a gift to me as it was to him. By holding a container of presence for him and listening to his pain, my heart opened. In my opening to him, I received the gift of becoming more fully myself, more present, and more openhearted.

We gain facility at listening and hearing what qualities of life are alive for another person with practice. The more we listen to others with empathetic presence, the more we trust ourselves to navigate conversations while caring about both of us. Listening in this way alleviates the tendency toward reactivity. It decreases the potential for misunderstanding and conflict while bringing a quality of connection that nourishes our daily interactions. Over time, we gain more confidence in speaking transparently and sharing our feelings and needs openly in the conversation. We will look more specifically into how this works in communication and dialogue in subsequent chapters.

Explore this Practice: Empathetic Presence with Another

1. *Breathe into yourself and find your internal coordinates.* Rest in awareness of the other person by coming back to your breath and body awareness frequently (refer to chapter 4 for review if needed). Your coordinates—your feelings, bodily sensations and the qualities of life wanting to be served—may change as the conversation develops.

2. *Bring your attention to the other person. Listen for what matters most to him or her* as he or she is speaking. As you focus on the other person, listen to what the person is saying and hear the essence of the meaning beneath his or her words. Some people will clearly verbalize their feelings and the qualities of life alive for them. Others won't put exact words to their emotions or the qualities of life that are relevant to their situation, but you'll get the gist of their meaning from the way they speak and their manner of expression. Either way, make a mental note of what you sense is central to what the person is expressing.

3. *Translate what you've heard into a simple guess*, homing in on what you sense matters most to the other person. Your purpose in guessing is to clarify for yourself that you have heard and understood the person accurately. It also offers him or her coordinates to take in and compare with his or her own internal experience. It is a verbal gift to the other, gleaned from your presence and attention.

4. *Pose a question.* For example, "Is it that you're disappointed because you wish you could have completed the class?" Or, "Are you upset with yourself because you'd like to have more kindness and understanding with your teenager?"

   When focusing empathetically with another person, there are no wrong guesses. You are offering a reflection, giving the person coordinates that he or she can take inside, check against his or her own experience, and then confirm or clarify your version of what he or she said. For example, someone might respond to your question with, "Yes, and ...," giving you more details. This means you're accurate; the person feels heard and has more to say about it. Or the person may respond, "No, it's more that ...," to clarify your understanding of what was said. In either case, your curiosity and attention have given the person feedback and an invitation to understand his or her own feelings and experience better.

5. *Keep listening, repeat the process of tender attention with curiosity while making simple guesses.* Interrupt the person as necessary to make sure you are fully understanding what matters the most to him or her. If the person says, "Yes, and ...," he or she feels heard and understood and is going further into self-exploration. In this way, empathic presence fosters deeper awareness, understanding, and compassion in the other person, as well as in you, the listener.

   When people have been heard and witnessed as needed, they will garner clarity and insights. At that time, they may naturally start to approach their

What Empathy Is Not

Empathy is not:

- **Giving Advice**—"You know, what I would do is … " Or, "Have you tried …?"
- **Sympathy or Commiserating**—"I feel so bad for you. I wish that hadn't happened to you." Or, "Yeah, that happened to me once, and it really took a toll on me."
- **Fact-finding**—"When did that happen to you?"
- **Psychoanalyzing**—"Why do think that happened?" Or, "What made you say that, anyway?"
- **Agreeing or Colluding**—"Oh yeah, I know exactly what you mean. I hate when that happens." Or, "I know someone who can get you out of this mess."
- **Turning the Focus Onto Yourself**—"Whenever that happens to me, I get so upset. In fact, the last time that happened I got really mad and wanted to scream."

situation with new perspectives and ideas. They might begin to see options about what to do next if they were previously in a quandary. They may feel open to exploring possible next steps.

6. *Keep your empathetic presence attuned to the person.* Ask if there is anything else he or she wants to say about the situation. If the answer is yes, continue with empathy as outlined above. If the answer is no, allow the person to continue to brainstorm possible things he or she can do. If you have insights about how the person might proceed, ask if he or she would like to hear your ideas before offering them.

The gift of empathetic presence is your tender attention and curiosity. *It is not about saying the right thing in just the right way.* Your focused presence creates a container of care from which insights can unfold. Authentic care and presence are your tools, and the desire to understand the other person is your impetus. It's simple but can be awkward at first because of the unfamiliarity of it. For clarification, it can help to look at what empathy is not.

The familiar ways of responding to another's pain outlined in "What Empathy Is Not" are well intended. We want to diminish the discomfort of those we love and care about. Although often meant to soothe uncomfortable feelings, such comments can subtly sideline the person's actual experience. This can create a knot of disconnection and sense of disapproval for the one who has shared something raw or tender about themselves. How we receive and respond to one another speaks volumes about our state of being and our own level of presence. When we are empathetically present with another person, we are very alive, aware of our internal coordinates, and curious to understand whatever the other person is going through. The willingness to feel our own emotions as they come up is fundamental to our ability to be in a state of empathy with others.

Specifics of Empathetic Presence

Notice that the empathetic questions above ask about what the person *wants to experience*, or longs to expand into. This is a subtle yet critical refinement from simply reflecting exactly what someone said. We can guess what is motivating someone by sensing what he or she might want to explore further or grow into, rather than just restating what is missing for him or her. When we reiterate what went wrong, the creative energies can deaden and inhibit further exploration.

To invite deeper insight and exploration, we state the quality of life we sense the person is longing to experience, whether or not he or she is experiencing it. That is to say, we voice our inquiry in the positive. For example, it is more productive to say, "So is it that you really want your expectations for the trip to be understood by her before you decide whether to go or not?" Rather than, "Oh, I see, she didn't understand what you meant and now you don't know what to do." This refinement to verbalize the desired possibility is uplifting. It energetically opens the person to a palette of options. In contrast, if we reflect what didn't work or didn't happen, it can have a leaden effect.

Let's look at an example. Someone says, "I didn't like that trip at all. There wasn't any music or anyone my age to hang out with." A simple reflection might be, "Oh, so it was not a fun trip because you didn't have anyone your age to hang out with and no music you liked." This is an accurate reflection but does not invite you or them into insight or options for greater understanding. The person's response could be, "Yeah. The whole trip was a downer."

Contrast this with a reflection that includes a guess as to what they would have preferred: "It makes sense that you would have liked to be with people your age. I imagine you wanted to go out, meet new people, and listen to music and explore the town together. It sounds like that would have been a lot more fun for you. Is that it?" In this case, the person's response might be to look at him or herself and his or her part of the equation more openly and respond with, "Yeah. I think it would have. I did meet a few people, but they were leaving the next day. I don't know. I could have explored a little on my own and maybe met people then, but I guess I wasn't feeling that adventurous. I had a headache too, so I just stayed in the hotel."

Often, a constructive reflection brings a thoughtful response and more information to light. Having been understood and witnessed, the person can take more responsibility for his or her experience and choices and potentially see other options to stretch in to.

Is it Empathy or Sympathy?

As we now know, we are endowed with the ability to understand our fellow human beings from their perspective via our mirror neurons. This capability bridges the gap between ourselves and others and forms the bond of understanding that leads us to accept one another. For clarity, it is helpful to make a distinction between *empathy* and *sympathy*. Although the two words are often used interchangeably, they are very different in their effect. Sympathy finds us getting drawn in when someone we care about is in emotional or physical pain, when they are suffering a loss or disappointment or even an affront. Typically, sympathy includes a feeling of pity or sorrow for someone else's plight. It often stimulates our own emotions and our own past experiences akin to theirs, and we can take the focus from them to us in a heartbeat, sharing our own troubles in response to theirs. There is a place for sympathy; it's just not empathy as we are defining it here.

In contrast, when we *empathize* with another, we see, understand, and come to know them by witnessing their experience, whatever it is, *from their perspective*, without judging it, trying to change it, or shifting the focus to ourselves. Their experience is not bad, wrong or in need of fixing; it *just is.* This is where courage comes in. It takes courage to simply *be with* others' experiences, including their possible discomfort, confusion, anger, or grief. But when we do, our presence and objectivity allow for the witness effect to occur. People who are witnessed feel seen and known by us for who they really are. No one is trying to change them, fix the situation, or soothe them in some way that diminishes their discomfort or any part of their experience.

Perhaps surprisingly, to be seen, heard, and understood in our own pain or any other experience, is the surest, most expedient way for the pain or distress to move through and to transform. When we repress, ignore, or try to change our experience (or that of another) without first acknowledging and accepting it as it is, we only prolong the angst. Famous psychotherapist Carl Rogers agrees, saying, "The curious paradox is that when I accept myself just as I am, then I can change." The same is true of accepting others just as they are.

When we don't let ourselves feel our emotions at the time when they occur but hold them locked in the body, the experience lives on in us, though we may not be fully aware of it. Nevertheless, repressed emotions pull at us from below our awareness, influencing our decisions and diminishing our energy. This is the very reason many of us try to "help" someone in pain by changing the subject or making light of a difficult situation. We are keeping our own feelings of discomfort at bay—because to be with your emotions might just uncork mine. If we are uncomfortable with others' feelings, we are well served to take a look inside ourselves. Freedom comes from looking into the jaws of our fears and by being with our discomfort. When faced, fears often evaporate like fog in the sun.

We can share our own freedom and expansiveness with others simply by having the courage to be present with *what is*. It's a wondrous thing to be seen and understood by someone else. At times, it is just the reflection we need to know ourselves better. Somehow, the more we let ourselves be seen and known, the more we discover about who we really are. In fact, this is exactly how we know ourselves—in the context of how other people see and respond to us. There seems to be a lovely loosening of skeptical layers that can lift off and drift away in the wake of sweet connections in our close relationships. Such interactions give us the feedback we need to reorient our compass or drop further inside and nurture the parts still developing or in need of healing.

Empathetic presence can be felt even when no words are spoken. Still and yet, when words are spoken, when one person says aloud in the form of an inquiry what he or she senses another is feeling and needing, something magic happens. That magic is the experience of being truly seen. This is where empathy becomes an invitation to stretch into greater possibilities, to discover options that become available only when we are seen and accepted just as we are in that moment.

CHAPTER EIGHT
Celebration and Mourning

All changes, even the most longed for, have their melancholy,
for what we leave behind us is a part of ourselves; we must
die to one life before we can enter into another.
—Anatole France

Our emotions offer information about ourselves in relation to the world around us. They are like a high-speed fiber-optics network continually transporting messages between us. And yet, residual thinking from the Age of Reason tells us to ignore or override our emotions. We learned early on that we shouldn't show them and certainly mustn't let our feelings run us. That would be chaos and fearsome to behold!

In fact, it is shameful in many settings to show our emotions much at all. For the most part, the only emotion men have permission to feel and express is anger. In general, women are permitted to show sadness. For a man to show his tears is commonly met with derision, and for a woman to be angry is usually met with disapproval. Even joy and happiness, although we all claim to want them, are looked at askance if expressed in public.

Emotional Intelligence

In recent years the term *emotional intelligence* has come to the fore. Social science now tells us that emotions play a significant role in our lives. Not just reason but feelings, too, are valuable assets. As Dean Koontz reminds us, "Some people think only intellect counts: knowing how to solve problems, knowing how to get by, knowing how to identify an advantage and seize it. But the functions of intellect are insufficient without courage, love, friendship, compassion, and empathy." To bridge the gap between our heads and hearts and connect our minds with our feelings can be surprisingly difficult for many people, but this short journey is worth the effort. With our emotional intelligence intact, we tap into a great reservoir of possibility for fulfillment, as well as better health.

Some people have trouble connecting with their bodies—that is, taking their attention inside and sensing what they feel physically, as well as emotionally. For many of us, it is challenging to navigate emotions constructively. This can create misunderstandings and even conflict because, in fact, emotions *do* run our lives. We are feeling beings. And, like any part of our nature that we try to suppress, emotions can come out unbidden if we don't address them at the time we feel them. We can become vulnerable to depression and anxiety, as well as unexpected outbursts when we deny our feelings. Trying to keep feelings in makes life ever so much more complicated and anxiety provoking. As T. K. Coleman says, "Our feelings are not there to be cast out or conquered. They're there to be engaged and expressed with imagination and intelligence." But because we may not be adept at expressing our feelings skillfully, let alone having full emotional awareness, we have some exploring to do. And we don't know what we'll find when we start to look.

When we approach ourselves and our emotions with tender attention, we allow for gentleness in our discoveries. Emotions are the lifeline of connection and understanding; they are the medium by which we know ourselves and others. They are also the ways we stay current with ourselves. Expressing the emotions we feel, keeps us clear and updated in the present moment. In this manner we can surf the ride of our daily lives and enjoy every moment of the adventure. In particular, the powerful emotions of celebration and mourning are meaningful and need to be recognized and expressed regularly. They have cleansing and transformative properties that can help us to stay healthy and connected not only with ourselves, but also with our family and community.

A Story of Grief and Celebration

The knock on the front door was unexpected. When I opened it, the man standing there looked friendly yet official. He said he'd heard there may be unpermitted buildings on the property. *So this is it*, I thought.

Ten years in the making, my beautiful hand-built, Zen-like eco-retreat center had been found out. *What a relief,* I heard myself exhale as I slumped into the couch after he'd left. I would no longer have to live in fear that the county would catch on. Now they knew. The county official made his report. It was determined that we would not be granted building permits because the retreat center was near a year-round creek—technically, a floodplain. Never mind that we'd built every structure three feet above ground and sturdy enough to withstand any weather conditions. All the materials used were also sustainable in nature; they were "green" structures.

The upshot of it? Every building had to be taken down and removed from the property. Every workshop we had on the calendar for the upcoming year had to be canceled. A year's worth of revenue flew out the window in that one encounter, and unexpected expenses loomed in front of us. My vision of a nature-based eco-retreat center had to be completely dismantled.

I chose not to spend my time and resources in a legal battle with the county. But I had a lot of grieving to do. One of my mentors, sound healer Karina Schelde, suggested I make time to grieve intentionally. It wasn't the first time her guidance had taken me out of my comfort zone. By now, I trusted her wisdom. I took her suggestion to give myself twenty-one days in a row to grieve this painful loss.

I went to the Big Yurt, the large group meeting space for retreats and workshops, elegantly welcoming with Japanese antiques, Turkish kilims on the floor, and silk kimonos draping the walls. I hunkered down on the rugs, pillows around and tissues nearby, and crossed the threshold into my grief. Tears flowed easily, punctuated with loud sobs, anguished writhing, and lots of nose blowing. Feelings poured through me until I felt the sweet release only tears of mourning can bring. My grief over the retreat center tapped into a well of sadness over other losses I had forgotten or had not fully grieved.

For the next twenty days I willingly went back to the Big Yurt to mourn and left each time feeling clearer, lighter, and softer. I felt cleansed and renewed after every session spent letting my grief flow. In my mourning, I honored the beautiful vision I'd held for so long; the love, devotion, and resources I'd put into its artful construction over the ten years previous; and the people who had come to the land to heal and grow in the peaceful, natural setting, which was also my home. I took time to appreciate all that had gone into the retreat center's construction, all who had benefitted from spending time there, and the purity of vision that had inspired it.

Over the three weeks of daily grieving, I did not gain clarity about what was next. What I did garner was the sense of spaciousness and peacefulness that letting go into grief affords. In the ensuing months as my next steps became clear, I was able to celebrate and even feel gratitude for the telltale knock on the door. In some strange way, the retreat center had served its purpose. It was time for me to write a book.

The force of our grief tells us how much what is now gone mattered to us. In this regard, the flip side of mourning is truly a celebration of life. They go hand in hand. To embrace our feelings of grief and to let go of what was is naturally freeing and expansive. It gives us full permission to celebrate what we have loved so deeply. To feel and to express our emotions truly makes us more alive; it makes colors brighter and our interactions more vivid. Psychotherapist and author, Francis Weller shares, "The work of the mature person is to carry grief in one hand and gratitude in the other and to be stretched large by them. How much sorrow can I hold? That's how much gratitude I can give. If I carry only grief, I'll bend toward cynicism and despair. If I have only gratitude, I'll become saccharine and won't develop much compassion for other people's suffering. Grief keeps the heart fluid and soft, which helps make compassion possible."[40]

A retreat center to be dismantled or any loss large or small, when mourned, becomes compost for new growth. Our inner life is fed and nourished when we embrace what happened, when we allow ourselves to feel our loss or heartbreak. In the process of surrendering into our feelings, we also nurture the seeds of what will come next. In the aftermath of mourning, we are left cleansed and open to welcome our unfolding into the next chapter of our lives. Continuity remains because the container, either our own presence or that of the surrounding community, holds us steady within the flux of our lives.

Explore this Practice: Surrender, Grief, and Praise

Overview

This practice is designed to cleanse and open our hearts. It also shows how to create a container to help hold the grieving process in a sacred way, meaning with a ceremonial aspect. Ceremony in this context simply means consciously preparing the space and naming your intentions. A simple template for how to do this is described in the first step below.

---

[40] Tim McKee, The Geography of Sorrow: Francis Weller on Navigating Our Losses. *The Sun*, October 2015. https://thesunmagazine.org/issues/478/the-geography-of-sorrow

It isn't necessary to know ahead of time what it is you need or want to grieve. This process is about giving yourself the time and space for grief to bubble up because, as sure as the sun rises every morning, it is there. When we put our feelings of sadness and grief off until later, we can end up with many regrets and grievances that need to be metabolized. As feeling beings, we need the time and space to allow for our grief to make us whole and to let go of past grievances, mistakes, changes, and losses.

If you do know what you need to grieve or to let go, it is a good place to start. If you have a recent loss of some magnitude, I recommend making a time to grieve daily for up to twenty-one days. If that isn't realistic, I suggest making the space to grieve from three to seven days in a row or once a week for three to seven weeks in a row and whenever you need more beyond that. At the very least, I recommend carving out time weekly to grieve, for as long as you need. Each time you do the practice, give yourself at least twenty to thirty minutes of uninterrupted time.

Create the container

Decide when to do this practice and set your time frame for how long you will do it.

I suggest allotting at least ten minutes to actively grieve. I plan twenty to thirty minutes in total, with ten to fifteen minutes of active grieving. You may have a clock nearby, although I don't recommend setting a timer because it may shock you out of your process if it goes off while you are in the throes of crying.

Prepare a room to receive your soft spilling of tears. Make it comfortable, private, and cozy. As you prepare the space, bring your intentions for clarity, release, ease, freedom and vibrant aliveness or other personal intentions that are meaningful to you. Bring beauty into your space in whatever way appeals to you—maybe fresh flowers or a beautiful tapestry. Bring in the sacred element if you choose, by lighting a candle and/or incense. Have water available and tissues nearby. Wear comfortable clothing so you can move easily as your body relaxes or expresses feelings in movement.

To begin

At the start of the grieving session, stand in your space with soft knees, feet firmly planted on the floor about hip distance apart, and state your intentions out loud. If you wish, invite in your spirit guides, helpers, and protectors, specifying those who serve your highest good and the good of humanity and the planet. Intend to receive the support and guidance you need. Feel your feet pushing softly into the floor or earth.

Feel the earth supporting you. Bend and straighten your knees gently, just a few inches up and down, to engage the sense of connection and support of the earth beneath you. Relax into standing with soft knees, slightly bent; soft belly; and relaxed hips, shoulders, and jaw. Feel your skeletal structure supporting you easily as you relax your muscles. If you can't stand comfortably, sit with your back well supported, feet flat on the floor, and push gently into the floor and release a few times. Offer gratitude for the support and the opportunity to do this work.

Take a few deep breaths into your belly and exhale down through your feet into the earth. Allow yourself to feel your breath stretch down into the earth, like roots growing from your feet. Inhale the energy of the earth back up through your feet, legs, and torso and into your heart. Exhale from your heart back down through your feet into the earth. Do the earth to heart to earth breath three or more times. Then take a big breath and exhale with an audible "aaahhhh" sound. Repeat the breath with an "aaahhhh" exhale a few more times. Let your awareness of your body and your breath bring you into the present moment.

1. *Open to your tears.* Put yourself in the position most natural for you to cry, lament, sob, or grieve. I find sitting on my knees, hunched over on my elbows with my head between my hands is conducive to surrendering into my tears. Start to make the sounds of crying. As the crying begins, remember what you are sad about. Something completely unexpected might come to you that takes you deeper into your feelings. Let yourself flow from one thing to another in a natural, fluid process as your grief takes you where it needs to go.

2. *Stay with it; trust the process.* Allow yourself to flow with the sounds, tears, body postures, or movements that naturally arise as the feelings move through you. If thoughts take you out of your grief, simply notice them and let them float by. Come back to your sounds of lamentation and crying. Bring to mind what you are sad about. As you surrender into your feelings, let your body move as is natural for you. Come back to your tears. Feel your losses and the changes, mistakes, and regrets you've had—any and all of it—and let your memories fuel your release of the grief inside.

3. *Follow your process.* If other feelings come up, allow them a place for expression. It is common for grief to be layered with anger. If anger comes up and it feels pertinent, express the anger by pounding your fists on a pillow, clearly stating "No!" or whatever words express your anger so you can release it. This can be a place to reclaim your power from a time when you felt helpless or victimized.

You may want to stomp, kick, or push against a wall, all the while stating your truth to the situation or person you are angry at.

However, I strongly recommend that you *do not* take your anger directly to the person or situation that stimulated your pain. Keep the anger in your ceremonial space and direct it symbolically to who or what you're angry about. To direct your anger symbolically to someone, as if they are sitting there, will have all the benefits to you of clearing, release, and empowerment without the possible untoward ramifications of doing so in person. (If you decide you must express your anger directly to someone in person, I recommend having a facilitated conversation with a professional counselor or mediator.)

Allow the anger to dissipate with your expression of it and move back into your grief, to another layer of surrender and acceptance, allowing for more heart opening and release. Grief will be the last, or bottom, layer of the grief-anger sandwich. From the final layer of grief, peace and calm naturally arise—the purified essence left from the alchemy of mourning your losses. As the grief subsides, acknowledge and honor your process. Dwell in the awareness of your relaxed, clear state.

Closure

When you are complete, sit quietly for a few more minutes, letting the experience settle inside. Notice how your body feels. What are you aware of inside, in your body, mind, and heart? Journal the experience if you wish, noting what you grieved and other emotions that came up and how you feel in the aftermath. Acknowledge and honor your process. Before leaving the space, stand again with softly bent knees and feel yourself connected to and supported by the earth. Take three deep breaths letting the "aahhhh" sound out on the exhale. Take a short walk to support you being fully grounded and present in your body. Be sure to come back to fully inhabiting your body before driving a car or operating machinery. Set your intention for the next grieving session by noting when and where it will happen.

Grief is the very natural process of letting go of what went before, maybe a loss or a significant life change. It is a way to honor what we have loved and to release it from our grasp. To mourn nourishes and makes us whole again after the disorienting, empty place left when someone dies, something dear is lost, or major life changes occur. To stay in tune with ourselves and with life moving around and through us, we must grieve and celebrate in equal measure. Francis Weller wisely relates, "A heart that does not somehow deal with grief turns hard and becomes unresponsive to the joys and sorrows of the world. Then our communities become cold; our children go unprotected; our environment can be pillaged for the good of the few. Only if we learn to grieve can we keep our hearts responsive and do the difficult work of restoring and repairing the world."[41] Feeling and expressing our grief makes us whole. It is the ability to accept *what is* and to surrender to the pain of loss that allows us to grieve and, thus, to live with greater vitality. This process opens us to the full spectrum of our emotional lives and inevitably leads to more freedom and joy.

There are numerous parts of our lives that require us to let go of what we're attached to, like an expectation or a dream that doesn't come to pass. A marriage or partnership that comes to an end falls into this category. Even to make a tough decision may demand that we delve into ourselves to see what we must let go of to make a wise, considered choice.

Earnest's Story

A client I'll call Ernest was unhappily married for over twenty years, yet he stayed in the marriage out of a sense of duty and obligation to his family. He overrode his personal needs in deference to his need to keep his family intact and to be seen as a happy family unit in the eyes of friends and extended family. It was the obvious choice to him, guided by his core values of responsibility and social acceptance. To make it tolerable to stay in the marriage with so many of his other needs going unmet, he held optimistic stories that put his wife in a more positive light than was accurate. The stories served his values of partnership and duty, giving him more ability to navigate many upsets and challenges along the way.

The overriding story that kept him going was that the two of them had shared values about parenting and marriage as partnership. In retrospect, he saw that he and his wife were not much unified in their parenting styles and had very different personal values. He later realized that he dealt with this by deferring to her wants to avoid escalating their numerous arguments, while nursing a growing resentment each time. He needed the story that they were in partnership and working together to help him achieve internal equilibrium, even though her actions frequently did not match his story.

---

[41] Tim McKee, The Geography of Sorrow: Francis Weller on Navigating Our Losses. *The Sun*, October 2015. https://thesunmagazine.org/issues/478/the-geography-of-sorrow

"I was so frustrated," he told me. "I worked a lot harder than I wanted to, both to get along with her and to make enough money for the growing family—I supported all seven of us and couldn't really make enough money to afford many extras. Because I had to work so hard, I didn't spend as much time with my kids as I wanted, but I kept my commitment to the marriage out of my sense of obligation to the family." Eventually, it became clear to him that the primary glue that held the marriage together was a value they did share—the need for social acceptance. From all appearances, they were the model family, and they upheld that facade in their community.

It took him a number of years after their separation and subsequent divorce to see the situation clearly. When his wife announced one day that she was done with the relationship, he was crushed. Life as he knew it fell apart around him. All he had worked so hard for and had sacrificed in the process suddenly seemed meaningless. Chaos reigned inside as he falteringly made attempts to regain a sense of purpose and integrity in his life. Eventually, he allowed himself to feel his monstrous grief. He mourned having stayed in a loveless marriage for so long, having worked so hard and given up so much of what mattered to him personally and as a parent, in deference to the supposed partnership. To give up his marriage and all he'd expected from it was a great loss to him. His grief was layered with anger, which he also expressed. To grieve was to honor significant parts of his life that he had left behind along the way and to celebrate the qualities of life he had chosen to serve throughout the marriage.

Had he ended the marriage two years into it when he realized it wasn't going to work out as he'd hoped, he would have grieved a different set of his needs as losses. He would have prioritized different qualities of life, other core values of his, such as self-connection, self-care, compassion, transparency, authenticity, intimacy, and autonomy. He would have made a change that went against the grain of his sense of commitment, duty, and responsibility to the marriage. And he would have had to let go of his need for social acceptance, as he thought of it then. In that case, he would have grieved the loss of his role of husband as he'd held it and the image of a happy family, while he embraced another set of values having to do with his integrity as an individual and his adventuresome spirit. But he'd been on automatic pilot, unable to see any other options then. To come back to himself and wholeness, he had to grieve what he had given up and acknowledge what he had given.

As it was, it took him a few years to sort through the changes and regain his equilibrium. "I was at rock bottom and needed a lot of time to come out of it. I knew I had to learn how to be in a healthy relationship. I explored lots of avenues to learn who I really am and what really matters to me. But as painful as it was, I'm so glad it happened. I am free to really be me now. And, I love my relationships with my kids."

If Ernest had had a container of acceptance and compassion inside of himself or if he'd been able to ask the community to support him and his family through their changes, continuity would have been preserved, even if the marriage wasn't. How? By holding the family members with care and understanding, giving them a time and place to grieve while supporting them to find their new ground.

The following practice can take a lot of the stress out of making hard decisions by embracing all of who we are and what matters to us, including what we leave behind when we choose one thing over another. I was first introduced to this process by Robert Gonzales, a very skilled nonviolent communication trainer and significant mentor of mine.[42]

Explore this Practice: Making Decisions Whole with Grief and Celebration

Overview

This practice offers a circumspect approach to making tough decisions. It is similar to delineating the "pros and cons" of a situation, but is values-based, which can more clearly elucidate what really matters to you, and thus, help to simplify decision-making.

To begin

1. *Think of a decision you made that was challenging because you had reasons to go either way.* Or use a situation where you still need to make a difficult choice.

    On a clean sheet of paper, put the options you are comparing at the top of the page, each in a separate column. Underneath each option, list the qualities of life that would be fulfilled by making that choice.

    For example, a couple years ago, I was faced with a difficult decision. I was stymied about whether to go to a big family reunion in Ohio that would be the last of its kind in my lifetime or to fulfill my commitment to the sound healing apprenticeship I had begun. The sound healing apprenticeship required that I

---

42   Robert Gonzales, www.living-compassion.org.

attend a weeklong training in British Columbia the very same week. The training was mandatory, but I had promised to attend the family reunion a year before, prior to receiving the announcement of the dates for the sound healing training. At first, both options seemed equally compelling in different ways. I put them each in a column on a blank page and wrote down the qualities of life that would be fulfilled if I chose that option.

Example list

The family reunion would fulfill these values:

- Family connections
- Continuity
- Belonging
- Remembrance
- Being seen and known
- Appreciation
- Fun
- Socializing
- Learning

The sound healing training would fulfill these values:

- Personal growth
- Camaraderie, belonging
- Companionship
- Learning
- Challenge—an opportunity to stretch myself
- Connections
- Nature
- Skill building for future facilitation with clients
- Contribution
- Expansion

2. *Make your choice based on the qualities of life*: Evaluate which list of qualities holds the most meaning and significance for you for this specific situation. When doing

the exercise, if clarity about your decision isn't apparent after simply reviewing your lists, give each quality of life you listed a numeric value from 1 to 5, according to how important that quality is to you. Add them up to see which option received the highest number; that one is your preferred choice.

Check in with yourself to find out if your choice resonates as true. An unsettled feeling inside or constriction somewhere in your body indicates you are not completely lined up with that choice at this moment. A sense of relief, ease, or lightness inside indicates that you are in alignment with the choice. Trust your gut feeling—your inner wisdom and intuition have your best interests at heart. If you don't feel lined up with your decision, make time to do steps 1 and 2 again. Take your time and then return here.

Looking at my list, I could see which option held more meaning for me, but it was still a tough decision. I chose the sound healing training. To make myself whole in the process, I needed to let go of the qualities of life, or the experiences I'd miss by not going to the family reunion. I made time to mourn them as I let go of the option I hadn't chosen.

3. *Let go of the option not taken.* Focus on the qualities of life in the column of the option you didn't choose. Allow yourself to feel the meaning and precious reasons you *did* want to choose that option. Celebrate their importance to you by acknowledging and honoring those qualities of life and let them go for now. You may feel sadness and tears come up or maybe frustration and anger. Be with your feelings until they subside naturally. In this way, you can embrace and honor what you are letting go of while remaining engaged and whole in the process. You will avoid resentment and stay current with yourself.

4. *Focus on the option you did choose.* Let yourself bask in the clarity of your decision and the importance of it for your life right now according to the qualities of life represented by this choice. Embody the qualities of life to be fulfilled. Take the steps to make the choice come to fruition, as indicated. Celebrate having made a clear, well-thought-out decision.

When we sort through and sift out what truly matters to us prior to making important decisions, we stay true to ourselves and bring commitment to our choices. It's like being in alignment with ourselves and fully aware of our motivations. This practice makes crystal clear what we value most and draws to us the experiences that will feed and mature us. To fully consider all of the options increases the likelihood of keeping our agreements with ourselves, as well as with others. To acknowledge and honor a core value that is not taking priority at the time keeps us in integrity with ourselves, even as we let go with tears. It leaves us open and able to fully embrace the decision we have made.

To Feel or Not to Feel

If your attitude about emotions is that some feelings are "good" and others are "bad," then you will be reluctant to feel the "bad" ones. But to feel our emotions requires us to be open to embracing all of them. There is only one switch—to feel or not to feel; those are the options. As Archbishop Desmond Tutu said in a conversation with His Holiness the Dalai Lama, "Discovering more joy does not, I'm sorry to say ... save us from the inevitability of hardship and heartbreak. In fact, we may cry more easily, but we will laugh more easily too. Perhaps we are just more alive.'"[43]

To shed the residue of our losses, we release them with tears of mourning. It is a way to celebrate what we hold as precious and dear. But more importantly, to let the powerful flood of heartbreak wash through us brings us back to life. In the moment when we willingly surrender into our emotions, we include ourselves in life's mutable procession. When we forgo the illusion of control and allow ourselves to feel truly alive, we tread in the territory of spirit. As Martin Prechtel points out, "This ... heart break ... [of loss] ... forces us to begin to learn how to court the Divine: the first grand step toward becoming a whole person, a person who can turn loss into grief and grief into a song of life-giving praise. This is the metabolism of grief into beauty."[44] When we praise our losses and acknowledge what is gone, the grief transforms our darker times into beauty and grace.

Authentic emotions bring a richness, immediacy, and passion to life, without which we are left less than fully alive. A healthy emotional life is like a flowing river. When we hold back our feelings, we curtail the flow of life through us and, like a dam, end up harboring the weight of it all. This results in constrictions inside and blocks our life force. Eventually, such blockages may cause illness and disease or leak out sideways

---

[43] HH the Dalia Lama and Desmond Tutu with Douglas Abrams, *The Book of Joy* (Random House, 2016).

[44] Martin Prechtel, *The Smell of Rain on Dust* (North Atlantic Books, 2015).

when least expected. To express our feelings is natural, but we sometimes need a container to help us normalize expressing our deep emotions. Without a community to serve that purpose, we can find a friend, colleague, or professional facilitator to hold that container for us. The following case study shows how holding the space and setting for another person to feel and express his or her emotions can benefit him or her.

Debbie's Story

A client I'll call Debbie came to me to explore the cause of a severe pain in her back, located behind her heart. Over the weeks we worked together, she discovered the original shock that created the blockage around her heart. It became clear that unresolved trauma from childhood was the cause of the acute pain. The betrayal of trust and heartbreak she'd experienced at the hands of her mother's physical and emotional abuse was lodged there. She expressed her emotions through metaphor when she said, "It was like my mother stabbed me in the back, and my heart broke." Out of necessity, she held her life together beautifully until well into her forties, acting as if she was perfectly fine.

It takes a lot of energy to hold an emotional wound of that magnitude for so long. It took tremendous effort—what Debbie called "a lot of backbone" to distance herself from the pain in her heart. Energy that might otherwise flow through her heart, allowing for joy and connection, instead formed an energetic black hole from which nothing could escape.

The remedy that helped her to open her heart involved accepting the pain of her childhood, as well as the losses that resulted from ignoring her broken heart. In her healing, she navigated a long and staggered process of mourning that featured expressing intense anger at times. Her process included acknowledging qualities she'd relied on since childhood, such as strength of character, fortitude, and tenacity. Acknowledging and honoring these qualities was critical to her healing, as they had served her throughout her life and continued to support her healing process.

To expedite her healing, we transcended talk therapy and included movement and sound therapy as well. We went beyond the intellect and directly into the energetic patterns via sound and movement, streamlining her opening and healing. The black hole slowly released its contents, both beautiful and terrifying in turn. It was a long and difficult road to wholeness that demanded immense courage and frequent surrendering into deep emotions. As Debbie delved into her feelings, the expression of which brought purification, and insight, she eventually found freedom from her past. As she released the stories that had formed and held the blockage in place, the pain in her back began to dissipate.

Through it all, she had a consistent container of support and understanding, not only from me, but also from friends and family. The continuity of the container for her grief and healing, along with her fortitude and courage, were significant ingredients in her process. Eventually, Debbie's holding pattern transformed into a lightness of being. As her heart released what it held, she opened to giving and receiving love as she'd never done before. Eventually, she beamed with an aliveness that touched anyone in her sphere. By facing herself and her emotional pain, she found true freedom and received a new lease on life.

Grief and Wholeness

A neighbor of mine whose husband had died recently apologized as she started to tear up while talking about clearing his things out of the house. Then she said, "I went into a bad depression yesterday when I walked the dog down to the creek, because we used to do that together." I felt sad that she thought she should not be feeling her loss or expressing her sadness with her tears. Not only did she have shame about her grief, but she also labeled it *depression*, a clinically diagnosable mood disorder. In fact, depression often results when we *don't feel* and express grief, anger, or guilt. As Martin Prechtel relates, "Grief is not depression; a griever is not depressed. Depression comes from not being able to grieve, which converts our losses into violence."[45] When we stifle our emotions, we derail the constant ebb and flow of the life force through us. To hold our feelings inside depletes us. It drains our energy reserves and thus we may feel depressed and irritable. To feel and express our emotions on the other hand, allows the energy to move through and to nourish us, the way a flooding river brings nutrients onto the land. To feel and express emotions keeps us open to life and to living vibrantly.

Many of us are hesitant to accept *what is* because acceptance of what we don't like or don't want can invite uncomfortable feelings. As long as we deny something's existence, or rage at its "wrongness," we can subconsciously avoid the discomfort of our more tender feelings about *what is* or what happened. But emotions aren't

---

[45]   Prechtel.

necessarily unpleasant in and of themselves. We avoid them in large part because we have learned that our feelings are socially unacceptable—in other words, because we *think* they are troublesome. Sadness, grief, and mourning—all aspects of acceptance and surrender—are often considered "negative" emotions, to be expressed only under duress, and even then, oftentimes with shame. And yet, "Any grieving we don't do stiffens our hearts and shuts us away from fully engaging with life."[46] Even joy, a "positive" emotion, can be taboo to express. In *The Book of Joy*, the Dalai Lama says that joy is associated with having a wide expanse of feelings. Archbishop Tutu follows this up with, "Yet as we discover more joy, we can face suffering in a way that ennobles rather than embitters. We have hardship without becoming hard. We have heart break without being broken."[47] To drop into our deep feelings is matter of choice, of surrendering into life.

Surrender, Acceptance, and Will

Surrender is not passive; it is not "giving up." It is active—a choice to move toward something that invokes our resistance, often the case with feeling our emotions. To surrender is a powerful act that can take us beyond the boundary of our familiar limits. When we take stock of ourselves, we see that resistance is usually due to fear, and often, it is simply fear of the unknown. In response, we constrict to protect ourselves. In surrender, we purposefully step toward our fear and into the unknown.

To move toward rather than away from the unknown, we notice where we feel constriction inside physically or emotionally, accept that it is there, and open to feel what is in the constriction. In other words, we use our minds to apply our will to walk through our resistance and step into surrender. When we surrender a constriction around our heart, tears are often released. Our heart softens and expands. This simple process reconnects you with your body-heart-mind, grounds and centers you, and facilitates the release of emotions held in your body. It will keep you up to date with yourself and more resourced to be the person you want to be.

To release our resistance and the constrictions it fosters in the body is accompanied by a palpable physical sensation. We can feel warm and expansive inside and experience energized, tingling sensations. To surrender through resistance brings us fully into the body, even if part of us had checked out or *dissociated*. And yes, it takes courage to

---

[46]   Miki Kashtan, *The Little Book of Courageous Living.* (Oakland: Fearless Heart Publications, 2013).

[47]   Dalia Lama and Tutu with Abrams, *Book of Joy.*

land fully in our physical body—it is inextricably entwined with our emotional body. It necessitates that we engage our will and ask ourselves to walk toward what we otherwise would shy away from or defend against. To surrender, we use our mind to allow our heart to open in the face of the unknown and to feel what is there. When we feel, metabolize and express what we have held in our bodies, then we can be present in our physical being.

Together, acceptance and surrender are the foundation of transformation because they guide us through our resistance and transmute the blockages that hold us back. Willingness and the courage to feel our emotions are needed to fully accept *what is*, which supports our presence. Every small act of surrender is a gift of aliveness in both body and spirit. It transforms what keeps us small and fearful. As feelings wash through us, clearing and cleansing the discomfort of an awkward or painful situation, we are left ready to move on to whatever's next. No residue remains to hold us back from being present to the next moment. No story is created that keeps us tethered to the past. In fact, when we are transparent with our feelings, a meaningful connection often occurs between everyone involved because we have shared the human experience that is our emotional life.

Emotions and the Body

The body is a brilliant, multifaceted organism with tremendous wisdom. As we continue the journey into deeper self-connection, we are likely to feel more emotions as our body unwinds holding patterns that have served us in trying times. Feelings live not only in the heart, but also throughout our physical being. We can stumble onto emotions when we focus on tight places inside, as one might do during meditation, massage, or yoga. In fact, to feel our emotions we must inhabit our physical body, which can be challenging at times for some. But the effort is worth it, as there is much to be gleaned from paying attention to our sensations, feelings, and intuition. To receive the wisdom we have inside, we must be willing to feel our emotions and, perhaps most importantly, to let ourselves grieve. In the end, grieving will open our hearts to the joy and the beauty of being alive.

CHAPTER NINE

Wisdom and the Wounded Child

The wound is the place where the Light enters you.
—Rumi

Have you ever heard your inner voice speaking to you and then completely ignored it? Not listening to that voice of wisdom can tempt mishaps, from physical injuries to unhappy marriages. It is our strident, rational mind that is the culprit in disregarding our intuition. Many of us need to focus diligently to reacquaint ourselves with our own internal wisdom, such that we don't override the still, small voice inside. The more we trust that inner voice, the clearer and stronger it gets. There is wisdom there for us, just waiting to be heeded.

Given how challenging it is to simply be attentive to ourselves from the inside, it is really no mystery that many of us feel disconnected from our body-heart-mind's wisdom. This is not serendipitous. We are products of our culture and upbringing, well steeped in paying homage to the intellect while marginalizing the rest of who we are. But to simply attend to ourselves with the presence and care we might offer a child in need, for example, can heal various offenses incurred in childhood, whether verbal, physical, emotional, or spiritual or any combination of them. In the healing process, we ask ourselves to open, to explore, and to be with whatever is there inside—with acceptance and compassion.

The exploration in this chapter rests on the foundation of looking inward. It includes our growing self-acceptance, following on the heels of kindness with ourselves and holding ourselves with compassion. A radical approach for many, it is a way to resolve patterns that hold us back, while, at the same time, to tap into our personal wisdom.

Carol's Story

A client I'll call Carol came to me to find freedom from her patterns of shame, low self-esteem, and self-sabotage. She realized she was feeling diminished to the point of being paralyzed from accomplishing her life goals. At that point, she was working on a college degree in environmental studies. She recognized that she undermined herself by "self-medicating" her emotional pain with alcohol, recreational drugs, or sex. She was worried she may be heading down a path of no return if she didn't seek help soon, so she summoned the courage to reach out for support. This is her account of her story of shame and self-discovery as she came to know it:

> I felt invisible as a child. From an early age, I spent a good deal of my time alone, quietly going about my days and staying out of trouble. I spent a lot of time outside and with animals, where I felt accepted and knew what to expect. I was well into my twenties before I realized that I am not invisible, and in fact, I actually affect people around me simply because I exist. It struck me then that I could choose to affect situations positively, if only I knew how. In therapy, I discovered that, having been invisible for so long, my need to be cared about and known was hidden even from myself. There were parts of me I feared to know and kept hidden where they could remain unknown and, really, disowned.

> During one psychotherapy session, I saw the image of a wad of sticky, black, steaming gunk somewhere deep inside of me. I was repulsed, full of shame and disgust at the discovery of what was there. My therapist invited me to stay with it, to accept the image as meaningful. I refocused and went in further. To my surprise, the sticky black gunk melted away, revealing a beautiful baby girl underneath. I wept at the discovery. It was then that I put the pieces together under the guidance of my therapist. I gave way to my tears and mourned the loss of that baby girl's innocence and sense that she mattered. She had been encased in the debilitating shame of being herself, having never been seen or

appreciated for who she was. She was ashamed, brokenhearted, and in so much need of being loved and cared about. With the vision of my inner child's shame and self-loathing, my therapist helped me realize that now it was up to me to give her what she needed.

Befriending the Inner Child

Carol's story of getting a clear image of her wounded inner child is not uncommon. Once we sincerely desire to know what's holding us back or keeping us only halfway here on the planet, our inner world will readily divulge its contents. Yes, she was skillfully guided through her process, but it first required her willingness to look inside and the courage to see and feel what she found. Notice that, as soon as she stayed with the shame image (the "black, sticky gunk" at her core), it morphed into something completely different. With curiosity and focused attention, our inner world will alchemically shift and change, almost miraculously recreating itself into its true image of innocence and beauty. Our inner wisdom-being wants health and wholeness and will show it to us in the way each of us is most likely to understand it.

Our subconscious mind works in symbolism. The symbols that come to us can be archetypal, those common to the collective unconscious, meaning all people. Or they can be specific to our own particular brand of imagery. Either way, they are gifts from an intelligent and wise part of ourselves. It behooves us to stay with an image that comes to our awareness, to observe and discover what is being offered up from our innate wisdom self.

Curiosity is a great friend to us. By its nature, curiosity invokes courage because it invites us to venture into the unknown. We often remain unaware of much of our internal landscape, the details of our past resting underground like seeds waiting for rain to germinate. With the influx of compassion and acceptance, the scars of childhood wounds rise up through us, shift as we attend to them, and alchemically become the voice of wisdom over time. The habit of listening inside soon unveils a cornucopia of pertinent insights and relevant information that support our evolution. Guidance comes when we listen and trust the wisdom of our inner voice.

Conscious Meets the Unconscious

Human infants are helplessly dependent upon others for their survival. We exist in a trancelike state from conception to age five, absorbing information directly from our environment. The amount of information we take in is staggering. At that age, we are unable to learn in a linear fashion through reason, logic, or didactic instruction. Rather, we learn through osmosis. As life goes on around us, we invisibly receive everything we need to know in order to survive. All that we take in becomes the template for life as we know it to be. These patterns run like software below the surface of our awareness, informing most of our decisions. It is our reliance on the vast programming within the subconscious mind that makes the complexity of living possible. Many of the patterns we absorbed are absolutely necessary, while others hold us back. Wisdom is the ability to discern which is which—to know what to keep and what needs revamping.

Our subconscious mind monitors trillions of bodily functions, keeping all systems working in concert, apparently effortlessly. As superbly complex beings, we rely on our subconscious mind to do the bulk of what it takes to navigate the terrain between our self and the external world. Without it, we wouldn't be able to do the myriad things that keep us alive and that we mostly take for granted. The subconscious mind is a double-edged sword, however. It serves to keep us alive and functioning while at the same time, keeping us in a psycho-neurological maze built in our past. The narratives we hold about ourselves and others keep these constructs in place.

To change our stories and ingrained reactions we need to understand how the subconscious mind operates and work with it on its terms. Our subconscious functions solely in the present moment. It has no self-reflective abilities; it simply reacts. This explains the infamous "triggers" or "buttons" that, when pushed, cause reactions in the present that are really rooted in our past. Our neurology uses neuropeptides to sequester our emotional experience as it was then, and whenever we are similarly alarmed, the neuropeptides are reactivated and that same pattern pops into being again.

Because the subconscious has no sense of time, the feeling that my needs don't matter, for example, kicks in *as if it were true right now*. My logical adult mind can see the difference between then and now, but the subconscious mind cannot. A trigger is the stimulus in the *now* that activates a pattern established *then*, causing a childlike reaction. This knee-jerk time jump is at the root of many interpersonal misunderstandings and conflicts. How, then, do we work with the preprogrammed beliefs that keep us locked into a past that undermines our presence in encounters now?

Having learned most of what we know about life and ourselves in an openly receptive, trancelike state, we can best address our subconscious in a similarly receptive state. This requires us to develop a conscious observer self whose job it is to remain open and receptive, to simply witness our thoughts and feelings without reacting. This skill comes with the compassionate observer self, the practice learned in chapter one. In the words of Bruce Lipton, "As a preprogrammed behavior is unfolding, the observing conscious mind can step in, stop the behavior, and create a new response. Thus, the conscious mind offers us free will, meaning we are not just victims of our programming."[48]

As Lipton points out, it is possible to make a conscious choice, rather than just react. We can enlist the conscious mind and use our free will to make different decisions based on our here-and-now reality. We can befriend the subconscious and work with it on its terms. Said another way, we can collaborate with subconscious aspects of ourselves. As with any successful collaboration, it helps to take a kind, respectful approach. Such universal qualities of goodwill quiet the mind and body and allow us to drop into a receptive state. From the state of calm compassion, we have better access to what lies beneath the surface of normal awareness. The kindness meditation practice, supportive of our compassionate observer, is very helpful here. The kindness and compassion we may have missed in the early part of life can be instilled at any time. This is called re-parenting our inner child.

Re-parenting the Inner Child

The practices shared in the handbook thus far set the stage to wisely and compassionately re-parent our inner child. Internalized compassion and the approach of kindness and empathy for ourselves forge the way. To re-parent, we proactively engage the clear, grounded, kind part of us. This is the healthy adult aspect of self that can be drawn upon to give our inner child what has been lacking. When we re-parent ourselves, we create trust between our adult, present time self and our younger wounded, or survivor self.

What we refer to as *the inner child* is the part of us who knows what we need, also called our wisdom self. As it becomes second nature to listen and attend to the wholesome needs of the inner child, we begin to hear a voice of wisdom from within. Every adjustment and contortion we made to adapt and survive childhood difficulties

---

[48] Bruce Lipton, *The Biology of Belief,* Hay House, 2008.

Dissociation Demystified

Dissociation occurs in a wide spectrum of instances. It means that our conscious awareness separates, or dissociates, from our body-heart-mind. Our awareness can either simply float away and hover nearby, or it can zoom back into a traumatic scene from the past. Daydreaming is a very mild form of dissociation—we let our mind wander to other places while our body stays put. Post-traumatic stress can include dissociation that shows up in a variety of ways depending upon the nature of the traumatic event. For war veterans, a sudden loud noise such as a door slamming or backfire from a car can cause them to dissociate and behave as if they are in a war zone. An extreme form of dissociation is the creation of a separate internal personality, as with someone who has multiple personalities. The creation of subpersonalities is a naturally protective response to severe abuse. When abuse is such that we can't stay present for what the body is enduring due to its threatening nature, the wisdom self may create a separate, discreet personality that "can take it" and, thus, protect the tender, helpless self that cannot.

Dissociation is how the body-mind-spirit protects itself from experiencing the full onslaught of threatening circumstances that we have no control over. In effect, our consciousness vacates the premises while the body undergoes the abuse. An individual with a history of severe abuse can find it extremely challenging to come fully into his or her body and live from the inside out. Such experiences are too painful, frightening, and possibly life-threatening to stay in the body at the time when they occurred. The child's ability to trust can be shattered, and the damage can take continued, focused efforts over time to repair. Once a child learns to dissociate, dissociation can readily become the go-to strategy in any stressful situation. Professional facilitation can support repair and integration of disowned parts. We all have elements or parts of our personality that are integrated to varying degrees. There are aspects of our personalities that serve different parts of life. They function in ways called for in specific times and can be referred to as *roles*. For example, we may have our office self, our home self, our party self, our responsible self and our playful self, and so on, each one performing a functional role. The more aligned with our authentic self we become, the less differentiation we will sense in how we function within our different roles and thus, the more integrated we are.

came from this aspect of our being. Our inner wisdom being's job is to care for and protect us. When we trust ourselves to connect with our inner world, we gain direct access to our inner wisdom's voice. At any moment in time, we can discover what we need, how best to care for ourselves, and how to navigate the environment under the protective guidance of our healthy adult self.

Explore this Practice: Re-parenting the Inner Child

Overview

Many facilitators utilize re-parenting to help people become more fully functioning adults and better integrated with themselves. The process can be deeply transformational and healing. It offers the opportunity to befriend your inner child, gain trust among the different parts of yourself, and heal childhood wounds. This is how to engage with parts of our internal makeup that may be sabotaging our efforts to make healthy choices or change debilitating patterns. Integrating our wounded parts allows us to become whole and to make conscious choices from and for the present and, thus, increases personal sovereignty. Please read through the whole practice first and then go back to the beginning to start.

Caveat

If you lose self-awareness or are unable to stay connected to your compassionate observer self during this exercise, consider that you may have dissociated. Your internal protective mechanism may be resisting pain that your inner child is holding. In any case, please honor your experience in the present moment. Embody your compassionate observer self and respond with kindness and care to whatever occurs. If you find you cannot stay aware of yourself as the compassionate observer during the exercise, please discontinue the process. Please seek professional guidance to continue with Re-parenting the Inner Child with support.

If you know you have childhood abuse issues, such as incest, sexual or ritual abuse, or physical or emotional violence, please seek a trusted professional to facilitate this process, if you haven't done so already. If you do not know this about your history but stumble upon it during the exercise, please seek professional guidance with someone who has experience with trauma, PTSD, and dissociative disorders. If you have abuse in your history, befriending and re-parenting your inner child is key to healing, and it may trigger memories and even a dissociative episode. *Please stop the exercise and seek professional guidance if this occurs.* Although this practice is significant to your healing journey, I strongly recommend forging ahead only once you have the support and safe container you need in place.

Transforming childhood wounds and learned limitations depends first and foremost on becoming fully embodied, both physically and emotionally. By metabolizing the emotional content of traumatic events, we release the neuropeptides holding the trauma and are freed to come into our physical bodies. To attempt to leap over and avoid emotional discomfort results in partial aliveness and, most likely, continued dysfunctional relationships and/or addictive patterns. It is by dropping into our internal lives that the painful experiences and wounds in need of healing can surface and be resolved.

Give yourself thirty to sixty minutes the first few times you explore Re-parenting the Inner Child. As you become more practiced, you can check in briefly, as short a time as one minute, to get needed information and reestablish self-connection.

Sit or lie in a quiet, comfortable place with no distractions. (Turn off your phone; tell anyone in your environment you'd like to be alone for up to an hour.) Breathe for a few minutes, allowing yourself to settle into relaxation. Bring in your compassionate observer self and breathe loving-kindness into your body. Once you feel relaxed, are connected with your body, and sense your compassionate observer self within, begin the exercise.

The practice

1. *Recall a recent difficult or painful interaction with someone.* This could be an argument or any interaction where you felt constricted, got defensive, or shut down your heart. Use your compassionate observer self to go inside and notice where you feel the constriction in your body. Bring your attention to that place and gently breathe into it. Relax into your breath and put your attention there for a few minutes. Notice the sensations in the area and allow yourself to open to receive images and information directly from that area of your body. Trust what comes.

   While connected with your compassionate observer and the sensations, emotions, and/or images inside, ask yourself, "How old do I feel when I recall this interaction?" Or ask, "When was the earliest time I felt this way?" Breathe slowly and deeply with your attention focused inside. Simply allow any images and sensations to come to you. You may find a scene with your younger self or simply feel it. Follow the sensations, colors, or images that come to you. Continue to breathe gently and hold a container of presence for whatever shows up. From the perspective of your compassionate observer self, notice the situation your younger self is in, her or his emotions, thoughts, and physical stance. Trust what comes to you. Stay present as the compassionate observer and simply allow your inner child to reveal him or herself. If you don't receive an image, words, or sensations of him or her on the first go, stay with whatever you do become aware of with the same compassionate presence.

The image might be an empowered, defiant stance of your younger self, the part that completely knew who she or he was before your self-connection began to crumble away. It might be an image of your child self being mistreated, disregarded, ignored, or hurt in some way. Trust the image that comes to you; view the scene with compassionate, objective presence, even as you feel your inner child's experience.

2. *Embody your compassionate observer self while sensing your younger self's experience.* Notice what arose as you focused internally. Become the "wise, compassionate parent" as an extension of your compassionate observer self and visualize yourself walking into the scene where your younger self is. Notice what she or he, the child self, is experiencing.

3. *Offer your compassionate presence.* Tell your younger self what you see from her or his perspective. For example you might say, "I see how much you wanted to be seen and appreciated by Dad just then. He was angry and frustrated and told you to shut up. He was upset about his own worries; it wasn't about you. I'll keep you safe. You are precious." Trust your wise, compassionate adult self. You will know what to say to your inner child. Speak to her or him while you are embodying your compassionate parent self. Trust what comes and stay connected to your body as the wise, compassionate adult.

4. *You have a choice. You can step in as the protector*: If immediate protection is needed, tell the hurtful person from the past to leave the child alone and to never do that again. Stand strong and protect your younger self. Remove the child and take him or her to a safe place if needed. Once the threat is gone, continue to be present and compassionate with your child-self.

Continue the process as follows *once the child self is safe. Or, if immediate safety and protection are not needed, you can ask your child self what she or he would like from you.* This is about building trust between your younger self and your present, wise, compassionate parent self. As the wise, compassionate parent you can also see or guess what the child needs and offer that. *However, do not make any assumptions about what to give the child part before getting permission to give it.* This is important for building trust with yourself. Be sure to establish communication and agreement before taking any action. Honor what your child self wants and needs.

5. *Verbalize your observation, offer what you guess is needed, and listen for your inner child's response before giving it.* If your child self has been neglected for years, it may take a few meetings before she or he is open to being held and rocked or even to just sit close by and enjoy being near one another. Listen attentively to what she or he shares with you. This is the voice of your inner self. The information is the truth about yourself and what you need in order to become whole and empowered. Trust what you receive.

Decide together what your inner child needs and wants and what you are able and willing to give. It may be sitting next to each other or walking together in a beautiful place. It could be holding and rocking her or him and crying together. Have a conversation about what that will be. Agree to a time and place to do what you have agreed you will do. If it is right then, go ahead and do it. Once complete, agree when to meet again and what that might look like. It might be a playdate, a bubble bath, a playful time with a good friend, or an outing in nature. Or it simply might be a one- to five-minute check-in to see how the inner child is doing and what he or she needs in the moment.

6. *At the end of each such meeting, before leaving the scene with your child self, make an agreement about when the next meeting will be and what you plan to do.* Be sure to be honest about what you are able and willing to give. Tell her or him when you plan to be back. Keep your agreement or change the agreement with your inner child as soon as you know you cannot keep it.

With this practice, we establish trust through honesty, integrity, and kindness—key ingredients for integrating lost and disowned parts. The more trust that you establish, the more wisdom you will receive when listening to your inner self. The voice of your inner child will soon be one and the same with the voice of your internal wisdom.

Continue with Re-parenting the Inner Child process formally until it has become a natural impulse to check in regularly with your inner world. Once you have immediate access to your inner self upon sitting and reflecting, use the exercise itself on an as-needed basis.

Continue to acknowledge and check in with yourself regularly. The invitation to friend and re-parent your inner child is a sweet way to make a habit of staying connected to yourself throughout the day. As you become more adept at listening to and responding to your emotional well-being, confidence in yourself and your inner guidance system will grow. You will garner immense wisdom, generosity and kindness for yourself as you deepen the connection with your inner child. Self-care, acceptance, and self-esteem are based on this relationship with yourself. The more you trust yourself to stay connected and tuned in to yourself, particularly with the embodied compassionate observer self, the more at ease you will be in almost every situation and interaction.

Hannah's Story, Part 2

When Hannah came to me wanting better communication and more connection with her sixteen-year-old son, they already had a long history of painful interactions. Despite her strong desire to communicate clearly and compassionately with him, Hannah found it nearly impossible to do so. Her son was consistently angry and aggressive in response to her admonitions. Hannah admittedly felt challenged to be the caring parent she wanted to be and acknowledged that she'd reacted with anger to her son at times. She hadn't looked into the source of her anger and wasn't in touch with the wounded child inside of herself.

Having divorced her husband some years earlier, Hannah felt helpless when she witnessed father and son yelling at one another in her yard one day. The stress of the situation caused her to disconnect from herself. She had enough awareness to observe what was occurring but could not find the internal resources to effectively intervene in the argument escalating before her eyes. She was paralyzed.

As I sat listening to her, I wondered if Hannah, like many people I've worked with, was inclined to dissociate from herself and her emotions. I asked her to take herself back to that scene and notice what she's feeling, as if it were now. She was able to identify tightness in her belly that seemed to be giving her a sense of distance from the situation. But she could not feel anything else—no emotions, no bodily sensations, and no thoughts as to what might help move the argument toward resolution. She was in a dissociated state. Dissociation is a strategy that our internal wisdom being naturally utilizes when we are powerless to physically escape a threatening situation. We all need a sense of safety to remain fully embodied and present. When we aren't safe and are helpless to do anything about it, our energy-body, at times including our consciousness, lifts up out of the physical body, in effect leaving "nobody home."

To get to the root of that tendency, I helped Hannah connect with her body through a technique from *bioenergetics*. (For more information, go to www.bioenergetic-therapy.com). She stood with softly bent knees, breathing into her belly, gently pushing against the earth as she bent and straightened her knees. This technique, called *grounding*, brings energy and awareness into the feet and legs. It allows us to feel connected to and supported by the earth, our natural place of safety and belonging. Coming into the physical body this way can move stuck energy so that we can better access kinesthetic sensations and emotions. In effect, we invite our awareness to descend back into the body.

Once Hannah was reconnected to her body, I asked her to go back to the situation mentally, check in with herself, and notice what was there inside now. She said she felt helpless and wanted to flee the situation. This confirmed what I'd suspected—we were dealing with a childhood pattern. Hannah had learned to protect herself by dissociating from her body.

I asked her to find her earliest memory of having this same feeling. She took a minute to go inward and then said, "I was ten years old, sitting at the kitchen table doing my math homework with my father. He was trying to help, but I was afraid he would get angry and call me stupid." She remembered it very clearly. "I feared his judgment and knew he would get angry at me if I didn't do it right."

I invited her to find her wise and nurturing inner parent and encouraged her to embody that consciousness. With focus and intention, we can summon and embody the compassionate state we seek when working with our inner world. Once embodied, I directed her, as the compassionate, wise parent, to approach her ten-year-old self in her mind's eye. I invited her to offer words of support or make physical contact with her child self—whatever she sensed the child part of her could receive. The compassionate part of ourselves naturally knows what to say and how to respond when we trust it. When we approach the younger wounded part of ourselves in this way, we evoke our more resourced adult self to offer what is needed.

The adult part of Hannah offered empathetic understanding to her ten-year-old self and asked if she could sit between her and her father. This process goes on inside as we intentionally connect with internal aspects of ourselves. As Hannah sat between her child self and her father, I suggested she have a conversation with her child self. She assured her younger self that she was not stupid. She made physical contact with the child, who was willing to hold hands with her adult self. After more conversation between her adult self and her inner child, Hannah made an agreement to check in twice a day, morning and evening, to see how the child part was doing and what she may need.

The interaction happened within Hannah energetically, which she could see in imagery. But it had the psycho-emotional effect of happening in reality, in the present. She could feel the sensations both of her child self and her adult self and thus began to bridge the gap between her wounded child and her wise adult counterpart. She embodied the healthy, caring parent she needed and, thus, gained the trust of her fearful child self. The more she heard and attended to her inner child's needs, the more her inner voice became her own voice of wisdom. It has helped her to know what she needs so that her adult self can attend to those needs and stay present in challenging interactions.

This practice has the power to transform patterns set in the past that were useful then but are self-defeating in the present. We come to understand what we feel and need by listening to our inner voice. This helps us repair the wounds of our inner child and release the energy that keeps the old patterns and limiting beliefs in place. From there, we can make different choices that support our current needs. It is important to honor the wounded child's fears and survival mechanisms. When we do, we rebuild trust with ourselves. Rather than castigate those parts or patterns no longer viable to us, we recognize the important job they performed by keeping our child self as safe as possible. With gratitude, we acknowledge their prior usefulness even as we let them go. The old patterns then disband and, like retooling, the energy is freed up and available for new endeavors.

Once we start listening inside and spend time conversing with forgotten or disowned parts of ourselves, a whole new world becomes available to us. When we befriend the inner child, we become more integrated and aligned with our authentic self. With immediate access to our internal world, we can hear what we need for self-care moment to moment. This increases our ability to trust ourselves, which brings the self-confidence we need to meet all kinds of circumstances with equanimity. In this way, we can embody care, understanding, protection, or whatever quality we need in the present moment, rather than getting triggered and allowing the wounds and patterns of the past to govern our actions in the present.

The Familiar and the Unknown

Familiarity, even if debilitating in some way, is commonly experienced as "safe." For us to go beyond what is familiar and into the unknown takes our willingness and courage, even when to do so is a healthier response. As adults, when things are finally bad enough, it's as if there is no choice but to make the changes needed to better ourselves and our situation, and it almost always entails stepping out of our comfort zone. But when we are ready to take the leap into the unknown, the courage and support necessary to proceed appear—*once we make the decision and commit ourselves to it.* Because there is no separation, unseen forces move on our behalf, and the way opens before us.

As adults, we have freedom of choice. But as children, generally there was no option to change our circumstances, dependent as we were on others to sustain us. Even so, the option to choose something different as an adult can seem like a distant, unattainable dream. As soon as we focus inwardly, however, we find that everything we are made of is malleable and, with a clear intention, will shift under the watchful presence of our compassionate observer.

Hannah truly wanted to communicate with respect and kindness with her son. But until she did her own inner child work, she treated him the way her father had treated her. It was a debilitating cycle that hobbled her relationship with her son. As she uncovered her own fear and confusion about how she was treated as a child and re-parented herself, she became more able to respond with empathy and kindness to her son. She was so committed to making this shift and becoming the parent she wanted to be that she had the courage to keep going inward. With time and focus, she was able to establish the compassionate, healthy parent to her own wounded inner child. This translated into kindness and understanding in her present-day relationships, including with her son.

We use clarity of will in tandem with our compassionate observer to navigate the inward journey. Depending on the severity of our childhood wounding, coming into the body and landing on the ground of physicality can be awkward or feel scary. And yet, physical embodiment is needed if we are to have access to our full life force, our passion and creativity. It is embodiment that offers us the possibility of freedom and empowerment to live true to ourselves and to tap into our inner wisdom. When we embody our physical container, then we can be present and fully engage with our purpose and share our gifts. When we are whole and integrated, we are filled to over flowing, and naturally want to give of ourselves to others.

CHAPTER TEN
Beyond the Blame Game

*It is not he who reviles or strikes you who insults you, but
your opinion that these things are insulting.*
—Epictetus

Blame actually serves a very useful, although primarily unconscious, purpose. It protects our feelings, thoughts and expectations—our sense of self—by focusing on someone else's part in our pain or discomfort. It is a reliable way to avoid taking responsibility for our part in upsets and disappointments. Given the ingrained habit to look outside of ourselves first, blame makes perfect sense. Although blaming others may take the initial sting out of feeling hurt, it doesn't make us happy.

The adage, "Do you want to be right, or do you want to be happy?" says it succinctly. It is difficult to be both in the context of our relationships. As with judgment, blame informs us that what's going on is impacting us—and not in the way we'd expected or hoped it would. In short, blame keeps our tenderness from being known and experienced. When we resort to blame, we lose connection with ourselves and create separation from others. And it usually increases the potential for escalating conflicts. In essence, blame is a detour that takes us away from *what is*.

It's simple to get back to self-connection but, again, not necessarily easy. The blame train can rapidly pick up steam and pull us right down that old track of disconnection. This is where the cumulative effect of having practiced embodying your preferred qualities of life comes in very handy. As with any tightness or constriction, we take our awareness inside first and seek our coordinates of presence. This shifts the responsibility for our experience back to ourselves and reveals the truth about what we're feeling and wanting.

The learning curve is cut short with a strong desire to live in more resourceful and resonant states, like generosity, kindness, gratitude, or acceptance, for example. That's what makes us happy. To do so requires that we be in touch with ourselves internally and know what motivates us, rather than reacting outwardly. The simplicity of the process lies in focusing on embodying the quality or state of being we desire by slowing our breath and going inside. Blame, judgment, and all our habitual constrictions and limiting patterns dissolve when we fill ourselves up with a coherent emotional state.

To be motivated from the inside out means aligning our subconscious mind with our conscious intentions. This way, our deeper values, the qualities of life that matter to us, become the impetus behind our words and actions. When we practice this, our choices coincide with our values and we are more likely to enjoy uncontentious, harmonious interactions. The nagging habit of blame, more fallout from right-wrong thinking, is automatically transformed when we respond from our true feelings and core values.

The qualities of life that matter to us are served almost seamlessly once we willingly feel what's uncomfortable and speak to that truthfully. There is no blame or shame for being us—for feeling and wanting what we do. And, when we are aligned with our values, we become better able to consider the effect we have on others.

The Blame Game

I remember feeling aghast when I heard Marshall Rosenberg, the originator of NVC, say that we often actually enjoy the suffering of others. I took a hesitant look inside to see if I could find it in myself. In short order, I was shocked to see that yes, indeed, it was true. I cringed realizing that I sometimes felt a certain glee at another's suffering, especially if I felt they "deserved it." It was gut-wrenching to admit this to myself, but I could no longer pretend it wasn't so. It became apparent that blame intends to relieve us of pain or angst, but it happens at another's expense.

The phrase "they deserved it" is a sad testament to a social system that encourages people to close off to others' difficulties. Just a step away is the desire for physical harm to be done. It isn't just that we don't often consider the effects of our actions on others. It is also that we wish them ill at times. How are we to overcome this habit of blame and castigation? How do we heal the ballooning sense of separation from one another that allows the perpetration of violence on each other?

To harvest the full benefits of the following exploration, we need clarity about the values that matter to us and choose to implement them to guide our decisions. For example, why is a shift from blame and resentment to inclusion and care important? You must understand for yourself what your values are and why they matter to you. Knowing this is key to having the internal motivation needed to make real change. When we agree with ourselves about what truly matters to us, then our conscious and subconscious are in alignment. That way, we don't sabotage our own efforts to change.

The Pain of Hurting Others

It can be very difficult to acknowledge and take responsibility for causing another person pain or hardship. Because of our tenderness, it is oftentimes easier to blame someone for his or her plight than to feel our own helplessness about it. Even if the harm we caused was inadvertent, to take responsibility for our part in someone else's suffering is so uncomfortable that most of us use blame to push it away before it even reaches our awareness.

I remember sitting in a group of about seventy-five people with my NVC mentor, Miki Kashtan, as she shared a story about her mediation work with Israelis and Palestinians. She spoke of facilitating a conversation between an Israeli woman whose husband had killed the Palestinian woman's husband. The Israeli woman was agitated; she insisted it was the Palestinian's fault for getting himself killed. Finally, having been heard with empathy and presence for some time, the Israeli woman collapsed in tears. Once she stopped projecting blame onto the dead Palestinian, she was able to admit that her heart ached over what her husband had done and that she felt helpless in the face of the pain it caused the Palestinian woman and her family.

While listening to Miki's story, I couldn't ignore my own tendency to deny my part in another's pain. Once the awareness really hit me, a loud sob burst out of me into in the otherwise quiet room. Miki acknowledged it with, "There's someone who got it." To be the stimulus of another's pain is hard to reconcile. The circular suffering in such cases is complex and demands insight as well as courage to accept our part in it. Blame is much easier, but it isn't the truth. The truth is that we care deeply about one another.

To attend to our inward experiences with care allows us to feel our emotions without blaming the apparent external cause. The true cause of our feelings is what we think about what happened, which stems from our beliefs and the values that matter to us. The ability to take responsibility for ourselves includes increasing our stamina to be uncomfortable, which for most of us means to feel our emotions. The compassionate observer self is well suited to this task. Gentleness affords us more willingness to witness, accept, and be with our true experience, including our feelings, without brushing it off, pushing it away, or projecting blame for it onto others. Once we embrace *what is*, we have access to more resourceful options in response. The following practice can transform blame, release constrictions of the heart, and allow us to open to our feeling states. Our emotions support our connectivity and allow us to live with more presence and authenticity.

Explore this Practice: Beyond Blame with Self-Empathy

Blame causes a contraction of the heart that can be felt as a tightening in the chest, constriction in the gut, or a hardening of the jaw. Condemning thoughts are often part of the internal scenario, fueling the tendency of the body-heart-mind to close. A cascade of judgmental and blaming thoughts can overtake us, as if to make a case to prove we are right and the other is wrong. To catch ourselves in this onslaught, we need to tune in to the discomfort or agitation that accompany these thoughts and feelings. Self-awareness is key to recognizing blame. The practice of self-empathy first will help to uproot the blame-habit and allow for more creative responses.

Self-Empathy first

1. *When you recognize you're blaming someone or something, stop and breathe.* Notice where the constriction is. Breathe into it.

    For example, if my daughter forgets to fill the gas tank after she borrowed my car, I might blame her for making my life more difficult when I have to dash off to work and the needle is on empty. Blame gives me an immediate sense of empowerment and righteousness, from which the thought of punishing her might arise. This is a sign that I have closed my body-heart-mind. I notice the tightness in my chest and feel anger rising.

2. *Notice the thoughts that feed the tightness.* Notice the automatic thoughts that feed your blame. Come back to your body. Breathe again. Ask yourself: what matters so much right now that it triggers me to shut down my heart and to be filled with anger and resentment?

For example, I want to drive right to work. That's all the time I have left by now. I'm angry that I have to get gas right away because I may be late for work. I rail at her in my mind for causing this upsetting situation. As I breathe into the tightness, I feel frustration, sadness, and helplessness and also, I start accepting that this is the way it is right now.

3. *Look to see what universal quality of life wants to be recognized and activated.* What is it in the situation that matters so much to you that it creates the blame reaction? Breathe into the quality of life that is up for you. Surrender into the energetics of the quality; embody it.

    For example, I wanted ease and expediency when I got into the car. I don't want to be late to work. Keeping agreements and integrity with my word matter to me. I also want to understand what happened that she didn't follow through with what she said she'd do. I notice I can go to "Why didn't she?" and it fuels my anger. I don't want to go down that wormhole, so I let it turn to curiosity rather than feed my anger. I want ease and integrity, so I bring that awareness into myself and breathe the energetics of them into presence. I notice my chest relax and I can suddenly see through the situation to doable solutions. I feel calmer and can focus on solutions.

4. *Recognize yourself as human with feelings and needs.* As you embody the quality that represents your desired state, notice that acceptance has allowed other possibilities to surface. Breathe. This is self-empathy in action.

    For example, as I feel ease and integrity washing through me, I realize that this isn't the end of the world. I see I may have time to stop for gas, or I may be able to get to work and get gas later. Or I can call in to say that I'll be five to ten minutes late.

5. *Make a request of yourself and carry on with your day.* Do what makes the most sense to you given the qualities of life you've embodied and the specifics of your situation.

    For example, I decide to drive right to the gas station. If I see that I'll be late, then I'll call in to let them know. I will have a conversation with my daughter about it later. I don't blame her for my experience, but I want her to think about me and my needs, too, and include me with consideration. I'll remind her to fill the gas tank when she borrows my car and find out what kept her from doing it this time.

This is an in-the-moment, on-the-go application of self-empathy. It reconnects me with my deeper values and I realign with them. I recalibrate my experience from anger and blame to presence and creativity. The practice allows you to continue what you were doing with acceptance of what occurred while transforming blame. It can lighten you up and open your heart-mind, thus allowing new solutions to show up. In the next chapter, we will learn how to communicate clearly without blame.

Making and Breaking Agreements with Integrity

To make an agreement with integrity means to include the other people's wants and needs equally with our own. And if we can no longer uphold our part of an agreement, we communicate about it with care for how our change of plans could affect the other(s). To break an agreement with integrity entails having a conversation, preferably beforehand, and then coming to mutually agreeable terms for the revised agreement or a new time frame for its accomplishment. This may disappoint someone or invite disapproval. It's uncomfortable to face the prospect of telling someone that we've changed our mind. However, to be honest when we are unable or unwilling to keep an agreement shows respect for the other person. We are taking him or her into consideration by addressing circumstances that have come into play after we made the agreement.

Integrity lies in our willingness to fully communicate our needs before making an agreement, as well as to communicate when we can no longer keep an agreement we have made. Blame and resentment are common results from broken agreements because most of us are not skilled at this sort of direct, attentive communication.

Steve's Story

A client, Steve, came to me confused and full of resentment toward his son. Steve is a big-hearted man who cares deeply about his friends and family. When he divorced his son's mother, he carried some guilt that maybe he hadn't been the good husband and father he'd expected of himself. Perhaps to compensate, he determined he would give his son anything he needed and wanted. Steve wanted to do things differently than his father had done with him and assumed his kindness and generosity would help his son to be generous and caring, too. When his son was old enough, Steve brought him into the family business. Soon after, when his son wanted to set up his own branch of the business in a neighboring town, Steve thought it was a worthwhile idea. Per their agreement, his son would be responsible for bringing in new clients, managing the new branch, and paying back the cost of the new infrastructure with the increased profits.

However, Steve's generosity backfired. Soon, his son left the business, abandoned the acquired debt, and left his father with a new business site that had no management or revenue. It was easy to blame his son for being irresponsible and lacking in integrity. Certainly, these assessments made logical sense—they formed the basis of Steve's sizeable resentment. Remember, our exploration here is not about funneling down into right-and-wrong mode. We want to see the whole situation, to zoom out to the broader perspective. Our aim is to gain clarity, find resolution and get to freedom from the confusion and discomfort that comes with blame and resentment.

There is no one to blame for the outcome in this situation. It is a natural consequence of all that went before and the established relationship patterns. Like so many of us, Steve didn't know how to have an inclusive conversation in which he and his son could both have their needs and expectations be a part of it. He didn't know how to help his son learn to take responsibility for himself and include consideration for the others involved.

If he'd had the ability to include himself and his needs all along, Steve would have modeled inclusion and caring for others to his son. He would have been able to discern when saying "no" was in his son's best interest. Their relationship would have had a different foundation altogether had Steve included his own needs in decisions and agreements from the beginning. His son would have developed an understanding that he was responsible for his part of the bargain. Most likely, he wouldn't have confused his father's generosity with free license to walk away from responsibility.

Just like Steve, most of us are well intentioned. But when we operate from the assumption that there is only room for one of us to get our needs met or that to give the best of ourselves we must leave parts of ourselves behind, we set ourselves up for blame and resentment. The ability to include ourselves equally with others is the antidote to later resentment. Developing the skill to notice and accept what we're feeling and needing will help us avoid blame and not accumulate resentment.

Explore this Practice: Turning Resentment into Acceptance

When you notice you're feeling resentful about something, this will help you come back to presence, clarity, and honesty with yourself.

1. *Notice your feelings*. When resentment comes up, notice what you feel in your body. Breathe. Allow yourself to feel the feelings about the situation and what is upsetting you. Write them down.

   For example: "I feel stuck. I'm angry she made me come along on this trip. I feel trapped and tight inside. I wanted to stay home and get things done. Now I'm worried about when I can get to them. I feel tense and resentful."

2. *Notice the stories you have about the situation*. Listen to the stories you're telling yourself about the situation. Notice how the stories feed your upset and resentment.

   For example: "I didn't want to come on this trip. Why did she force me to come? She never listens to me. She always makes decisions without me and then expects me to go along. She gets angry if I don't go along with her plans."

3. *Notice your emotions*. Name the emotions you feel when you note the stories you have.

   For example: "I feel angry and frustrated. I feel constricted and upset. I'm mad at her. I feel helpless and resentful."

4. *List the universal quality of life within the stories*. Note what really matters to you, free of the stories. Name at least one quality of life that is feeding your resentment.

   For example: "To be heard. To be understood. To be included. Respect. Consideration. To matter."

   Take out your personal list of universal qualities of life to help you find what is fueling your upset and concerns in the statements, if it is helpful to do so.

5. *Name the universal quality of life served by the decision that led to your resentment*. Write down the universal quality of life you were serving when you said yes or agreed to do what you now feel resentful about.

   For example: "Harmony. Ease. Expediency. Acceptance. Security. Peace. I was afraid if I didn't go along with her that she'd be really angry at me."

6. *Use your compassionate observer self to understand and accept* what you were prioritizing (the universal qualities of life identified in step 5) when you made the decision and agreed to do what you did.

   For example: "I was afraid to say no. I wanted peace and harmony."

7. *Notice and feel your emotions*. Notice the immediate relaxation inside when you name and own your part in what happened. You may be aware of sadness, regret, or anger about not having included your other needs (the qualities of life identified in step 4) before agreeing. Note that you did the best you could,

given the skills and self-awareness you had at the time. Breathe. Use your compassionate observer self to accept and feel the disappointment or regret of not including yourself fully. This is taking responsibility for your part in the experience.

8. *Make a request of yourself.* Decide what, if anything, you want to do about the situation. You may want to leave it alone for now and simply enjoy having transformed your resentment into acceptance. Or you may want to have a conversation and discuss changing the agreement that fostered your resentment or see if there is time and space for further discussion about it before the agreed upon situation happens.

     For example: Request of yourself that you speak with her. Embody the quality of life mattering to you before engaging in the conversation, for example, harmony.

     You might say to her, "After thinking more about it, I realize that I need to get stuff done here, and if I go with you, I'll be stressed about it. What is that like for you to hear?" This is an opening for further discussion with the intention of taking both sets of needs into full consideration before agreeing. Or, if it has already happened, you can bring it up too. You might say, "I realize I agreed to come with you because you said you wanted me to come and not because I really wanted to. I'm feeling stressed about getting work done now. I'd like to talk about me staying in to finish up this work on my computer while you go out today. How is that for you to hear?"

When blame and resentment are disabled, their energy is freed up for more constructive interactions. Life seems easier and less abrasive and becomes more enjoyable. Facility with tracking and connecting with our inner world gives us the information necessary to feel out whether we are fully on board with something before agreeing to it. Any sense of constriction or hesitation before saying yes is reason to pause and take time to reflect before entering into an agreement. You can even take time to write out the qualities of life you want to include in the decision-making process and bring them to the table. You can express your hesitation by saying something to the effect of, "I want to say yes, but I notice I'm a little hesitant. I want to honor that and include both of us by taking more time to discuss it. I want to find out what I'm concerned about or what I need before I agree." We will discuss in more detail how to have this type of conversation in the chapters that follow.

Blame and resentment have deep roots in our psyches. Simply put, blame is the resistance to feeling our discomfort by projecting it onto others. In the next chapter and in part three, "The Way Together," we'll learn more about how to communicate with transparency and authenticity while taking others into consideration too. This alleviates the tendency to project blame or make decisions we may resent later.

CHAPTER ELEVEN
The Heart of Communication

Your vision will become clear only when you can look into your own
heart. Who looks outside, dreams; who looks inside, awakes.
—Carl Jung

Heartfelt communication lands as balm on the soul. It satisfies our deep longing for truth and kindness. Their sweet infusion wraps us in wings of compassion that lift us into our own generosity of spirit. When it comes down to it, generosity is at the heart of resourceful communication, by which I mean communication that generates connection as well as understanding.

Connection and Understanding

A successful exchange of information is when what we intend to transmit is what is received, resulting in greater understanding and/or connection. This often is not the case, however. Hurt feelings and conflicts frequently result from misunderstandings. We can't ensure beforehand that what we want to get across will land as we'd like it to. However, we can have clarity about our intentions. When we uphold connection as our primary intention, understanding is more likely to result from the interaction. This is a shift in orientation for most. Most of us assume that the words coming out of our mouths and their meaning to us is what the other person will hear, regardless of whether or not we are tuned in to one another. Although it seems logical, it doesn't encompass the breadth of factors that go into communicating.

Every interaction, no matter what kind, is a form of communication. Communication is simply the transfer of information. In that sense, communication is constantly occurring in one form or another at every level of life by way of waves or vibrations, as well as sounds and movement. We live in a soup of microcurrents and magnetic fluctuations that weave in and out of existence, gathering and depositing information every nanosecond of the way. This awareness gives us a broader perspective on things. It also makes communication more expansive than we normally think of it—talking is just the tip of the iceberg.

In fact, the energy we emit by the attitude we carry precedes our physical body by three to eight feet or more. Before we even open our mouths, a great deal of information has passed between us through the energy waves from our body-heart-minds. As the vibrations of others come toward us and mix with ours, what happens next unfolds as if it has a life of its own. We have reactions and make decisions before we're consciously aware of it happening. It follows that we sometimes say or do things unexpectedly or unconsciously. We can greatly increase our chances of being heard and understood as we'd like to be by front-loading the conversation with a clear intention. Intention informs our attitude and thus the energetics of what we say and do. It is on such subtle levels that much of our communication is actually happening.

Our attitude is comprised of so much—our level of presence; our hopes, fears, and expectations; our wants and needs; and our feelings and beliefs. Our tone of voice and body language reflect and transmit our attitude, our energetic imprint in that moment. The simplest way to hold the attitude most conducive to successful communication is to embody the quality of life you desire in the situation. Clear, heartfelt communication will be expedited with the intention to experience connection and understanding. I consider this to be a spacious and generous approach. It naturally allows us to hold the outcome of the dialogue lightly as we focus first on mutual understanding. When we hold the outcome lightly, we are more likely feel connection between us, and thus, to want to understand each other.

We may have a clear picture of other needs of ours too, the qualities of life we'd like served by the dialogue and its outcome. It may seem contradictory to know what we want and also to not be attached to the outcome. If we can stretch our awareness to include the other person fully, however, it makes perfect sense. To do so demonstrates generosity of spirit. Our focus shifts from convincing someone to agree with our position to making space for all of our needs and feelings at the same time. This is a very resourceful approach; it invites creativity into the space. To have the presence to hear whatever is true for one another boosts connection because the conversation is heartfelt and honest. With connection, understanding comes naturally, as does collaboration. With mutual understanding, genuine care about one another arises. When we care equally about our self and the other person, we often find more flexibility in our priorities. This is the course that supports the shift from me to we. The dominant paradigm changes the moment that we include others equally with ourselves before taking action or making decisions.

Getting to the Heart of Communication

Nonviolent communication (NVC) gives a specific format for speaking and listening that is designed to bring our naturally compassionate attitude to the fore. When practiced skillfully, NVC has the potential to alleviate as well as dissolve conflicts and to restore connection, as was Marshall Rosenberg's explicit vision in its origination. About developing NVC he says, "I have ... identified a specific approach to communicating—speaking and listening—that leads us to give from the heart, connecting us with ourselves and with each other in a way that allows our natural compassion to flourish." His innovative idea was well thought out and clearly presented. He researched how people steeped in living nonviolently communicate, like Gandhi and Martin Luther King, Jr., and he sought to apply those same attributes in a duplicable way. He created a template for communicating that, when adeptly practiced and applied, indeed increases mutual understanding and connection, both facets being intrinsic to conflict resolution.

The consciousness of compassion can be cultivated intentionally or remembered and embodied, as we have practiced. When we bring a formula for speaking into the equation, however, we can easily fall into old habits. Trying to do it right, fear of doing it wrong, and comparing ourselves to others are common hiccups. This can become distracting and bog us down in rules and the slippery slope of "should" and "shouldn'ts." To alleviate that sinuous detour to our hearts, I redirect people to their own internal "NVC consciousness." To me, NVC consciousness means to be in empathetic presence with yourself and others at the same time. It includes everyone's feelings and needs equally. When I share the direct route to this consciousness, bypassing the formal NVC template, people tend to come directly to their hearts. This shortens the learning curve substantially while offering immediate results. Rather than learning a new and somewhat stilted way of speaking, we speak more naturally, but it is informed by a fresh consciousness—compassion. To learn the original version of Nonviolent Communication, please read Marshall's book, *Nonviolent Communication: A Language of Life.* It is a wonderful look at a whole new way of being and interacting in the world. Or look into taking classes with a certified NVC trainer.[49]

If you have read and done the practices thus far in this handbook, you have already experienced embodying consciousness as energy in an intentional way. It bears repeating here that the embodiment practice outlined in chapter 3 is the surest, fastest way that I have found to empathetic connection with ourselves and others. It sets our intention while simultaneously allowing us to hold a flexible attachment to the outcome. Embodiment of qualities of life engenders an attitude of compassion and brings us into the state of empathy and inclusion quite naturally. All of the qualities of life are part of the spectrum of love, hence, to embody any of the qualities invites easy access to other qualities, like empathy, compassion, and kindness. When we speak from that place, we naturally speak from the heart. This skill is a major cog in our turning from separation to connection. And it is a defining tool for assuming leadership in a new world.

Components of Communication

The components for openhearted communication have been shared in the previous chapters. We will string them together here to illustrate the complete process. When you know your internal coordinates, meaning what you're feeling and what you're seeking (as your need, value, or quality of life) and listen and speak with empathetic presence, you naturally invite connection and understanding. Understanding is an expectation intrinsic to most conversations. But without establishing connection, we might miss mutual understanding and unintentionally incite conflict in the process. When we intend and practice bringing both connection and understanding into our conversations, cooperation is engendered. At the same time, the likelihood of having a conflict is minimized significantly.

The potential for conflict is further diminished by embodying qualities of life relevant to the conversation. Another key skill is making requests after speaking to confirm you both are being heard and understood as you'd like. We will apply these skills further in Part Three of the handbook. Below is an exploration of the components to the heart of communication, also called "the empathy dance."

---

[49]   See cnvc.org for more information or go to "Further Resources" at the back of this book.

The Empathy Dance

The empathy dance is a way to stay tuned in to yourself while venturing out to focus on another person throughout the conversation. This is a practical way to hold a conversation that prioritizes connection and understanding. We are developing an athletic sort of awareness that uses mental agility and flexibility of focus. I picture it like the keen yet fluid flight of a hummingbird hovering midair, darting in to reach a flower and then drawing back and hovering midair again. The point is to stay centered and engaged with yourself while sending your attention to another person and coming back to yourself in fluctuating intervals.

To summarize, the empathy dance is when we let our attention stretch between our own internal state and our presence with another person. We pay attention to our feelings and universal qualities of life as well as theirs, flowing back and forth between the two as in a dance. The universal qualities of life give a very down-to-earth way to recognize and name our human experiences and longings. As such, they are the purveyors of mutual understanding and connection between us.

Explore this Practice: Empathetic Listening and Self-Expression

Use this practice for an upcoming conversation or to redo and repair a previous conversation that you wish had gone differently. To start, come into self-connection by noting your internal coordinates. Notice what you are feeling, both physically and emotionally, and wanting—the essential quality of life that is up for you in the situation—before you start the conversation. This will help you to be present and empathetic.

For an example, I'll use an imaginary couple who both live and work together, Mary and John. After the completion of a particularly long and grueling project, they both have needs that were put on the back burner in order to meet their deadline. Mary wants to drop into connection with John by taking time away together. John, however, needs time to himself to recharge and reconnect with himself. Notice how the conversation between Mary and John flows through the steps.

The Empathy Dance

1. *Self-connect and self-express.* Take your attention inside. Find and express what you are feeling and wanting.
2. *Listen with empathy and reflect what you've heard from the other.*
3. *Follow with a request to ensure mutual understanding.*

MARY. I'm exhausted now that we've completed this project and really want some time together to connect and relax. Let's go away for the weekend, just you and me; leave the kids at my parents; and have some time to ourselves, okay?

JOHN, *hearing this, realizes that they are in very different places after their big push and expenditures of efforts over the last couple of months. But he is adept at empathy.*

That sounds really wonderful, Mary. I'd love to spend time alone together, relax, and reconnect. I'm also noticing that I'm so fried and depleted from how hard I worked over these last few months that I need to replenish and get recharged by having some time to myself first. Will you please tell me how that is for you to hear?

MARY. Oh. Shoot. I'm disappointed because I want to just drop into us now, after all the distractions we've had. I feel sad. I really want to connect with you. I get so nourished when we spend unscheduled time together, just you and me.

JOHN. Yes, I get it. I see that you're disappointed and I know how much it means to you when we can be relaxed and enjoy free fun time together. I love it too. And I don't have anything left in me right now to bring to it. I am so depleted I don't even have energy to think about connecting for the weekend. Please tell me what you hear is going on for me.

MARY. Okay. I get that you are totally drained and unable to even consider going away together this weekend. You need something else first, time to yourself or something that isn't with me. Is that it?

JOHN *hears Mary's pain and disappointment that her wishes aren't also what he wants and needs right now.*

**The Heart of Communication:
Components for Connection and Understanding**

self-connection. Know your internal coordinates—your bodily sensations, your emotions, and the quality of life mattering to you in the moment.

self-expression. Express yourself in terms of what you are feeling and what you are seeking.

request. Follow your statement with a question to get the information you want from the other person after you speak.

empathetic listening. Listen for what the other person is feeling and seeking. Ask a question that includes what your sense is of what he or she is feeling and what quality of life he or she is seeking to experience. Your curiosity and focus on the person form your empathetic presence.

Interesting fact: The other person does not need to know how to communicate this way for it to work. Only you need to use it, trusting yourself to hold empathetic presence for both of you.

Yes, pretty much. And I hear your sadness about it. It isn't that I don't want to spend time with you, as you know. I do want to spend time with you—but when I have something more to give. I'd rather take time to myself first, to get replenished, and then make time to do something together, when I can really be present with you, with both of us. What are you getting about where I am with this?

MARY *feels the empathy John has for her, and it helps her through her disappointment. She is met and understood by him and feels connection in this way. She has more room to accept and honor John's needs too.*

All right. Thank you for being so clear and present with me through all of this. I see we do have different ways of dealing with getting replenished right now. You do want to spend time with me but need time to yourself first. I respect that you need time to yourself. I can take the kids to my parents and hang out there with them. Maybe I'll visit my girlfriends while I'm there. Let's go out to dinner by ourselves tonight then and take the weekend apart. Does that work? We can debrief from the push to finish the project and make plans for the weekend, me with the kids and you chilling.

JOHN. That sounds perfect. Thank you for understanding and supporting me this way. It means a lot that we can work things out so we both get our needs met without the other one feeling neglected. Where do you want to go for dinner?

That example is a pretty ideal conversation. It represents the culmination of learning the skills shared thus far. Integrating these skills is a matter of continuing to drop in to yourself more and more deeply and to unabashedly and openheartedly speak your truth. Acceptance of *what is* allows our honest feelings of disappointment or whatever they are to come up. But it isn't an indictment of the other person being in a different place. It just *is*.

Connecting beyond Judgment

Heartfelt communication is, in effect, empathetic communication. It rests on our own self-connection, our awareness of the emotions we're feeling, and the essence of what is mattering to us—the value or quality of life in play. The technical part is the fluid dance of speaking and listening with our empathetic presence and the intention for connection and understanding between us. The most significant factor, however, may be what is missing from the conversation. We sense something familiar is missing in the above example conversation but can't quite name it. Or can you?

The missing element is judgment. Every practice in this book is directed toward unraveling and dismantling judgment as it occurs inside of us and insidiously spreads from our thinking and speaking. If John had construed that he was "wrong" for needing and wanting time to himself or that Mary was "wrong" for wanting time together, then an argument could have ensued from Mary's suggestion to go away together. But John knows and trusts himself. He trusts his consideration and compassion for Mary, too. He does not judge her for what she needs and wants; nor does he judge himself. There is no right or wrong in this conversation. There are simply two human beings expressing their feelings and needs and responding with empathy to one another. Read through their conversation again and let yourself sink into the sweetness of a heartfelt conversation without judgment. Listen between the lines for the qualities of life they are prioritizing.

The absence of judgment, both internally experienced and outwardly expressed, brings freedom. Such unencumbered interactions need not be rare. Judgment is not a natural component of the human condition. It is learned. It is a signature of the patriarchal paradigm and, as such, is the root cause of conflict. It foments disconnection and condones punishment. In effect, freedom from judgment signifies the departure of the dominant culture and the shift from me to we—that is, from separation to connection.

To implement this paradigm shift we don't need to combat what's here now. As Buck Minster Fuller said, "You never change things by fighting against the existing reality. To change something, build a new model that makes the old model obsolete." Cooperation and kindness aren't new, but we are in desperate need of remembering and employing them. They are agents instrumental to our new social model. When we choose to make the internal shifts of the practices given, the new model emerges while at the same time, the old one naturally dissipates.

To further widen the scope of an inclusive and compassionate attitude, two specific ways to re-establish connection are explained below. They are practical methods that support us to gain freedom from judgment. As directly and simply as possible, they help illuminate the consciousness that the partnership paradigm implements. To step directly into the consciousness of compassion brings us to the heart of communication and simultaneously transforms judgment. We transform the paradigm inside and outside of ourselves at the same time.

Shift versus Compromise

As I sat in a counselor's office with my then husband, in my mind, it was clearly time to sign the divorce papers. I was beyond the let's-make-this-work stage; our four-year relationship had been painful and contentious the whole way through. To me, it seemed that we consistently brought out the worst in each other. But he obviously needed more time. He wasn't ready to let go of the dream, and he said so in no uncertain terms. We were at yet another impasse.

I was desperately attached to the outcome I wanted—to finalize the divorce and be free of the stress of interacting with him. But in a moment of insight, I surrendered to what was clearly true for him—he wasn't ready to let go of the marriage and sign the papers. I felt myself relax and said, "I see this is hard for you. Just take as much time as you need and let me know when you're ready." I was truly no longer attached to my time frame and trusted it would work out. The counseling session ended, and we went our separate ways.

Prepared to wait a few weeks or more to get the papers signed, I stopped thinking about it as soon as the session was over.

Unexpectedly, he phoned the very next day and said, "I've thought it over and I'm ready to sign."

❦

Most arguments are resolved by negotiating a compromise. In a compromise, each party gives up something he or she wants in order to come to an arrangement that both parties can live with. No one gets exactly what he or she wants, and everyone loses something. As logical and fair as compromise seems, it can be a setup for resentment and broken agreements later. In order to reach a full yes from both parties, a different strategy altogether is required. With a full-on yes from both people, buy-in is complete and agreements are much more likely to be kept.

How do we resolve conflicts without compromise? How do we get to yes when there is disagreement? As with any successful conversation, through connection and mutual understanding. When I dropped into full presence inside and realized my former husband was in a completely different state of readiness than I was, my stance shifted. It was also the path of least resistance as I accepted *what was*. I had a true attitude shift; I went from holding tightly to my desired outcome for the counseling session to letting go and acting in support of his needs in that moment. I willingly chose to support his need for more time. I shifted from *my need for completion* to *my need to support* him. With nothing for him to push against or resist, his freedom of choice inadvertently allowed him to shift, too, and thus to go through with signing the papers.

A dialogue that supports connection and mutual understanding opens our hearts. To do so, we bring all of our respective needs to the table for consideration. We allow one another's concerns and desires to be taken into account, which acts as a catalyst for collaboration. The guiding principle for decision-making becomes a shared desire to make things work for everyone concerned. This is what makes a shift possible. A shift is far and away more beneficial than a compromise. When we shift rather than compromise, our agreements have a solid foundation that makes them stick. It may take a little more time up front to get there, but it will save time and angst later by eliminating misunderstandings and the potential for broken agreements. As Miki Kashtan points out, "True dialogue can only happen if I enter the conversation willing to be changed by it. If I am unwilling to change, to be affected sufficiently to consider options new to me, on what grounds am I expecting the other person to change?"[50]

Conflict resolution becomes an adventure rather than a painful battle the moment we let go of needing one particular outcome to achieve success. To do this, we can approach it with the generosity of spirit and willingness to make a shift. For a shift

---

[50] Miki Kashtan, *The Little Book of Courageous Living.* (Oakland: Fearless Heart Publications, 2013).

to happen, we move out of the polarization that results when we focus solely on our differences. Rather, we go for the mutual understanding that happens when we seek our common ground. We become partners who want the best for each other, rather than adversaries who work to out maneuver one another. In this way, we look at the issue together and partner to find solutions that work for us both. When we get right down to it, most of us prefer to work things out amicably and not to get our needs met at someone else's expense.

Explore this Practice: Making an Internal Shift

Shift happens when we are open to the unknown and welcome the unexpected. It isn't about giving up what matters to us, giving in to pressure, or giving away some part of ourselves. A true shift happens almost involuntarily. It is a natural result of listening with curiosity and truly caring about the other(s) involved, as well as letting go of attachment to a single possible outcome. It is a pure act. It is an act of flexibility that takes everyone into consideration. To do so invites in the creative process. It is not an obligation, but it is an option that can make life and relationships more spontaneous and fulfilling. It is a very resourceful and creative approach to problem solving.

The next time you find yourself having a disagreement with someone, suggest that you take time to listen empathetically to each other. Or implement it yourself spontaneously. Empathy is an excellent strategy that supports us to find clarity and connection. It opens our hearts and brings to light the common ground between us—in other words, mutual understanding. Finding your common ground is simple with fluency in the language of the universal qualities of life.

To Begin

Name what you want to discuss and verbally acknowledge any concerns or apprehension you may have at the outset. Invite in an intention to let go of attachment to a particular outcome or a specific strategy to fulfilling your desired outcome. If you aren't willing to let go of a particular outcome, choose a topic that is less charged for this exercise.

1. *Take turns listening and responding with empathy.* Focus on expressing and reflecting the feelings and the qualities of life up for each of you regarding the issue at hand. This invites connection an understanding.

2. *Dance in the gap of uncertainty.* Take as much time as necessary to fully understand one another. Stay in touch with your feelings and needs as well as the sensations in your body. Communicate transparently what's going on for you during the dialogue as you both share honestly what matters to you. The outcome is completely uncertain at this point.

3. *Make a list of the needs, or universal qualities of life up for both of you.* Add or delete items that gain or lose relevance as the conversation continues. This is a sign of flexibility, a crucial element required for shifting perspective.

4. *Look for the stretch.* If a clear common ground for resolution hasn't yet appeared, pay attention to your body, to where you know you tend to constrict when in a disagreement. Breathe and let it soften. Try on the other person's quality of life, the resulting experience that matters most to them. Can you stay openhearted, relaxed, content? Or do you tighten and constrict somewhere inside? If you constrict, then this isn't the time to make a shift. Continue the conversation until you both find a satisfying solution. If you stay open and feel expansive when imagining the other person's need getting met, you may be on the verge of a shift.

5. *Shift.* If it is a natural step, allow yourself to shift to prioritizing the quality of life, or need, up for the other person. You will feel goodwill and generosity of spirit with a true shift and happily choose to support the other person's need getting fulfilled.

   Please, do not attempt to fake a shift! Stay in integrity with yourself and shift only when it feels true and real to you.

A shift is a possibility, not a necessity. It is much more likely to occur in an empathetic dialogue than in a conventional argument that pits us against each other. In general, there is more common ground among us than there is disparity. We just aren't used to looking for it. When we get beyond polarization, the space between us opens onto a very broad playing field. When we trust that we both matter, when we know our needs and concerns as well as theirs are being taken into account, magic can happen.

Do-Overs

In any relationship, we will necessarily make mistakes along the way. A mistake in this regard means we react—do or say something that invites disconnection or hurt. I have found that a good remedy after making a mistake is a *do-over*. A do-over gives us the opportunity to show up with our fallibilities and to take responsibility for how what we said or did affected the other person. In a do-over, we include what we would have liked to do instead. This is particularly useful to do with children. It demonstrates personal responsibility and the humility to admit we made a mistake. But with anyone, it will help to reestablish connection and trust between the two parties. This process models taking responsibility for how we affect others and gives us the opportunity to verbalize the values we would prefer to have expressed.

Explore this Practice: Do-Overs

A do-over is a way to repair damage and to restore connection. It is a form of apology, but not the usual kind. Rather than simply to say that we are sorry, a do-over is a way to express regret for what we did and for how it affected the other person and to review and restate our intentions for how we would rather communicate or behave.

1. Open the conversation. *Express your discomfort. Empathize with your sense of the other person's upset, pain, or disconnection. Invite him or her to talk about it.*
   For example: "I don't feel good about how I spoke to you last night and what I said to you. I know it was hurtful and that's not how I want to be. I bet it was hard for you to hear and uncomfortable to be with. I'd like to hear anything you want to share with me about how it was for you."
2. *Make room to hear the other's pain or whatever is up for him or her; empathize with him or her.*
   For example: "Yeah, it really sucked. I was scared to see you like that. I was really hurt after you said that to me. I just shut down because I didn't want to lash out at you and exacerbate the whole thing."
   "Yes, I understand it was not only scary to see me like that, but you also got angry. You didn't want to make things worse and lash out, so you shut down. That must have been painful to do. You did it so the whole thing wouldn't escalate. Is that it?"
   "Yep, that's right."
   "Is there anything else you want me to know about how that was for you?"
   Continue with empathetic responses until the other person has shared everything he or she wants to about the situation.

3. *After the other person has been fully heard, share how you feel about your part in it and what you wish you had done differently.* This is showing up with true accountability and integrity in the relationship. It is *not* an explanation of yourself about why you did or said what you did or said to them—no blame, no explanation, just authentic humility and presence.

    This is an expression of your feelings, usually including regret, *about how your behaviors affected the other person*. You can also include what you wish you'd had the resources to say or do differently at the time. You can then indicate how you would prefer to do it in the future and what your intentions are if it occurs again.

    For example: "Thank you for telling me how it was for you. I really regret how it played out, and how what I said hurt you. It's painful for me to know that I hurt you, that I lost control like that. I really wish I'd been able to just tell you how I was feeling about the whole thing and not act like it was your fault. I don't want to blame you for my feelings. I want to be responsible and express my feelings honestly. I want to remember to be considerate and kind and to speak with respect always, especially to you. You matter to me so much. I want you to know how much I love and care about you."

4. *Make a request to find out what they are experiencing right now.*

    For example: "I wonder how you are with what I've shared. Will you tell me how you're doing right now with all of it?"

    "Well, I'm sad for what happened and still hurt by it. But I'm glad you came to me to talk about it. I'm feeling better and more connected again. But I'm worried it could happen again."

    Continue reflecting what the other person said with empathy until they are complete.

5. *Then, if you'd like to be heard and understood about how the situation was from your perspective, ask if the other person is willing to hear how it was for you.*

    For example: "I really appreciate you sitting and talking with me about it and getting it cleared up. I have stuff that went on for me about it and things I learned from it that I'd like to share with you. Are you willing to listen to how it was for me?"

    Or, if you feel complete, then simply say so.

    Sometimes there isn't enough energy for both people to stay focused on this kind of conversation for as long as one or both people might like. If you want more discussion and the other person doesn't, request to talk later and make a time that works for both of you.

In general, the goal in do-overs is to take responsibility for a mistake, to repair damage, and to reconnect. This practice reestablishes and deepens our connection and by extension, can deepen trust. Of course, it is following through with what we say we want to do that paves the road to trust. As ever, the more access we have to our empathetic presence, the less likely we are to say and do things that stimulate discord, disconnection, and hurt. Together, co-creation of the relationships and life we want is expedited here, at the center of our being. The heart holds the story of our common ground and is the seat of generosity. Generosity of spirit allows us to move out of defensiveness and into curiosity, the doorway to mutual understanding.

In the third part of the handbook we will put into practice what we have learned in parts one and two. We will explore how to do this in the context of interpersonal relationships and groups.

PART THREE

The Way Together

One of the sayings in our country is Ubuntu—the essence of being human. Ubuntu speaks particularly about the fact that you can't exist as a human being in isolation. It speaks about our interconnectedness. You can't be human all by yourself, and when you have this quality—Ubuntu—you are known for your generosity. We think of ourselves far too frequently as just individuals, separated from one another, whereas you are connected and what you do affects the whole world. When you do well, it spreads out; it is for the whole of humanity.

—Bishop Desmond Tutu, 2008

CHAPTER TWELVE
Meeting in a Container of Care

Regardless of what we call it or how science and religion define it, it's clear that there's a field or presence that is the "great net" that connects everything in creation and links us to the higher power of a greater world.
—Gregg Braden

Imagine a pebble dropping into a mirrored pond. As the ripples on the water's surface expand from the center outward, more and more volume is included in their circumferences. Think of your heart as the center where the pebble first entered the water, and you have an image of the direction we're heading. You may have already felt the expansion through your chest and relaxation throughout your body-heart-mind with the embodiment practice. This movement of energy travels from our center outward, and just like the ripples on the pond, spaciousness fills our hearts, and calm pervades our body-minds. When you inhabit this state as the ground of your being, confidence and ease are yours.

We begin part three with a kinesthetic summary of what we've learned so far. We are gaining internal authority with the practices, as well as freedom to bring a new energetic into being. In shorthand, we've learned to bring kindness to ourselves, to sense our internal coordinates, and then to embody the coherent quality of life we want to activate. When we bring that energetic as our intended attitude into the world, we are being the change. The HeartMath Institute's e-book, *Science of the Heart*, concludes with the perspective that, "being responsible for and increasing our personal coherence not only improves personal health and happiness, but also feeds into and influences a global field environment." Integral as we are with the field (see chapter 3), when we increase our personal coherency, coherent energy is amplified globally. Each one of us has the potential to contribute to strengthening and stabilizing not only our personal lives and relationships, but also to anchor that coherence worldwide.

The electromagnetic waves of heart-brain coherence vibrate at 0.1 Hertz. The electromagnetic field of Earth also vibrates at 0.1 Hertz. We are at optimal synchronization with our own internal resources, the combined intelligences of our heart and our brain when we slow our breath and focus on embodying gratitude or compassion, for example. At the same time, we are coherent with the vibratory cycle of the Earth. This is a tangible way to increase harmony both inside and in relation to those around us.[51]

Until recently, the brain and heart were considered to be separate organs. But research has shown that the heart communicates with the brain and the body in four proven ways—1) neurologically, via the nervous system; 2) biochemically, via hormones; 3) biophysically, in pulse waves; and 4) energetically, via electromagnetic fields.[52] It is the electromagnetic fields of our cells, particularly potent around the heart, that interface with the Earth's geomagnetic fields, as well as one another. As it turns out, the heart and the brain are interdependent and their interactions affect our whole being and the world around us.

Expanding Ripples of Influence

The coherent energy we hold for ourselves and our close relationships reverberates in ever widening circles beyond us. We know from the science of oneness and the all-pervasive field that our sphere of influence spreads far past our rational comprehension. By now, we have activated energetic states of coherency in ourselves and gained firsthand experience of connecting with the field. At this point, we can make practical the shift from me to we by applying our experience and holding a similar energetic field in a group setting. The intention is to expedite local efforts within a global context. Because the intention is to hold all of us with equal care, I call it the *container of care*.

---

51   Gregg Braden, "Human By Design," Season one, Episodes 1, 2, 3. June 2019. Gaia TV, www.gaia.com.

52   The HeartMath Institute Research Staff, *Science of the Heart Volume 2: Exploring the Role of the Heart in Human Performance*, 1993-2016. Retrieved from, www.store.heartmath.org/books

The container of care practice is a way to have a collaborative group dialogue with a purpose. As leaders of our lives, each one of us is the expanding heart at our own center. The heart comes into play as our compass for navigating the world from the inside out. When we look at the world through the lens of our heart, we see with the eyes of compassion. When we know ourselves inwardly and are self-connected, ease and self-confidence deepen in us. We live by our values and readily recognize our inner authority, as well as our interdependence. Kindness with ourselves and others becomes more natural, giving credence to our ability to beneficially affect the world around us. In this light, we are also speaking to the confluence of leadership, to working together for the betterment of all.

When we use the skills we've learned so far to intentionally hold a space that includes all of us, we shift the paradigm in the world. As we shift internally, we inevitably affect what happens around us. Applying this knowledge purposefully to create the container is a way to support our own and others' empathetic presence and to manifest our creative intelligence while in conversation. When in dialogue with others while embodying a coherent state in resonance with the "all-pervasive, super-charged backdrop," Lynne McTaggart's description of the field, seemingly magical openings and astonishing insights can occur.

I consider the following, more collaborative practices to be quite athletic in timbre, requiring a certain mental agility. As with learning any new sport or skill, the cumulative effect of consistent practice allows it to become second nature. The following component skill sets are valuable to all manner of interactions, especially where group decisions need to be made.

Explore this Practice: Weaving a Container of Care

Overview

A *container of care* is an invisible, energetic field of intention and awareness that holds all participants equally to enhance collaborative dialogue. Mutual understanding is a key component to successful collaboration. Our motivations and intentions for mutual understanding generate goodwill. Goodwill is reciprocated when others trust our intentions and know that they, too, matter. Goodwill is a subtle and pervasive effect of personal sovereignty, of being the leader of your life. Generosity of spirit is goodwill in action for the good of all.

Refer to the descriptions of component practices, "Dancing in the Gap of Uncertainty" and "Making Clear Requests", at the end of the chapter to clarify how to implement those steps where indicated.

1. *Tap into the field that includes and yet transcends you and the others present.* To do that, first embody the quality of life motivating you to be in the conversation. You can get clarity on what you are motivated by when you imagine the outcome that you'd like. To first know and embody the quality up for you will empower you to navigate the situation with self-connection and an open heart. Reflect on how you would most like the conversation to go. At the early stages of dialogue, curiosity and mutual understanding are at the top of the list. These qualities set the tone and lay the foundation for what will follow.

2. *Expand embodiment to include the field.* When we are tapped into the field, the fact of our interconnectedness is tangible and inspires us to co-creative action. Our interdependence is clear and undeniable from this perspective. Here, we are naturally empathetic and communicate authentically from the heart. This is the foundation for peaceful conflict resolution and inspired collaboration. It also could be considered the ingredients for *mystical activism*. (See box, "What Is Mystical Activism").

3. *Maintain self-awareness and self-connection using your personal coordinates and pay attention to the others with curiosity.* This can seem a bit "mentally athletic" at first. Check in with yourself periodically to update your coordinates and stay self-connected. Return to empathetic presence with the others, particularly those speaking, once you've reconnected with your current coordinates. When someone speaks, ask if he or she would like what was said to be reflected to him or her. This is to ensure that the person has been heard as clearly and fully as he or she would like to be. Reflecting each speaker can also expedite the meeting, even though it takes a minute or two longer at the time.

4. *Hold clarity of your intention for mutual understanding, while "dancing in the gap of uncertainty."* Trust that we can hold all of us with care at the same time comes into its own here. To navigate the dialogue with its uncertain outcome requires our internal stability, or self-connection, and the fluidity of empathetic presence. Dance with the conversation to-and-fro until those involved have been heard and understood as they would like. Refer to "the empathy dance" if needed (see chapter 11).

> ### What is Mystical Activism?
>
> Mystical activism is an integration of mystical realization with effective social activism. In his award-winning book, *The Conscious Activist*, James O'Dea reveals how the integration of activism with mysticism can powerfully and permanently change the current social trajectory, waking up humanity from its downhill slide into self-destruction. According to O'Dea, mystical activism is the most expedient way through the archaic structures of power over, domination, and materialism and into a secure and abundant world that works for all. The container of care practice exemplifies combining transcendent awareness with applied activism.

5. Make clear requests when expressing yourself. When you share something, what do you want in response? A reflection of what someone heard you say? Information? Agreement on an action? State it succinctly and direct it specifically to the person you want to hear from. Invite others to make requests as needed by asking them what they want back and from whom after they've spoken.

Self-awareness, self-connection and our facility with embodying coherent qualities are fundamental ingredients to our empathetic presence and holding the container of care. Add to that tracking the conversation, hearing the essence or qualities of life mattering to the person speaking, and choosing how to respond, and you have a lot to attend to. Facility with the constellation of skills at play naturally increases with practice. Use any interaction as an opportunity to practice self-connection, empathetic presence and mutual understanding. With the container of care specifically, the beneficial effects are uplifting for the whole group. I recommend making decisions this way to include all those affected by the outcome.

The components to the container of care weave fluidly in and around each other. Your center point, the ground of your being, is the gift of presence and willingness to hold space for the best outcome for all concerned. This is assuming leadership in an unassuming way.

Most importantly, our intention is to remain connected to our hearts throughout. The brain is a polarity organ. The heart is a non-polarity organ. With the heart, we can be fully present and no longer be attached to the outcome. Compassion begins in the heart. As we are able to utilize our minds to support our heart connection and infuse it with compassion, a new world awakens within and around us. We begin to live a template of healing and wholeness in our interactions and relationships.

Master Desire

The centerpiece of conscious intention is clarity about what we want to experience. Clarity of intention, coupled with confidence in its unfolding, are necessary ingredients for manifesting our desires. The platform by which manifesting our desires occurs, curiously enough, also includes holding the outcome lightly. When we are firmly attached to one particular result, we tend to constrict in fear that it might not happen, inadvertently blocking the possibilities. Fear comes from lack of confidence and creates separation from all that is. It inhibits our creativity. To utilize the beneficial effects of no separation, we release the attachment to our singular viewpoint and trust the process—that is, our co-creative potential.

This is a way to recognize and honor the unknown, or the great mystery, the aspects of life that remain uncertain and beyond our control. This approach invites humility as we accept the uncertainty of our sought-after outcomes. At the same time, we have absolute freedom over what we desire and long to experience. Whether a strongly held belief, an unconscious expectation, or a newly created idea, our expectation coalesces the energy of creation. To embody the feeling state that what we long for already exists is the code to our creativity. It is the depth of our integration with the experience—as if it were already true--- that brings forth its manifestation. The knowledge that we aren't separate from the creative life force gives us the freedom and power to dream into being the life we want.

When we assume that we alone are responsible for manifesting our desires, on the other hand, we separate ourselves from the infinite creative potential of all that is. The subtle yet powerful difference between *your attachment* to and *your trust* in it happening is the key distinction to manifesting what you desire. Attachment to an outcome unintentionally limits the myriads of other possibilities available, one of which might be even better than what you had imagined. To focus on one sole option takes us out of the realm of co-creativity by cleaving us from the field of possibility.

Sufi elder and teacher Murat Yagan taught his students to use what he calls *master desire* to fulfill their dreams. Master desire is knowing with your whole being that what you want is already yours. Because there is no separation from yourself and the creative life force, or the holomovement, when you know without a wisp of a doubt that your dream is true, then it is so. Our attachment, on the other hand, begets the need to control events and to take things into our own hands, which is based in the belief of separation. It may seem paradoxical. But when we know there is no separation, what we sincerely long for with purity of intention indeed manifests, because it already *is*.

To engage master desire, you take the steps needed both internally and externally to accomplish what you want to happen. You use your rational mind to inform your subconscious mind exactly why this result is best for you. With your rational and subconscious minds aligned, let yourself feel the fulfillment of your dream with all your being, knowing that it has already happened. Then, with your master desire front and center, simply pay attention to how life unfolds while continuing to live as if your desired result has manifested. What you desire with your heart's clarity longs equally to unfold for you. With the knowingness that you are inseparable from the creative force, what you intend can't *not* happen.

The Uncertainty Principle

To shed more light on the topic of uncertainty as it relates to the creative process, we return to quantum physics. The uncertainty principle was developed by one of the architects of quantum theory, the German physicist Werner Heisenberg. He introduced it in 1927. "Simply put, the principle states that there is a fundamental limit to what one can know about a quantum system. For example, the more precisely one knows a particle's position, the less one can know about its momentum, and vice versa."[53] This simply means that an electron's location in space and its velocity cannot both be measured at the same time.

An electron is a tiny sphere of light vibrating at very high speed. As Lynne McTaggart points out, quantum particles are continually popping in and out of quantifiable existence, and therefore how fast it is going and in what direction are uncertain.[54] We can only measure one of those coordinates at a time because, at the quantum level, consciousness affects potentialities, meaning the various possible outcomes. The quantum field explanation for this is that the observer of an outcome participates in that outcome by the fact of being an observer. Here again, science supports the mystical notion that we are interdependent with the world around us, such that our consciousness affects what occurs, whether we are aware of it or not.

The uncertainty principle determined that quantum particles are never at rest but are constantly in motion due to the ground state field of energy, the zero point field, that

---

[53] Geoff Brumfiel, *Scientific American,* Sept 2011, accessed on August 15, 2019. https://www. scientificamerican.com/article/common-interpretation-of-heisenbergs-uncertainty-principle-is-proven-false/

[54] Lynne McTaggart, *The Field* (New York: HarperCollins, 2008).

ceaselessly interacts with subatomic particles.[55] "What quantum calculations show is that we and our universe live and breathe in what amounts to a sea of motion—a quantum sea of light."[56] This means that everything exists in a state of constant flux with the potential for myriads of different outcomes every moment, the specifics of which are dependent upon all the input known and unknown coming to bear. A familiar colloquialism sometimes used as a proverb states a similar understanding in idiomatic language: "It ain't over till the fat lady sings." This means that we can only know the outcome of an event *after* the completion of its unfolding.

Folk sayings reflect the hidden truths of universal laws discovered not by scientists but by average people living their normal lives. Sometimes called common sense, these truth-revealing statements transcend linear thinking. What the uncertainty principle explains and the folk saying implies is that a vibrating sea of potential pervades all of life. Because of this, nothing is solid or certain, and the outcome of any situation is unknown—until all the pieces influencing the outcome have played out. In quantum physics, this effect is called *collapsing the potential*. This means that all the other potential outcomes are no longer viable; one alone has manifested. This illuminates the vastness of potential in any moment and the relevance of our participation in but not control over situations and outcomes.

When we put together what we've learned thus far with the science of our interconnectedness, we have a sound formula for manifesting the world we want. Cooperation is natural to the process. The container of care synthesizes the practices introduced so far and integrates them for successful collaboration. The following two practices, "Dancing in the Gap of Uncertainty" and "Making Clear Requests," are components of the container of care. They are spelled out here for clarity on how to implement the practice of holding a container of care.

A Component Practice: Dancing in the Gap of Uncertainty

When in a conversation or dialogue, the ability to pay attention with empathetic presence is a gift to everyone involved, no matter the situation. Empathy and self-connection give us the opportunity to be clear and confident yet flexible. The metaphor of the martial arts stance—grounded, flexible, and aware of self and other at the same time—is an accurate depiction of how to "dance in the gap of uncertainty," a term

---

[55]   McTaggart
[56]   McTaggart

coined by NVC trainer, Miki Kashtan. To dialogue co-creatively, we must learn to play with uncertainty, a discomfort we normally attempt to override.

1. *Find your internal coordinates and come into self-connection.* Become aware of what you are feeling in your body, what emotion you are feeling, and where you are in the spectrum of love, the specific quality of life up and alive for you in the situation.

2. *If the other person speaks first, respond to him or her with an empathetic guess.* That is, after listening with curiosity to hear the essence of what is up for the other, find out if you understood him or her accurately. This is for your own clarity. It also serves to reflect to the other what you heard and lets the person you're engaging with know that you are present with him or her and that you want to understand—in other words, that what he or she is saying matters to you.

3. *If you speak first in the conversation, share your coordinates, followed by a request of what you want back from the person.* To openly and transparently share yourself invites others to speak honestly and openly too. It is an act of courage and strength to step into transparency, which serves as an invitation to connection. Your request will add structure and focus to the conversation.

4. *Allow the conversation to unfold as you dance these steps together.*

True dialogue is an exploration. To accept and embrace *what is* can be an adventure. We practice staying self-connected to support navigating our feelings and qualities of life as we go. At the same time, we hold a container for both of us. As philosopher Martin Buber says, "Dialogue is a conversation whose outcome is unknown." This form of dialogue generates creative juices and is extremely satisfying. We increase our chances to be known to each other while creating connection, trust, and goodwill as our vulnerabilities are revealed. Making a clear request after we speak improves clarity, connection, and expediency in conversations.

Making Clear Requests

A clear request creates connection and understanding, guides the conversation purposefully, and invites pertinent information forward. It is an extremely potent and phenomenally underutilized skill. The following descriptions and terminology of requests is gleaned from Nonviolent Communication (NVC). For more information about NVC, go to cnvc.org. Specific organizations that teach NVC are referenced in the Further Resources section at the back of the handbook.

Descriptions and purposes of types of requests

connection request. A request to find out what the person heard and how he or she understood what you just shared.

A connection request helps significantly to clarify understanding. The answer to your request gives you information about whether you are on the same page or not and can increase the sense of connection. The purpose is to find out how what you said was received and understood. A request follows immediately after you speak. Find words that are natural to your way of talking.

Examples of connection requests: How does that land with you? What's that like for you to hear? What goes on for you when you hear me say that? I wonder how you are with that. I'd love to hear what you think/feel about what I said. Will you tell me how you feel after hearing that? Before I say more, I want to make sure you got this part; will you please tell me what you heard me say?

informational request. This kind of request is used to expedite or orient a conversation specifically to get the information you want or need to move forward. This is useful when making decisions, making a proposal, or when you want specific information back after you speak.

Examples of information requests: Is that something you'd be willing to do? Is this something we can explore further together? Do you want to go to the 4:00 or the 7:00 movie? Will you tell me your thoughts on the topic? What do you think about that? Do you prefer this, or that? Do you like the idea of doing this together, or not?

action request. An action request is a simple, uncharged statement with a clear explanation of what is being asked of someone. It's a way to find out if someone will or will not do something specific that you'd like him or her to do. The request is a doable action, not a wishful expectation. The difference is explained in the paragraphs that follow.

Examples of what an action request is not: Will you please be patient? I wish you'd be quiet. It would be fun if you went with me tonight. If you do that, I won't go with you. Boy, it's cold in here with that window open.

Although these statements may sound familiar, none of them is a clear request. They comprise implied desires, or wishful expectations, but the actual desire isn't being verbalized. An action request is not a wishful expectation, which, as distinct from a request, has the verb *to be* in it. Although we often hear it, to ask someone to be a certain way is not a doable request as we define it here. How to be is always open to interpretation. It is subjective—there isn't something universally and specifically doable to comply with. With unspoken assumptions, the listener is saddled with the responsibility of figuring out what is being asked of him or her and deciding what to do about it.

An action request *is a doable action*. It gives the other person the gift of clarity of what is needed and wanted, from which he or she can easily decide whether he or she can willingly do it or not. The request voices a specific, desired action. A yes or no answer is often adequate to an action request.

Examples of action requests: Can you give me five more minutes, please? I'd love some quiet right now—are you willing to go into the other room to make that call? Will you accompany me this weekend? Will you drive me to my appointment on Thursday? I'm cold. Will you please close the window? I'm concerned. Please tell me what I can do to help you over this hurdle. If you can't be there on time, then let's go another day, all right?

request versus demand. A request and a demand sometimes use the same language. However, the tone of voice and intention behind the words are very different. A request simply means that we are willing to hear a no after we ask it. We don't have the tension of demand in our voice when making a request. The tone of voice and energetics are quite different with a demand because we are unwilling to hear a no. However, to reiterate Marshall Rosenberg's insight, a no is really a yes to something else. Therefore, no is an invitation to dialogue about what matters more to the other person right then than what you've requested—that is, to discover what the person is saying yes to when he or she says no to you.

Request versus demand can be a particularly thorny topic in parenting or other relationships with inborn power differentials. Soul-searching in terms of our core values, the qualities of life we most want to embody and to express, as well as what we want to model to our children, will help guide us in this regard. Although making demands on others, especially children, is common, demanding that others do our bidding does not take them into equal consideration. And, it often backfires with resentment and unwillingness later. When children are approached with respect and consideration of their needs and wants, they learn to address and include others with respect too. This engenders internal motivation, a strength integral to inner authority. When children's wishes cannot be granted, we simply respond to them with sincere empathy and hold them with love and care for their disappointment or their anger. The container of care has room for all that shows up.

CHAPTER THIRTEEN
The Adventure of Resolving Conflict

We are not afraid of the other person freaking out; what we're
afraid of is that we won't know how to handle it.
—Marshall Rosenberg

Throughout our childhood, my sister and I were embedded in conflict. Sharing a bedroom made our differences all the more pronounced. She stayed up late into the night; I went to bed not long after dinner. I woke up with the birds; she slept until the last possible minute and then dragged herself out of bed. She played with dolls; I played with horses. I had straight, bleached blond hair; she had dark, wavy hair. She rebelled against authority and frequently got into trouble; I played the "good-girl" game and avoided trouble at all costs. She was a girlie-girl; I was a tomboy. It never occurred to us to allow each other to be ourselves or to enjoy our differences. No. Back then, we hated each other and fought about everything. For us to get along wasn't an option.

When I look back on it, we were steeped in conflict from all sides growing up. My stepmother was twenty-one when she married my father, who already had three children under seven years old. She had no experience whatsoever with children, and no one guided her in her new role as stepparent. In her frustration, she resorted to yelling and even got physical with my sister at times. When she'd had enough, she would lock all three of us out of their little rental house to get some needed peace and quiet.

Duking It Out

Like many people, my sister and I had no modeling for cooperation. Not only that, we were actually encouraged once—at my father's direction—to duke it out. When we were about eight and ten years old respectively, my dad set up a boxing ring in his tiny living room and scheduled a match. The winner would be the champion once and for all—there would be no more fighting thereafter. At least, that was how the story was supposed to go.

Dad used furniture to set up the boundaries for the boxing ring. He had a timer and set it for each round of the fight. As I recall, there were no stated rules, but I was prepared to fight to the finish. Younger and smaller than my sister, I mustered all the force of my will to defend myself. Determined to the point of frantic, I was not going to let her get the upper hand. We went about three rounds and in the third, I managed to pin her down. I sat on her chest, her head in both of my hands, and with her hair tangled in my fingers, frighteningly, I banged her head up and down on the floor. At that point, the bell rang, and my father called the fight. I was the winner.

Looking back, I would have much preferred to get along with my sister. I did not like hurting people, and underneath all the conflicts we had, I did love her. Often, when we were out as a family, and my sister was moody, I would try to humor her. But no one ever encouraged that behavior or taught us the value of concern for one another. Rather than being shown how to work things out, when looking for help from our mother, she told me to ignore my sister and just stay away from each other. In our home, disagreements easily led to anger and conflicts. Take other people's needs into consideration? Respect our differences? That would require empathy, a totally foreign experience in our family home. We learned that we were in it for ourselves. There was only room for one of us to win or get what we wanted. We lived in a world of scarcity; there wasn't enough love to go around.

The Discomfort of Confrontation

To a considerable extent, the disquiet of our differences plays out in the culture at large. We hear it reflected in our language. Simply to have a difference of opinion is often referred to as a conflict. When we disagree with someone, we use language like, "I'm going to have to confront him about this." For many people, the default setting when conflict arises is to fight and conquer. The possibility that there is room for both people, for varied opinions and needs, doesn't happen automatically. Neither does the ability to problem solve creatively. Rarely do we hear people working their issues out thoughtfully with consideration for one another. When the overriding assumption is that one of us is right and the other is wrong, it makes sense that we are afraid of conflict and having different needs.

The cornerstone of collaborative conflict resolution is to make *room for both people* with their differences and with respectful consideration for both. When we remember empathy for the other person, even in the midst of disagreement, we can approach conflict as a problem-solving adventure. Holding ourselves and the other person in empathetic presence streamlines making the shift from me to we. It allows us to show up present, resourceful, and with the impetus to work together.

More often than not, conflicts between people aren't the result of irreconcilable differences or incompatible needs. Frequently they are what Miki Kashtan refers to as "contradictory images of satisfaction."[57] That's a fancy way to say that we imagine divergent ways to get our needs met. To transcend these contradictory images, or different strategies to resolve the issue, we need simply to shift our priorities. We focus on making a connection rather than on winning the argument. As Kashtan points out, "What's needed for creating connection and transcending such differences is the capacity to sustain an empathetic understanding of our own and others' needs even in times of conflict and disagreement."[58] To do this would make an adventure out of resolving conflict because we willingly step into the unknown.

Viewing Conflict as Adventure

What if we decided to approach challenging interactions as an adventure, rather than as a confrontation? How would a situation change if a conflict or disagreement led us to wonder: "What will I discover if I open to hearing this person?" A number of questions come up with this attitude. What can we learn about each other by simply being present and listening with curiosity? What does it take to stay true to ourselves and to be transparent with someone else? How do we meet the challenge to expand and accept "what's so" rather than insist that we already know what *should* be so? When we have a difference of opinion, is there more to understand than we currently

57 Kashtan, *Spinning Threads of Radical Aliveness* (Oakland: Fearless Heart Publications, 2014).
58 Kashtan.

know? Is there more information to gather before decisions can be made that affect all of us? As ever, curiosity is an important element for coming to mutual understanding.

The ability to adopt a curious attitude depends on our willingness to be with *what is* and to maintain our presence. Curiosity increases our capacity to stay present to whatever emotions come up in either of us, including fear or anger. Such focus affords us a sense of inner spaciousness and balance that is delicious. It's like having a big armchair inside that we can settle down into and view what's going on with presence and without reactivity. Presence, a kind of internal spaciousness, grows with trust in ourselves—trust that we do care about the other person and that we are able to hold us both with consideration. Fear comes from not trusting that we have room for both of us and from thinking that only one of us can get what we need from the interaction.

We often attempt to deny, repress, or conceal our fear when facing a conflict. This results in anxiety and internal contraction that makes it difficult to speak our truth. Often, when we try to sidestep our fear, we come across as angry or defensive. In fact, anger often has its roots in unacknowledged fear. Anger and defensiveness introduce additional tension that makes conversing with equanimity even more challenging. On the other hand, when we are authentic and voice our feelings, tension brewing below the surface is relieved. This kind of transparency invites more openness from others and translates into trust.

How does sharing what we're really feeling encourage trust? When we are seen as human and vulnerable, it is easier for others to be open and honest with us in response. Transparency means to share our inner worlds with one another. When we open the window to our hearts, it is an invitation for the other person to do the same. Trust grows when we cross the threshold of fear and share ourselves honestly. When we are received in kind, connections are woven.

Conversely, we introduce tension into a conversation when we have a strong attachment to a single outcome. When we enter a dialogue intent to get our way, we are constricted and can exude fear and defensiveness. Our position prevents us from being with *what is* and has a polarizing effect. The default is for each to make a case for his or her side while neither one of us truly hears the other. Little can come of this scenario in terms of mutual understanding and conflict resolution. The best outcome we can hope for is compromise, which is often an unsatisfying result for both people. A common occurrence is to use "power over," such that one of us dominates with aggression and the other one submits to avoid escalating into conflict. Resentment is likely to follow when we give up on what matters to us. When we carry resentment, we resist telling the truth about ourselves and find it hard to care about the people we resent. Truth telling --- with kindness --- is the antidote to resentment.

What does it take to arrive at a satisfactory outcome for both of us? Most often, we have disagreements with the people closest to us. We obviously care about the people in our lives and optimally prefer that they be satisfied with the results, too. By speaking our truth and focusing on mutual understanding, we set the stage to work things out together. When we really hear and understand each other, we may even find ourselves shifting our original desired outcome in support of the other's needs. When we feel understood, then we trust that we matter and want to collaborate, to make it work out for everyone. In truth, we'd prefer not to get our needs met at others' expense. Our tribal ancestry continues to call from the past, asking us to include others with care and consideration. Somewhere inside we all have the knowing that we need one another.

When we look at an issue from the desire for understanding, many rewarding possibilities arise. Rather than seeing one another as obstacles to getting what we want, we are uplifted by a shared intention. Collaboration is creativity in action. It functions to benefit everyone's needs and highlights our ability to co-create.

Connection through Conflict

No doubt it is much easier to be the kind and caring person we'd like to be when other people are respectful, kind, and caring toward us. Connection feels natural when kindness and consideration come our way. In an empowered state, however, we need not wait for others to show kindness in order to bestow it. With self-connection, the internal experience we want is available to us at any moment. What we desire is available when we remember to embody the quality of life we want activated. Our internal shift to coherence effects the whole, meaning both of us and, as ever, includes the field. Connection with ourselves facilitates connection with others.

Let's look at an example of how this works in the following case study. This was a conversation I facilitated between a couple stuck in a conflictual pattern. Facilitation by an unbiased third party supports both people to listen to one another and helps to ensure that both people are heard and understood. It is also very possible to achieve being heard and understood without facilitation—with clarity of intention and utilization of the skills learned. An explanation of how to approach conflict as an adventure follows.

Andrew and Rita's Story

Andrew and Rita came to me in severe distress. They had established a pattern wherein Rita would anxiously focus on something Andrew wasn't doing the way she'd expected and then get angry and criticize him for it. In turn, he would be hurt, get angry and defensive, shut down, and retreat into himself. Despite their love and affection for one another, at times, they could not break out of this debilitating cycle.

I asked them to take turns telling me about the situation and to speak specifically about the pain it was causing. I listened to them blame each other, essentially saying, "You're doing it wrong!" The message was inevitably interpreted as, "I'm not good enough." This exacerbated the resentment and pain between them and built a looming wall of disconnection. They could not see one another openheartedly. Nor could they call to mind their reasons for being together in the first place. They both shut down and could only see what the other person needed to do to fix it.

I reflected what I had heard from each of them, empathizing with their pain. I noted that at this point, neither of them could see the qualities they loved and admired in the other. I invited them to shift their focus and, one at a time, tell each other what they appreciated about the other one. I then asked each of them to share how it felt to hear those things. They both noticeably softened at the other's expressed appreciations. The shared sweetness in that moment allowed their hearts to begin to soften.

Once the overt tension had dissipated, we took a deeper look at what was instigating the disconnection between them. We looked at their respective triggers and the body-based kinesthetic cues that accompany those triggers. We examined the stories of blame and criticism that looped in their heads when the other did something triggering. We acknowledged that these stories are learned habits developed in childhood, survival mechanisms that had helped them to cope. I reminded them that the unresourceful patterns were being recreated in adulthood because, historically, they had worked for them in threatening or overwhelming situations. The problem is that those stories had turned into habits of thinking and behaving that narrowed rather than expanded their perspectives and options as adults. This, in turn, had led them to shut down, resulting in disconnection, resentment, and tension between them.

One at a time, we explored the experiences they would prefer. Rita wanted to feel calm, centered, and loving and to be excited about spending the evening with her man when he came home. I invited her to embody those qualities for a few minutes. As she sat quietly with eyes closed, breathing the qualities she longed for into herself, I could see her face soften into enjoyment and her body relax. She became infused with a lightness of being previously out of her reach. Once she made the energetic shift, those qualities became a felt reality for her.

From her new perspective, I invited her to share what she'd like to do when Andrew walks in the door after work. Her demeanor, now sweet and openhearted, reflected the energetic shift that had just occurred. She described welcoming him home and inviting him to make dinner with her and to sit down together and talk about their day. She was surprised at how good it felt to take responsibility for creating her desired experience by embodying the qualities she valued. It seemed remarkably simple to her. This freed her partner to express his love and appreciation for her in return.

We then explored how Andrew could make a similar change. He knew that blaming and judging her fueled the resentment between them. He was clear about what he would prefer to experience—loving-kindness. Rather than shut down and get defensive, he wanted to bring acceptance and strength to the table. He took a few minutes to embody these qualities. He too, noticeably relaxed and became a wholly different version of himself—clear and open-hearted, kind yet empowered. Once the energetic shift had occurred, his every word and gesture communicated care. The shift allowed him to be openheartedly interested in her, rather than defended against her. The two of them sparkled with their renewed love for one another.

When we embody the qualities of life we seek, rather than falling back into patterns of blame and resentment, everything about us changes. We become more lined up with ourselves. It even affects our physical countenance and can change our posture. Our disposition changes for the better. The light starts to shine from our eyes, and our voice can go from strident to melodic as the tension in our vocal cords relaxes. We are enabled to speak from the heart, rather than from our reactive mind.

To make this shift doesn't require a lot of time, only a clear intention to align with the qualities we truly value. Resonance with the "higher vibration" of coherent energy fills us and ripples out into the environment around us. Others can't help but be gently impacted by it. Moreover, we no longer need the other person to provide the experience we want. We bring that quality into play intentionally, naturally inviting them into that state with us. Desperation and conflict drop out of the equation. The experiences we want and have embodied then positively influence everything that happens between us. We are enlivened and empowered by embodying the coherent state of our choice.

To embody the quality of life we want to activate is a potent way to approach any conflict. We bring ease and flow to conversations rather than weighing down the dialogue with our unspoken (and often unconscious) expectations or demands of the other person. Our position is "I am here to improve this situation," rather than, "This is what I need from you if this situation is going to improve." It is a practical step into being the change and a sign of internal sovereignty. This is leadership in action.

Should we forget to initiate embodying a coherent state before or at the inception of a disagreement, we can easily implement it at any point. By remembering to focus on connection and mutual understanding, we automatically bring these qualities into being. We naturally slow down the interaction and establish our common ground. This intention invites camaraderie, rather than contention. Now companions with a shared goal, we much more readily find mutually agreeable solutions. Choice is always available; we can go down the old road of reactivity upholding the need to be right, or choose the higher road, where conflict becomes an adventure in creating connection and coming to mutually agreeable solutions.

Explore this Practice: Conflict as Adventure

Overview

To see conflict as an adventure in connection and understanding makes it more approachable. To be transparent with each other can be a stretch, which is part of the adventure. We don't know how someone will respond when we share our thoughts and feelings honestly. In the process, we hold a clear intention to prioritize mutual understanding and empathy. When we hold the assumption of innocence rather than blame, we have more spaciousness inside to field misunderstandings.

Reference points for resolving conflict peaceably

Refer to these bullet points when holding presence and care for both of you in a conflict or disagreement. An expanded explanation of the steps follows.

- Know your personal internal coordinates—what you're feeling and wanting— throughout the conversation. This will shift as the conversation progresses.
- Embody the quality of life that is up for you—the experience you want.
- Prioritize mutual understanding before looking to find solutions; discover what both of you are feeling and wanting. Remember, understanding someone does *not* mean having to agree with him or her. Understanding invites open

heartedness and connection and thus, is a precursor to finding mutually satisfying solutions.

- Hold empathetic presence and reflect what you hear the other person saying *before* responding with your thoughts, feelings, or wants.
- Assume innocence of intention on the other person's part.
- Express emotions without blaming the other person for your feelings.

Explanation of steps

Use the following steps as guidelines for resolving conflict. Each step may be returned to more than once as the conversation unfolds, and they may occur in a different order. Choose who will speak and be heard first, or speaker number one will self-select if the conflict arises spontaneously. Come to the conversation with as much self-connection and presence as possible and breathe throughout to help remain centered and self-connected.

1. *Express emotions without blame.* This can be the most challenging part. Because we are steeped in a culture of blame and judgment, to hear someone's strong emotions can bring up the sense of being judged or blamed. I find that looking away from the other person when expressing strong feelings helps. To take personal responsibility for your feelings is very important. Avoid using the word "you" when expressing intense feelings. For example, turn away from the other person to say, as loudly as feels right, "I get so angry and frustrated when this happens!" Rather than, "I'm so angry and frustrated that you did this again!" To say "you" is pointing the finger and invites blame and judgment, rather than connection and understanding. Or express anger while looking away and say, for example, "I'm feeling really angry and hurt about this right now. Ugh! I just don't want to have to deal with this!" Rather than, "I can't believe you did that! I hate cleaning up your messes!"

2. *Own your trigger.* After expressing your feelings, stop, breathe, and take stock of yourself. Own your trigger by speaking your version of, "I know this is my issue. And I want to take responsibility for how it affects me. This hurts a lot, and I'm not blaming you for how I'm feeling about it." Ask for reflection from the other about what he or she sees and hears is going on with you. Or empathize with him or her if you have the resources available to you. The conversation continues back and forth with the next steps.

3. *Listen and respond with empathy.* This can be challenging when we are instrumental to the upset or disagreement or are having strong emotions about it. In that case, we are susceptible to blame and judgment flying both ways. The remedy is simple, although perhaps not easy—assume that the other is innocent. If you're having difficulty being empathetic, simply focus on reflecting what you've heard and follow that with a question to make sure you heard it accurately. If you get triggered, take a time out and follow the guidelines below for "Choice Point—To Get beyond a Trigger."

4. *Ask if the other person is ready to listen to you now.* When the person you're engaging with seems to have completed what he or she is currently sharing, ask if there is anything else he or she wants you to know. Or if your capacity to listen is tapped out, say so and ask if he or she can/will listen to you now.

5. *Engage in the empathy dance.* Dialogue as much as needed, flowing between listening with empathy and speaking your coordinates transparently, also called self-expression. Focus on the universal qualities of life with curiosity, both yours and the other's and the feelings that are coming up. Listen to what is mattering to the person and reflect that in simple words. Include what you sense he or she is feeling and wanting. For example, make an empathetic guess such as, "Are you upset because you wanted more input about where we went last night?" Your self-expression might be along the lines of, "I'm sad about what happened because being connected with you matters so much to me. I really thought we had decided together on where to go. I do want to make these decisions together. What's that like for you to hear?" Continue the dialogue in this vein until you understand each other clearly—from one another's perspective. Agreement is not necessary, but understanding is.

6. *Complete connection and mutual understanding; brainstorm solutions.* The tension subsides naturally once mutual understanding is achieved. Once you both feel heard and understood, begin creative problem solving. Make sure to take into consideration both of your needs and values as the relevant qualities of life that surfaced. Once mutual understanding and connection are in place, hearts have softened, and solutions often present themselves quite readily. Part of the solution is included in the next step.

7. *Take responsibility for your part in the disagreement, as well as the solution.* With humility, we own what our part was in bringing on the disagreement or conflict. Follow that with what you see as your part to remedy the situation—what you will be responsible to change or do differently. For example, "I realize I was

triggered by you choosing what we did last night. I felt so left out and small in my family growing up and always had to do what everyone else wanted. I will be clearer about making sure I give input on decisions that affect both of us from now on."

8. *Make agreements*. Decide on the solutions that work for both of you. Be clear as to the specifics. Make sure that strategies are doable action steps. You might go a step beyond a verbal agreement and write it out. Check in later (a day to a month later, depending on the issue) and modify the agreement if necessary. For example, "Okay, I will be more careful too, when we're figuring out what to do and make sure we're hearing each other."

In summary, to transform conflict into adventure we make mutual understanding our first priority. Finding solutions is secondary. Cultivating the compassionate observer self and knowing our internal coordinates help us to focus and stabilize in a conflictual dialogue. Empathetic presence is also a big player. It helps with the internal stretch to make room for both perspectives at the same time. To resolve conflict this way feeds relationships. Even if only one person seeks mutual understanding before problem solving, he or she can guide the conversation with empathy and presence. This will help infuse the interaction with creativity and everyone involved will benefit.

Getting beyond a Trigger

As we become more adept at tracking our inner states, we can recognize *choice points* when they occur. Before self-awareness, we had no choice but to slip into the wormhole of reactivity, as our old stories and fears ran the show. To know we're at a choice point can make all the difference. The choice we face is to look inward first rather than react to the outer circumstances. When we are triggered by something "out there," we instantly turn our focus inward to see what is being triggered, noting our physical sensations, thoughts, and emotions. The habit of somatic tracking becomes extremely valuable here. That moment of self-awareness arrests the knee-jerk reaction to spew first and think later. It is the change of focus from outside to inside that gives us the power to choose something different. In that moment, we have the option to shift from reaction to response. In making that choice, we gain the freedom to choose how we want to show up and to take responsibility for our impact on the interaction. This is taking a leadership role.

A trigger is an instantaneous reaction ignited in the present that originates from a wound in the past. When triggered, we normally react with anger or blame at something or someone. The reaction exacerbates fear and defensiveness for both people, and conflict escalates—we no longer have clear access to the person we want to be. Whereas the ability to respond means we can show up as the person we'd like to be. We can take responsibility for our feelings and experiences. Making the choice to respond rather than to react means that, in all likelihood, we won't regret later what we do or say in the moment. Let's tease out the process to get beyond a trigger.

Explore this Practice: Choice Point—To Get beyond a Trigger

Overview

When we get triggered and an old reactive pattern rears its head, we are at a *choice point*—a juncture that determines what will happen next. We can choose presence or allow ourselves to shut down. We can choose to be empathetic or stand in judgment. Choice points occur many times throughout the day, especially in an intimate partnership or family where our vulnerabilities tend to be at the surface. When at a choice point and we first notice we feel upset, we focus internally, breathe, take stock of ourselves, realize that we're triggered, and settle into self-awareness. With self-awareness and somatic tracking, we can stay self-connected, rather than default to old reactive patterns. This process allows you to make your choice with full awareness.

To Begin

To have access for making a different choice depends heavily upon the habit of self-connection. That means to look inward first before reacting to a trigger. Use these steps as a guideline to practice creating the internal space to allow for a Choice Point.

1. *Recognize the signs and symptoms of a "trigger" reaction as soon as possible. Notice your thoughts, feelings, and bodily sensations.*

    Awareness might show up as tightness in the chest, belly, jaw, or shoulders. You might feel anxious or defensive and notice yourself shutting down or getting angry. Listen to the messages looping in your head. Learn to identify key words—a "trigger alert"—that let you know you're in reactive mode. Be particularly aware of words like should, shouldn't, always, and never. Your triggering thoughts might be, *She always does this to me!* or, *I shouldn't have to do this all myself!* or, *I'll never be good enough for him.* These alerts indicate stuck feelings and old tapes running—the thinking that causes reactivity.

When we allow our thoughts to run our feelings and vice versa, emotions and tempers escalate. Intensified emotions compound the effect, and it becomes ever more difficult to get out of the trigger loop. The first and most important step is to stop and notice what's happening internally. Breathe and then engage your compassionate observer self.

2. *Gain space from the trigger reaction. Engage the compassionate observer. Find your personal coordinates.*

Breathe and invite your compassionate observer self to witness your internal state. Find your internal coordinates (see chapter 4). Take time out to look inward with kindness and acceptance. What exactly are you feeling? What do you want right now? Name your feelings and longings, the qualities of life up for you.

If anxiety starts to mount and your body gets constricted, stop. Breathe. Name it. Say what you're feeling aloud, both to yourself and to the other person. Identify what's happening inside you. If necessary, take some time to yourself, five to ten minutes or longer. When you're alone, track your internal experience by breathing into tight places as you allow what's there to be observed without judgment or trying to change it. As the tension subsides, choose the experience you'd rather have. Find your personal coordinates and choose the quality of life—the experience you want to engender. If strong emotions are roiling inside, allow yourself to express them outdoors or in a private space. Once completed, come back to somatic tracking and notice your internal experience until the tension dissipates. Find and name your coordinates of presence.

3. *Embody the desired experience energetically.*

Once you've found your internal coordinates, embody the quality or qualities you want to experience. For example, qualities may include calm, understanding, loving-kindness, respect, consideration, or any number of other qualities. Whatever it is, fully embody it. Breathe it in and let it infuse your whole being. Once fully embodied, you will feel relaxed, expansive, and centered. Clarity and compassion will be available to draw on. Then go back and continue the conversation or decide together on a time to come back to it later.

4. *When you reengage, use the empathy dance model for conversing, prioritizing connection, and understanding.* (See chapter 11.)

With the practice of getting beyond a trigger reaction, you are essentially learning to intervene on yourself when you're triggered. Once you've connected with yourself and regained a sense of equanimity, continue the conversation. Remember the goal is to turn conflict into an adventure, to explore the unknown with curiosity and come to mutual understanding. To hold onto the notion that you need to be right or that you must win the argument will undermine your attempts to resolve disagreements peaceably. It will also keep you lost in disquiet and internal conflict, unable to access more creative resources.

A handy shortcut to equanimity when triggered is simply to make the assumption at the outset that the other person is innocent. Innocent of what? Innocent of *intending* to trigger or "do you wrong" in some way. With the assumption of innocence, there is no blame for your experience. There is simply your old wound being triggered and you taking stock of that with circumspection. When we trust our own intentions of goodwill, we are better equipped to approach others with the assumption of innocence and come back to the conversation with a neutral attitude. This allows our goodwill to further guide the conversation.

Expressing Emotions in Disagreements and Conflict: No Blame

There are times when, even with the best of intentions, emotions flare. What do we do when strong emotions arise during a conflict? How do we handle intense feelings and not allow them to exacerbate the situation? When approached consciously, strong emotions can play a transformative role in conflict. By consciously, I mean to *not blame* the other person for our upset. To do that, we *accept* that we have strong feelings when someone says or does something that triggers or upsets us. To not fall into blame, it is helpful to remember that the pain we feel was already inside of us and in this moment, it simply has been reawakened. It was slumbering, but now it is up and activated.

Our feelings point to the pain, to the trigger inside, and therefore, are of the past in most cases. There is nothing wrong with that. It *just is*. The past lives on in us until we change our patterns by resolving the wound. We can use our feeling states to increase connection by simply letting the other person know what's going on in us. We can even raise our voice, express anger and disappointment out loud, or stomp around in frustration. The skill is to know, and to say out loud, that our feelings are not being expressed in blame. The release of tense emotions brings us back to the present. This is a benefit of transparency. When we reveal ourselves transparently, rather than obscuring the truth with defense and blame, then empathy and, thus, connection, are welcomed into the space.

The practice of self-acceptance and self-compassion is fundamental in this regard. Invite the compassionate observer self to notice your feelings and internal states. The internal space we create with self-awareness gives us perspective, allowing us to choose what to do next.

The more habituated we are to remember our compassionate observer and to find our internal coordinates—our feelings and quality of life desired—the easier it is to be present and empathetic in the moment. When our subconscious mind has integrated kindness and compassion as our default mode, we naturally trust ourselves to show up as we would like to. We trust ourselves to be able to handle whatever happens and to be responsive rather than reactive. This is true whether a disagreement comes up suddenly or if you plan to sit down together and resolve a conflict. Finding our common ground is a resourceful strategy for resolving conflict harmoniously.

Finding Our Common Ground: Mark and Shannon's Story

A couple came to me in a stalemate about going on a vacation. Shannon was a very adventurous woman, and she'd married Mark later in life. He tended to be more sedate, a homebody who enjoyed puttering in the garden. She was clamoring after a full-blown travel adventure, the kind she had taken frequently before getting married. Mark didn't see the sense of it; he was quite content to stay home.

As they listened and came to understand each other, I could see their minds open and their hearts soften. Mark valued the qualities of ease, comfort, connection, relaxation and financial security. Shannon valued adventure, play, connection, rejuvenation, and expansion. Although they shared all the qualities to some extent, their strongest common ground was connection. They loved each other and wanted to share something special.

The conversation brought Mark to a shift. He heard the deep longing in Shannon when she expressed how much it mattered to her to go on a vacation adventure with him. He opened to considering going on a trip together. The excitement and creativity that arose once Mark shifted was palpable. They both put their creative efforts into envisioning their travel adventure. At the outset, they didn't have a clear picture of what they would do, but as a start, they made a list of what they wanted to experience. With open hearts and relaxed minds, the room was sparkling with energy as they discussed their ideas.

Eventually they agreed that they wanted to experience fun, connection, nature, relaxation, and rejuvenation. They then decided on a budget and explored where they could go. They decided to rent a cabin on a river not far from their home. Shannon could hike, swim, and read, while Mark could read, work on the computer, relax in the sun, and go for hikes with Shannon if it fit his mood. They had time to cook meals together and hang out without the everyday distractions of home. The conversation allowed their good temperaments to return and increased the richness of their connection. They were genuinely excited at the prospect of sharing the adventure they envisioned.

There are additional benefits to making decisions this way. Showing care and consideration for each other fosters trust and intimacy. Creativity lights up the space for unexpected insights and solutions to appear when we open to the unknown. Joy lives inside the vibrant sparks of creativity. When the creative life force plays through and between us, something ancient and potent is ignited in us. We engage with purpose, we feel meaningfully utilized, and our efforts serve our common good. In doing so, we experience genuine fulfillment.

CHAPTER FOURTEEN
Coming Home to Tribe

It is time to speak your truth. Create your community. Be good to each other. And do not look outside yourselves for your leader ... The time of the lone wolf is over. Gather yourselves! Banish the word "struggle" from your attitude and your vocabulary. All that we do now must be done in a sacred manner and in celebration. We are the ones we've been waiting for.
— Hopi Elders[59]

I was a horse logger in the woods near Eugene, Oregon, in the late 1970s and early '80s. Horse loggers use horses to pull logs, the way logging was done before machinery. It was the hardest physical labor I'd ever done, and I'd grown up doing lots of hard physical work. It went the smoothest when the horses would lean into their collars together and the log behind would move forward without a hitch as we slowly gained momentum going down the hill. We then used peeves, long-handled tools with a swinging hook on the end, to rachet the logs into a stack by the roadside to be picked up by the self-loading log truck. Sometimes one of our Belgian draft horses, Billy, would jump into his collar with a jolt out of sync with Burt, his teammate, and the logs wouldn't budge. In fact, the harness would often snap, and the operation would halt while we made repairs. I think Billy knew what he was doing, anticipating the downtime. It became very clear how important it is to pull together; without teamwork, the show could not go on. To be fruitful, all parts must work in concert.

---

[59] *Message from Hopi Elders,* Hopi Nation, Oraibi, Arizona. September 28, 2001. Accessed August 2019; http://www.angelfire.com/moon/fae/hopi.html

Giving the Best of Ourselves

It isn't always easy to step up to the plate and give our best. If we're tired, drained, stressed, confused, or overwhelmed, it can be hard to muster the resources to show up as we'd like. What does it take to find the equilibrium and ground support to be the person we really want to be? And how do we maintain that consistently?

In a needs-based existence in which meeting needs is prioritized over performance or privilege, our stress and overwhelm are minimized. Comparisons to an external scale that determines whether we'll be rewarded or punished is no longer a viable metric. In a needs-based community, we look inside for our sense of accomplishment based on integrity with our values and those of our community. In a tribe or community, we orient around interdependent, mutually supportive relationships. The immediate and meaningful connections with people around us serve as the measure of our success. Needs are met not because of our accomplishments or status, but simply because we *belong*. Consequently, we feel more satisfaction, largely due to knowing that we're all pulling together.

In their heartfelt book, *We Need Each Other*, Bill Kauth and Zoe Alowan delineate the anatomy of a new culture. They see the necessity for building what they call *gift community*. As with indigenous tribes, connection is the currency of wellness and abundance in such a community. As Kauth points out, "Our task is to re-tribalize our culture in a way that is appropriate to who we are today."[60] They go on to suggest that authentic community gives individuals the deep sense of security needed to function optimally. True security follows from belonging. I agree with Bill and Zoe that, "People are capable of so much depth. Humanity is an untapped resource just waiting for a mythic purpose and integrity to call them to their greatest joy."[61] Our mythic purpose is poignantly clear—to create a new story to live by based on the fact that we need each other.

We need each other because we can't do it alone. We need each other because connection is our real longing and fulfillment. And we need each other to celebrate the life we share and all that weaves together the beauty of the world. As the world becomes smaller, it becomes more evident that, indeed, we are all in this together. Together, we can create heaven on earth, once we know how.

---

[60] Bill Kauth and Zoe Alowan, *We Need Each Other* (Ashland, OR: Silver Light Publishing, 2011).

[61] Kauth and Alowan.

The sense of being "a lone wolf," wherein we are in this solely for our own personal gain, causes separation and, thus, stress and anxiety, which incite aggression. We are not independent creatures. We are social beings who need one another to survive, as well as to thrive, meaning to exert our efforts to become more fully who we truly are. We feel a lightness of being when we know that we have each other's backs. This simple yet significant support is necessary at times. A great deal of ease settles over our lives when we trust the community around us to lend a helping hand, to fill our reserves when depleted, and to whom we can give of ourselves. Ms. Kashtan emphasizes that, "Trust is to a collaboration-based social order what fear is to an authority-based social order. Trust, then, is the glue that binds everyone together in a large-scale society or organization."[62]

We feel purposeful and get the most satisfaction when we trust that we matter— that is, when our strengths and abilities contribute to both ourselves and to others. In a community's spontaneous reciprocity, we also receive support and enjoy the security of belonging to our tribe. Within such a circle of feeding and being fed our utmost longings are fulfilled. We trust that we are needed and that our needs matter.

Social Capital and the Gift Culture

Social capital and the gift culture are themes instrumental to writing a new global story of cooperation and abundance. The values inherent in social capital are fundamental to a culture built on sustainability and restoring balance. For a sustainable future, we need to make a radical shift in how we view ourselves and our resources. We can repair damaging relationships with the Earth when profit is not our highest motive. Rather than financial capital as the sole strategy to get needs met, we grow social capital. It is up to us to reweave the social fabric into a tapestry that serves life.

Social capital is gained through connections that bring trust, contribution, community, cooperation, and abundance. The way through our social and environmental predicaments is in partnerships that hold a vision of well-being for all. Those of us who use a higher proportion of the Earth's reserves will necessarily move toward using fewer resources. At the same time, our true wealth increases exponentially with the richness of our relationships and in living meaningful lives. In this new world vision, simplifying our life-styles may be the most significant pathway to our thriving together.

---

[62] Miki Kashtan, *The Little Book of Courageous Living.* (Oakland: Fearless Heart Publications, 2013).

To understand the relevance of growing social capital, let's contrast those values with more familiar ones—the world of financial capital. With financial capital, we make exchanges. We exchange money for goods and services, including food, shelter and health care. Those with little money may not have enough food, safe shelter, or access to health care. Without the resources to live comfortably, people become desperate and often destitute. Some people may tell themselves that those with little means deserve their lot, and therefore, it isn't necessary to consider them fully. But it is our habitual lack of care that is at the root of our problems. Lack of care for one another translates into lack of care for the Earth, and vice-versa.

Charles Eisenstein, author of *Sacred Economics, Money, Gift and Society in the Age of Transition*, reminds us that money is used to buy commodities and services that once upon a time we got directly from the Earth for free, or from each other.[63] The global economy is based on taking something from nature and selling it back to us. Or creating and selling a service that community historically fulfilled for us. Our economy is built on taking, not on reciprocity with the Earth or on the values of sustainability. A quantum leap in our priorities is required of us. We must see the Earth as a living being whose generosity is exemplary. We can look to peoples of the Earth who still hold her as sacred and who know how to live in harmony with her cycles. We can remember the wealth of our connections with one another and rekindle community intentionally.

To make this leap, we can assume leadership in unassuming ways. We can learn to create our own tribe. If this idea excites you, explore Bill and Zoe's invitation at https://timefortribe.com. The natural tendency toward community is apparent when dire need arises. The existing social conventions of separation and isolation fall away when disaster strikes—everyday heroes show up as if out of nowhere. People help each other, regardless of race, religion or social status. Sometimes it takes a calamity to invoke our true capabilities, but it doesn't have to.

As the Earth moves to regain dynamic equilibrium, our innovative abilities naturally kick in. We are the face of evolution. As such, we are the ones at the helm spawning solutions to the problems surrounding us. The constructive approach demands that we embrace the ideological shift from conflict to cooperation. The story of separation must give way to the story of connection and belonging. When we recognize life as sacred and each of us as integral members of our home planet, then the turning away from destruction and toward recovery begins.

---

[63]   Sacred Economics with Charles Eisenstein – A Short Film, https://www.youtube.com/watch?v=EEZkQv25uEs Accessed October 12, 2019.

The most direct route to recovery follows nature's lead. We remember respect for ecosystems' natural harmony and regenerative abilities and refer to our ancestral wisdom. When we take the whole picture into consideration, we can more accurately name the issues. Groups of people in obscure corners of the world are finding elegant answers to problems and forming pockets of collaboration. We are required to ask ourselves, "What makes living sustainable?" And, "How is there enough for everyone?" The wealth afforded everyone within the gift culture offers true abundance to all members. In so doing, we collectively honor the Earth as our ever-giving life-support system.

Referencing Bill and Zoe's book, *We Need Each Other*, five clear distinctions illustrate a set of radical values and their signature actions in a gift culture.

1. Rather than monetary *transactions,* in a gift culture we *trust* in the community around us for the support we need.

    When monetary exchange is the medium for meeting needs, there will always be limitations for many people to get their basic needs met. Dependence upon money as a strategy for freedom, ease, and happiness inevitably creates lack. Money, whether we have a lot or a little, is at the core of isolation, poverty and domination of a few over many.

2. Rather than the *consumption* of goods, we *contribute* our gifts to the community in which we belong.

    When we joyfully give our gift, personal skill, talent, or ability to someone who needs just that, we find fulfillment.

3. Rather than living in *isolation*, we live in *community*.

    In general, men experience more isolation than women, as women naturally tend to connect with one another regularly, although perhaps not consistently or plentifully enough. Community is bonding, trust building, and connecting. It brings the deeply meaningful sense of *belonging* that we all crave. With belonging comes the sense of *security*.

4. Rather than *compete* with one another, we *cooperate*.

    The cooperative business approach is being revived out of necessity, from farmers sharing equipment to airlines sharing customers. Collective partnerships benefit all of their members, bringing their overheads down and increasing their returns. Cooperation illuminates our unique abilities while serving the collective. Cooperation is the predecessor to *collaboration*.

Collaboration serves to creatively administer diversity into solutions that work for all concerned.

5. In community, rather than living in *scarcity*, we live with *abundance*.

In a world based on consumption, we rarely feel fulfilled. We think that something else will finally assuage our cravings. But consuming more will never be enough because material things do not satisfy our true desires. We need to revise our definition of abundance to find satisfaction. Fulfillment is possible with social capital and inner wealth—by knowing who we are, our place in the world, and by contributing our gifts to benefit the whole. The internal experience of abundance is the natural outcome of belonging, having meaningful connections with others, and living our purpose.

More of us will be sharing the gift culture lifestyle as we create local economies and rely on our communities for sustenance. Naturally, we can expect challenges in the transition process. Many of us will be learning to embrace diversity. We often create stigmatism about our differences, focusing on people's personality quirks and external characteristics. When we rely on one another's strengths instead, the common ground we share is a given. Our differences become unique attributes that are recognized as advantages, rather than liabilities. As in bioregions---the greater the diversity of life forms the healthier the ecosystem, so it is with people---the greater the variety of viewpoints, talents, and abilities, the more expansive are the opportunities for creativity, innovation, and success. This is collaboration—interdependence in action.

Collaboration within Diversity

One endeavor of this handbook is to uncover the leader in each of us. We are the founders and citizens of the networks of communities to come. Collaboration is what we do. Inclusion is how we do it. Diversity is what makes it rich and beautiful, a panorama of color, texture, and design. Collaboration within diversity brings the highest possible potential for innovation—the application of co-creativity to much-needed solutions for our current dilemmas.

As a diverse community, we won't always see eye to eye. There necessarily will be differences of opinion. We all have ideas and varied strategies for living, relating, and working things out. How, then, will we find our stride? How will we make decisions, agreements, and plans together? A balance of flexibility and stability

Living in Intentional Community: The Cohousing Lifestyle
Contributed by the author's sister, Susan Swift

Many forward-thinking people have sought to live collectively or communally, sharing resources and land in an effort to live more sustainably. As a result, there are many models to choose from, including ecovillages, communes, coops, and cohousing. Each community adopts its own guidelines and principles for decision making, what types of resources will be shared, and which will be held by individuals and families. It's all negotiable.

Ever since my college years, I yearned for a return to living in a connected community. When I went to university, the surrounding town was a community incubator of sorts—an interlocking web of deep friendships developed among those of us who were engaged in one aspect or several of the community's economic, political, spiritual, environmental, and artistic life.

After my husband and I met, one of the things we discovered we had in common was our interest in intentional communities. I learned that he had spent four years living in a monastery.

Our big question was whether to join an existing community or start our own. We signed up for a multiday workshop about intentional communities and, after considering the options, began searching for a cohousing opportunity. We didn't step into the process blindly; we had some previous experience, and we did some research before choosing this lifestyle.

We knew that there would be challenges to living in community, especially for those of us who came from single-family households and cultures that didn't emphasize connection and cooperation. For those of us who were raised in systems where strong individualism and competition were rewarded, the learning curve was steep. But, we surmised, by learning to live harmoniously within a group we would also be helping our planet, our intimate relationships, and our own personal growth.

Reflections and Snapshot Learning

It is often said that intentional community is the shortest path to self-knowledge. That is because in a community where you

makes for a successful community. Frequently, communities share an ideology or set of values that define why they came together. A shared vision transcends any one individual and simultaneously includes everyone. Continuity of community, or maintaining a social structure over time, depends on every individual making his or her contribution to the group. Sustainability is enhanced through the accumulation of social capital, that which is gained when we give back to the whole. The focus is necessarily to remember our common goals while accentuating our individual strengths and skills.

Cohesion and Reciprocity

Community is about interrelationships. Many decisions must be made to start a community, interact with more people about daily living concerns, you are likely to bump into your own assumptions quite frequently. You think, *Well, of course, this is the way it is done*, or, *The choice is obvious*. Such thought patterns emerge in meetings when a group is considering adopting a new policy or deciding to rearrange furniture in a common area. In matters big or small, a community of people will rarely agree completely.

At our monthly meetings, the facilitator reads aloud one of our ten operating principles. The mission statement and operating principles serve to remind us of our shared values. Revisiting them helps us to embrace our diversity as we go along, making decisions together and getting work done.

Decision making can be a stumbling block, because, again, it forces one to confront assumptions and to listen to others and be flexible. These are not traits we, especially European Americans, were raised to embrace. Even after five years of living in cohousing, we are refining how to make decisions, how to define consensus, and when to employ it.

Intentional communities often attract like-minded people with similar backgrounds. This is not necessarily the place where multiculturalism thrives. On the other hand, it is amazing how many seemingly small differences are cultivated and strongly held. These divisions are revealed when people live in close quarters and make decisions together. Such differences (or sense of separateness) are fertile ground for self-reflection and building bridges and acceptance.

Over time, this process of confronting one's own assumptions during meetings and interactions has helped me to become self-reflective and more flexible. The alternative, holding firm to one's own way of seeing things, inevitably puts me face-to-face with the Buddhist adage that says, "Attachment is suffering!"

The cohousing group we joined had land and had hired some consultants, but the buildings weren't built. The community, as it would become, was just forming. Compromise or coming to a place where all parties were satisfied with a decision was key. Whether it was about how to finance the project or whether or not to include heated floors or solar energy, these early exercises in decision making laid the foundation for trust and communication. The skills and relationships we built in those early meetings are even more useful now that we are living together in a community we share.

and the need continues as we live and prosper together. The agreed-upon principles of the community will offer guidelines on how to approach both decision-making and conflict resolution. A key element for making a comprehensive decision that sticks is to ensure that all stakeholder's needs are represented. Of course, the more people involved in a meeting or group, the more time it will take to complete the process to make a decision. For expediency, a committee representing the stakeholders can be employed to make proposals to bring to the larger group. When forming such a committee, it is important that all community members' perspectives are represented. Alternatively, all stakeholders can choose to represent themselves

In the end, we have created more living space than any of us could have afforded individually. We only need one lawnmower for thirty households. We have smaller homes because the shared guest rooms and common house kitchen can accommodate larger groups, when we need them. Our main dining room has become a community-wide resource for gatherings of all types, and our members have, likewise, become community resources with an array of talents, skills, and wisdom to offer.

We enjoy living on several acres with gardens, a workshop, and a children's playroom. We have our own complete living units, which we own outright and can sell or rent if we choose. But sometimes one of us gets frustrated when we notice something that needs to be done or we wish to express ourselves creatively only to realize that we need permission to make changes to an outdoor space or any areas that are held in common.

Whoever suspected that we'd need to have so many meetings? Or that some people would find meetings a place to build community, while others just want to get the business done with so that they can get back to their private lives?

Who would have thought that the topic of pets would be required discussion during eight or ten meetings? Or that yard work could be so quickly accomplished after sending out an email request for volunteers?

On the positive side, we are a greater force for good, catalyzing change and growing the idea of interdependence and sustainable living. Living in community feels like an exponential process—we are synergistic, more than the sum of out parts!

All in all, living in intentional community teaches us to be respectful of each other's different needs, desires, blind spots, and vulnerabilities. We are here for each other when illness or hardships interrupt daily life. We water each other's plants, bring soup when needed, and mind the animals when neighbors travel. It's not utopia, but it is fulfilling. And perhaps learning to embrace differences and work together with common purpose are just what's needed for human survival.

in a decision-making process.

In a circle of leader-members formed to make a decision, we begin by gathering perspectives. Once all differing perspectives have been heard and acknowledged, there are some options on how to come to agreements and/or to resolve conflicts. One model for collaborative decision making is explained below. A method for resolving conflict within community is described in the next chapter. Both processes are based on inclusion of and consideration for all involved. There is great strength and resolve in our decisions when those affected by the outcomes have contributed to making them. When we experience our relevance to the group, our sense of mattering increases and binds us together.

Group cohesion is woven this way, when each person recognizes his or her part in the creative process. The natural pride of doing and giving to the group and of being acknowledged for it is a simple yet significant aspect to cohesion. Reciprocity is the substrate of cohesion. We are hardwired to give of ourselves for the benefit of what and whom we care most about. We care about our own well-being and that of the others in our lives, and vice versa.

Wisdom Circles: How and Why

How a circle is set up and held can influence the level of trust and goodwill among its participants. Whatever role each person has in the meeting, the group will reap greater benefits if everyone in attendance assumes leadership for him or herself. This means to take responsibility for what you need to be present and to show up in integrity with your values. To assume the role of leader can help us to hold ourselves and the process with tender attention. Tender attention, along with curiosity and respect, offer an energetic signature that will beneficially affect the weaving of the container. As leaders, we practice self-connection and focused presence with *what is*. We hold others with consideration, inquisitiveness, and empathy at the ready. This attitude will engender goodwill and trust in the process, which will have the effect of a more efficient, fun, and successful meeting.

The configuration of a group meeting also plays a big part in its potential success. Connection and openness are engendered when we circle up and can see everyone in the group. A circle shape more readily invites our participation than a classroom-like setting with rows of chairs. In that familiar configuration, we tend to go passive and wait for someone to tell us what to do. It is easier to participate and harder to hide in a circle. Sitting in a circle together disbands a would-be hierarchy and creates a level playing field wherein everyone is both a participant and a leader. As leaders, we speak our concerns thoughtfully and listen with curiosity to understand.

For decisions to last and follow-through to occur, all stakeholders—meaning those affected by the outcome—need to be included in the decision-making process. When people have a say in decisions that affect them, there tends to be much greater buy-in. This fact harkens back to the significance of being heard and understood in any conversation—it softens our hearts and gives us a sense of belonging. Being heard brings us into alignment with those around us by the trust and connection it generates. We are not only more willing to do our part, but also may find ourselves willing *to shift* our perspective (see Shift versus Compromise in chapter 11) if doing so gives what is needed to benefit the whole community. A leader serves the whole, knowing that we are better off when the good of all is maximized.

A purposeful circle can be created with the people invested in the decision to be made. Although each person in the circle shall be considered a leader, meaning to take personal responsibility for your voice to be heard, your needs to be represented, and your presence in the circle, it is useful to designate one person to facilitate the meeting. The roles of timekeeper and recorder are important to fill also. The following description of the group meeting process will be given from the facilitator's perspective. Play with the idea of being in the facilitator's shoes while reading the guidelines for the process. We are always at choice, so imagining yourself as the facilitator will give you an opportunity to find out whether that is a choice you might like to make at some point.

The following exploration is an adaptation of the work of Miki Kashtan, a significant mentor of mine and co-founder of Bay Area Nonviolent Communication (baynvc.org). For more information on Miki's innovative contributions to social change, please go to baynvc.org and her blog, *The Fearless Heart*. She calls her format for making decisions collaboratively "convergent decision making."[64] Kashtan offers workshops and materials on the entire process here: http://thefearlessheart.org/product/convergent-facilitation-primer-packet/. Her materials are available on a gift economy basis. I highly recommend reviewing her Convergent Facilitation Primer, available at the link provided. I share my understanding of the model as an example below.

Another practical model for decision making used in organizations is, sociocracy. Sociocracy is, "A social ideal that values equality and the rights of people to determine the conditions under which they live and work; and, an effective method of organizing associations, businesses, and governments, large and small."[65]

Setting Up a Circle Meeting

• *Find a good meeting space.* Qualities to look for are space and seating for the number of people in attendance; heating and/or air-conditioning if needed; tea, coffee, or kitchen facility if needed; whiteboard or blackboard to track the process visually; bathroom; parking if needed; a space where everyone can see and hear one another and is also private.

---

[64]   Miki Kashtan, http://thefearlessheart.org/product/convergent-facilitation-primer-packet/

[65]   *Sociocracy*, August 16, 2019. Retrieved from, https://www.sociocracy.info/what-is-sociocracy/

- *Decide on the specific questions or topic to be discussed.* To get clarity on the exact issue and how to word it succinctly can be a task in itself. Other times, it is obvious. Make the topic known to the others involved and propose a meeting to discuss it. Propose the place, time, and duration of the meeting.

- *Decide on a facilitator, a recorder / note taker, and a timekeeper.* This can happen beforehand or at the start of the meeting. Along with a designated facilitator, designate a recorder. The meeting minutes are a good way to track what happened; to view the progress of the decision-making process, especially if it takes more than one meeting; and to make agreements clear. The recorder can use the notations on the whiteboard as the outline for his or her notes. Use of a laptop computer makes it easy to rewrite or correct and send out the minutes to others. A timekeeper is also an important role for the meeting. Keeping time agreements goes a long way to building trust and goodwill. Agree on how much time the meeting will take. If more time is needed, note when the time is nearly up. If desired, anyone can request that the meeting continue for ten, fifteen, or thirty more minutes, depending on what is needed and with agreement to continue. Or agree to adjourn and reconvene another day to complete the process.

- *Do a check-in at the beginning.* Depending on the familiarity of group members, the check-in might include some personal information but not necessarily. The check-in can also be used for each person to give his or her general ideas and thoughts about the topic so everyone can hear others' perspectives. However, the check-in is best accomplished if timed, so that those who tend to talk readily and longer than is warranted can have a time frame for their sharing. This will help the group container to be held with integrity, facilitate trust and goodwill, and keep the meeting to the agreed upon time frame. Establish the parameters for the check-in at the outset and include the topics to be addressed and the amount of time for each person to speak.

When deciding how much check-in time will serve the meeting, determine the relevance to share more or to keep it short, depending on the meeting agenda and needs of the group. Depending on the group needs and issues, a short check-in is from one to three minutes. A longer check-in to share more information is from four to nine minutes. Also decide on how much time the meeting will last and when to take a break. Invite everyone to take care of his or her own bodily needs throughout. The group can contract for more time if needed, but it is very important to hold to the time agreements unless the whole group agrees to change them together.

Explore this Practice: Wisdom Circle for Decision Making

This is an overview of how to come to agreements and to make decisions together as a group. The topic can range from innovative ideas to mundane logistics. Greater facility with wisdom circle meetings will occur as more time is spent in such decision-making circles and also by facilitating them. As we grow in our abilities to stretch into full inclusion of all pieces of the puzzle—that is, all people and parts involved in the process—our facility with the circle meeting will increase.

Facilitator role

Gather perspectives

1. *Listen attentively to each person who shares; capture the essence of his or her words.*

    Write down the essence of what each person is saying on the white board. The essence can be gleaned by paring the words down to the universal quality of life to be served, including the "how" or "why" if it's there in what they're sharing. Put it into a short, descriptive statement.

    For example, if the group is discussing whether to make a community garden or not, a conversation between one member and the facilitator might look like this:

    GROUP MEMBER. I'm not sure I like the idea of a community garden at all, because I don't really like to garden. I'm afraid I'll be an outcast if I don't help somehow, and I think it will be expensive. Will there be a required amount of time or money people have to give to it?

    The facilitator will respond with empathy first, so the speaker knows he or she is heard and then narrow his or her words down into a succinct statement elucidating the member's core concern. It may take a few exchanges to get to the nugget that fits his or her exact concern.

    FACILITATOR. It sounds like the community garden idea is not one that inspires you. You're not a fan of gardening. You're concerned about the expense and worried you might be required to give time and energy when you aren't feeling called to. Is that it?

GROUP MEMBER. Yes, that's pretty much it. And I don't want to be disenfranchised just because I'm not into gardening like everyone else is. It matters to me to participate in the community, but not in this way.

FACILITATOR. I understand that you very much want to be a participating member of the community and want to still be included even if you don't choose to be part of the garden project, right?"

GROUP MEMBER, *nodding in agreement.* Yes.

FACILITATOR. Okay. So, if the garden project gets the go-ahead, is it that you want to make sure people have a choice about whether they participate or not? And that the choice to not participate doesn't cause a sense of isolation or separation from the community?

GROUP MEMBER. Yes, I want to be at choice, and I also want to belong fully. I wonder if there is some way that I can be useful even if I don't do any gardening.

FACILITATOR. All right. Let me see if I can capture this accurately. You want there to be choice about the level and type of participation in the garden and to remain an integral member of the community even if you don't choose to participate. Does that capture it?

GROUP MEMBER. Yes. That sounds good.

FACILITATOR. All right. I'll write this down. *The facilitator writes on the board, "To have choice about the amount and kind of participation in the garden project," and, "To remain an integral member of the community even if not part of the garden."* Who else shares these concerns?

A few people raise their hands.

FACILITATOR. Okay. Are your needs addressed accurately in these statements?

The facilitator then acknowledges the other group members whose concerns are spoken to in the statements written down and added to the list on the board. (See step 2 for further explanation.)

2. *Ask if anyone else shares this idea, perspective, or opinion.*

Every circle member does not need to speak during the gathering perspectives phase, but every perspective does need to be voiced and clearly noted. If someone has voiced a *shared* opinion or perspective, expediency will be served by others not verbalizing the same idea. Acknowledge anyone who raises his or her hand, so each person knows he or she has been heard and understood and, thus, included. The facilitator might even say out loud the names of the members who agree that the captured statements serve and speak for them, too, to punctuate their inclusion.

Continue with 1 and 2 until all perspectives have been heard and captured.

Name disagreements

3. *Ask for conflicts and disagreements to be voiced.*

   Disagreement is best addressed directly and early on in the dialogue. As a facilitator-leader, hold the whole group with kindness and attention. When you hold space for everyone, meaning to have awareness of everyone and openness to all ideas and perspectives, it serves to stimulate that same attitude within the group. The more individuals who also hold themselves as leaders in the group and who also hold space for all perspectives to be heard and understood, the more dynamic and streamlined the meeting will be. In effect, there will be less contention and conflict.

4. *Request that each person with a disagreement share more about his or her perspective or idea.*

   Continue to listen and respond with empathy to what everyone shares. This will increase meeting effectiveness and potential collaboration as all are heard and understood. Collaterally, hearing and seeing that differences are held with respect and consideration will also help anyone who may be hesitant to participate to gain trust and courage to speak up. This will increase group cohesion by modeling that each group member matters to the process. As all differences of perspective are heard and understood, the statements on the whiteboard may shift, be added to, or removed. This is a very fluid part of the process.

5. *Rework the captured statements to include new stated needs and concerns or to remove obsolete statements.*

   As facilitator, you can knit together some of the statements to include more perspectives. This will help everyone to know his or her common ground and elicit hope that we can resolve the issue good-naturedly. Then find out how close the group is to agreement on the statements captured as described in step six.

6. *Optimize captured statements.*

Point to each captured statement on the board and ask for a show of hands of all people in agreement with it. Ask for a show of hands of people who disagree with it. If there are dissenters, ask for a show of hands of those who can live with it. The specific but slightly different questions highlight participants' level of willingness, or threshold, to come to agreement. For everyone to have full agreement is a high threshold; to be able or willing to live with it is a lower threshold of agreement and, thus, makes agreement more accessible. To find a low threshold is more constructive than dissent. Continue the process as delineated in steps 2, 3, 4, and 5 above until all people can live with the captured statements. The statements define the needs and concerns to be included in proposals for solutions. Take breaks and agree to reconvene as needed.

Proposals for implementation

7. *Engender proposals to implement the agreed upon decision or project.*

Action steps, the strategies to implement the ideas and desires from the captured statements, can be worked out now. Ask for proposals that include as many of the stated needs within the captured statements as possible. There are various ways this can happen. And this can be a good time to take a break from the meeting if the group energy is low. Verbally acknowledge the work and successes made together thus far. If taking a break, agree when to reconvene.

It is not necessary for everyone in the group to be a part of making proposals. As mentioned above, a smaller committee or task group can be entrusted to come up with proposals for implementation. If you decide to go about it this way, ask for volunteers to form a task group to make proposals. The task group will be most effective if the members in it reflect the greatest differences of opinions or needs to be addressed. If there are too many captured statements for one group to handle or if there are clearly delineated topics in the captured statements, ask for another task group to take half the captured statements or the other topic.

8. *Reconvene to approve proposals.*

Decide when to reconvene as a group to hear the proposals for implementation. The task groups will present what they came up with. During this meeting focus on what proposals meet most needs, make sense to everyone, and people agree with. Use the facilitation tactics above to come to agreement on which proposals to implement. Make an action plan with time frames incorporating the agreed upon proposals.

Make agreements

9. *Make agreements. Designate who does what and by when.*

     Ask people to self-select what part they will take to implement the agreed upon action plan. If all parts are not spoken for, request volunteers to take the remaining parts. Remember, this is about choice, not coercion. Support everyone to joyfully choose what most inspires him or her. Trust the process. Most likely, everything will get the attention it needs, even if it isn't fully clear how right now. As facilitator, it is not your responsibility to make sure everything gets taken on or done. It is your job to speak to and name what is happening, to reflect the agreements, and to invite action. If you notice yourself feeling stressed or constricted, make sure you are not assuming a story that you are responsible for it all to play out successfully. That is everyone's job; everyone here is a leader.

10. *Decide when to meet again to see how the plan is working, what needs modification, and what needs to be added or removed from the plan.*

     This can be done anywhere from a week to a month or more later, depending on the plan and group needs. You may also take time to decide on who will take on the various roles for the next meeting. That way, the next designated facilitator can send out an email before the next meeting to remind people it's coming up and give folks an opportunity to think about how the action plan is working from their perspective.

The more we trust that our needs matter and that we will be taken into respectful consideration, the easier, more fun, and more expedient meetings will be. When we work together in the "power-with" model, the fears of hierarchical separation and exclusion begin to dissolve. Collaboration becomes second nature to us as we reap the many benefits of working and living together harmoniously. However, we will not always be in a state of peace and harmony. We can count on disagreements and conflicts to arise.

To address conflicts and to repair fallout from broken trust, acts of aggression, or when one person acts to benefit him or herself alone, another type of circle meeting can be utilized. This format is called *restorative circles*, a term and process coined by nonviolent communication trainer Dominic Barter. The next chapter will describe this process. Dominic has had great success in Brazil and around the world repairing and restoring damaged community relations with restorative circles. For more information about this potent work, please go to restorativecircles.org.

CHAPTER FIFTEEN

Restoring Connection and Integrity in Community

Peace cannot be kept by force; it can only be achieved by understanding.
—Einstein

I want to say upfront that I have minimal experience facilitating restorative circles, the focus of this chapter. However, I believe the information is relevant and important enough to include my summary of what I learned about the process from Dominic Barter. It is a complex set of moving parts that is reliant on and reflective of the specific situation and people involved. The process originated in Brazil, evolving from Dominic's significant experience with Nonviolent Communication (NVC) and its expansion into applications in the field of restorative justice. The process arose as a response to the needs of communities he was engaged with and as such, is a community-based under taking. It follows that the beneficial effects of restorative circles are more fully gleaned within the context of the community setting in which the process occurs. My hope is that those forming or joining communities will become inspired to explore the deep social transformations possible that this process points to.

Refreshingly, restorative circles create the opportunity for people to speak and listen to one another in a safe container that provides clear guidelines and equality for all voices. This in itself is a shift from the familiar model of retribution, wherein an external authority has the power to guide as well as punish. Restorative circles intend to restore power, connection and dignity to those people involved from the perspective of the community effected. Such circles are versatile in that they can be used proactively to develop relationships and build community, and they can also be used to respond to wrongdoing or conflicts.[66] They are currently used widely in classrooms and various community settings to encourage mutual understanding and support collaborative efforts. I believe the circle format has the potential to draw out of us the wisdom and insight that both rely on and strengthen our human connections.

Individuals Reflect Community

As social beings, we are in constant interaction with one another. Our interconnectedness shows up in many ways and types of relationships. Overall, the health of the community we belong to is reflected in our individual relationships—that is, in how we interact one-on-one. When an event happens that causes harm or threatens another's person or property, it is a reflection of a tear in the fabric of the community itself. Miki Kashtan contends that, "When people have done significant harm, it takes enormous courage to traverse the sea of shame that separates them from their own weeping soul."[67] This degree of pain and separation can be tenderly held within the context of a community circle set up for that very purpose.

To most eloquently restore integrity and connection, the affront is taken to all members whose lives have been affected by that event. In the circle format, the shape of community meetings over eons, we share our stories of what occurred and how it affected us. To speak openly to one another brings our tenderness to the fore. When the hurt we may have participated in creating is seen and felt, our hearts melt and open in empathy. Our humanity is highlighted when both the actor(s) of the event and the receiver(s) are held in circle by their supportive and protective community. The natural response is to grow through our personal stories of separation and into the desire to restore safety, dignity, and health for everyone.

Restorative Circles

Restorative Circles are an integration of restorative justice concepts with Nonviolent Communication as developed and taught by Dominic Barter. The premise is that an individual or gang aberration, such as cheating, robbing, or physically harming

---

[66] Marieke van Woerkom, Edutopia. *Building Community with Restorative Circles*, March 12, 2018. https://www.edutopia.org › article › building-community-restorative-circles

[67] Miki Kashtan, *The Little Book of Courageous Living.* (Oakland: Fearless Heart Publications, 2013).

another person, is a statement of malaise within the community itself. Rather than giving away the power of retribution of an individual to the state or criminal justice system, power is put back into the hands of the community members affected by the offense. The relationships of those involved in the act, the author of the act, and the recipient, as well as those affected, can be repaired by coming together in a circle meeting to hear one another. In this way, solutions that include everyone's needs can be sought. Such circles help overcome the illusion that we don't live together, that our actions are somehow discreet and don't affect others, and that we are powerless to find solutions at the community level. The circle brings us back into connection as a community and empowers people to engage personal responsibility and integrity.

The function of a restorative circle is to use circle-council practices in which all involved in an offense, including those affected by it, meet as equals. It represents horizontal power, rather than the familiar hierarchical form of power over. With a specific format for speaking and listening to one another, detailed below, the intention is to repair harm done, to restore dignity to those affected, and to reintegrate everyone affected back into peaceful coexistence. In this model, the community is recognized as indirectly responsible for the offense, and thereby indirectly benefits from the circle process. The process is based on the wisdom circles of our indigenous predecessors, and as such, resonates with our ancient memories.

Remembering Community Power

The circle-council meeting is a way to embody the strong human value for heartfelt justice among people. It takes justice out of the realm of legal institutions and empowers people to restore balance and safety among themselves by making visible the crucial roles of relatives, neighbors, witnesses, and others affected. It puts the receiver of the conflict or offense at the heart of the resolution process with the community's support. To sit in circle together seems to rekindle our shared tribal inklings, no matter who we are. "Long term results of Restorative Circles have shown them to be effective regardless of the nature of the conflict and irrespective of the age or education of the participants."[68]

---

[68]   Dominic Barter, Restorative Justice Training, San Francisco, CA, December 2007.

The Circle Format: Horizontal Power Structure

The circle format is truly about revealing our common ground. The restorative circle naturally dismantles labels and social roles by establishing a horizontal power structure. Mutual understanding is supported to flow from the simple, direct questions asked and the responses reflected to the person asking the question. The web of human connection within the affected community is made clear in the process. Each person speaks his or her truth and is heard and understood from his or her perspective. People begin to gain clarity about why they did what they did. If their actions caused harm or damage, they can strategize new ways to meet the reasons for what they did. As the needs-based interpretation of the actions of all participants comes to light, the wisdom in the circle becomes clear. Once all those affected have been heard and understood, connection and care naturally emerge as the motivators in members' responses. The desire to contribute to repairing damaged relationships arises unbidden for most people in the circle.

Overview of Restorative Circle Meetings

As I learned from Dominic, he defines three parts in a complete restorative circle process. It starts with the *pre-circle*, in which each person to participate in the circle has an individual conversation with the facilitator. The effected individual, the "receiver" of the offense, identifies the facts of the act or offense that was committed and is offered empathetic listening to the consequences, how the act affected him or her. Then the facilitator gives the receiver information about the restorative circle meeting process and invites him or her to participate. The receiver tells the facilitator who else was affected by the offense and these people, too, are invited to the circle. Each circle member meets with the facilitator and shares his or her story of how he or she was affected. Then they can agree to participate or not, and they also can make suggestions as to who else to include. Next follows the *circle meeting* itself, which has three distinct phases, described in detail below, followed by the *post-circle*. People reconvene in a post-circle to evaluate how the agreements made in the circle are working out and to make modifications if indicated.

The suggested role of the facilitator is described below within the context of each phase of the restorative circle meeting. In restorative circles, the facilitator is there to support the natural wisdom inherent in the circle itself. As Dominic Barter shares,

"Something in the form of the circle has its own wisdom that reveals itself. It's a process that does not depend upon the skills of a certain person." The facilitator is there simply to make things easier. He or she isn't the director so much as the navigator, the one who holds the map and points the way, according to Barter. The intelligence is within the design of the process itself, not in the skill set of the facilitator. This makes the process easily duplicable. In fact, the greatest skill the facilitator needs to know is what not to do, rather than magically knowing exactly what to do. The degree of explicit leadership of the facilitator lessens in each of the three phases of the circle process.

The Restorative Circle Meeting

The intention of the circle is to illuminate the interrelationships of the *context*, or the community setting in which the *conflict*, the offense, or a severing of communication, happened. There are three phases of the circle meeting that make this visible to the participants—*mutual comprehension, self-responsibility, and agreed action*. As mentioned, this approach wisely functions to establish horizontal power structure or a power-with format, wherein each of us is equal in importance. In the hierarchical power-over formula, we agree that some people have more power and matter more than other people. Our dominant hierarchical social structure makes conflict inevitable and resolution doubtful. Here, on the other hand, we establish something very different, the phases of which are described next.

To gain *mutual comprehension* among the group members, the facilitator asks participants simple questions to reveal each person's intention in creating the conflict or what he or she wants to accomplish by the actions he or she took in response to it. After each person speaks, what he or she said is reflected to him or her. Speakers experience being understood by the person they want to hear them. It is set up in this way so that *shared meaning* about the event is communicated. The purpose isn't to talk about what happened, so much as to understand how what happened affected each person. When we sit face-to-face in a circle and hear how a rift in the container of the community has affected others of us personally, we have a naturally empathetic response. Our hearts open to the hurts people have sustained. This sets the tone to openly grieve the painful effects of the event. Those involved are inspired to take responsibility for their part in response to what happened and how it affected their community.

Self-responsibility is an investigation into understanding what each of us did within the larger context. It takes us beyond the familiar categories of right and wrong, where a person or an institution has the power to punish one of us. When we put the power of communication at the center of the circle, along with those who caused hurt and were hurt by the event, the wisdom of the circle brings us back to our hearts. It awakens our humanity. In this setting, people can get in touch with the motivating forces that impelled them to do what they did and to understand the consequences of their actions on others. This phase invites mourning, to feel grief and sadness for the harmful actions taken out of desperation to get needs met.

Specifically, awareness of the values, or the qualities of life at play, are explored representing underlying needs people attempted to get met. Because we share the same universal needs motivating our actions, to voice them makes the reasons for our actions transparent to others and, as such, makes visible our humanity. If we incurred violence or damage in our attempts to get our needs met, then we can see and feel the disturbing consequences for ourselves. Mourning can occur on all fronts, both from those who were hurt by transgressions and by those who transgressed. To take personal responsibility for how we affected others becomes a natural step. To grieve relieves us of holding onto the pain any longer and, thus, allows it to transform. When we sit together in a circle and hear painful consequences of desperate acts, we tend to be inclined to want to help repair the damage or to support people to overcome their losses and restore dignity to their lives.

The third phase of the circle is *agreed action*. This is generally an easy follow-up to hearing the needs people were attempting to meet by their actions and reactions to the event. The group focuses together to find constructive ways to respond to people's unmet needs. Everyone in the circle will come up with an action to repair damage and/or restore dignity. All actions offered will be agreed upon by the whole group. A time frame is then set up to revisit the agreed actions and to adjust or modify them as indicated.

The following are questions to be asked by the facilitator in each phase of the circle. If no one self-selects to begin sharing, the facilitator sees who is in the most discomfort and invites that person to start.

Mutual comprehension

The objective is to discover how we are now, in the aftermath of the event.

Facilitator to the first person: "What would you like the other person to know about how you are now, in relation to the event and its consequences?"

The facilitator encourages the person to speak directly to one person, whoever he or she most wants to be heard by, and to share where he or she is now, in the present, and the significance to him or her of what he or she is experiencing. The facilitator then asks the person listening to the first speaker to reflect what he or she heard.

Facilitator to the second person: "What did you hear her say?"

After the second person responds, the facilitator goes back to the first person.

Facilitator to the first person: "Is that accurate? And is there anything else you want her to know?"

This format continues until everyone who desires to share with someone in the circle about his or her experience has done so and has been understood as he or she would like to be. As each member is heard and understood for the event's effects on them personally, the group begins to have shared meaning about what occurred. A container of understanding is woven in which every member is held with equal care.

Self-responsibility

This step involves retroactive rehumanizing of one another by verbalizing underlying motivations for actions taken.

Facilitator to first person: "What would you like him to know about what you were looking for at the moment you chose to act?" The facilitator can support people's sharing by holding awareness for the possible values, principles, or needs (qualities of life) that might have been in play and motivating their decisions and actions.

Facilitator to second person: "What did you hear her say?"

Facilitator to first person: "Is that accurate? Is there anything else you want him to know?"

After she responds, the facilitator continues with the same questions to the second person.

Facilitator to second person: "What would you like her to know about what you were looking for at the time you chose to act?" This process of asking questions and responding with reflections will continue until all who wish to share in this phase have done so.

Agreed upon action

Here we have the practical steps of reparation and restoration.

Facilitator to all: "What would you like to see happen now? When would you like this to happen?"

All participants who want to share a response to this and the next two questions can do so in this last phase of the circle meeting.

Facilitator to all: "What would you like to offer and to whom? When?"

Facilitator to all: "What would you like to request and from whom? When?"

The facilitator or another group member can write down the agreements that come out of the third phase of the central circle meeting. This part of the conversation may have a tone of concern and compassion for those who have suffered from the incident. It may be lighter than the previous two phases of the circle and bring a sense of hopefulness to the community. The last part of the central circle meeting is to set a time to reconvene for the post-circle.

The Post-Circle

In the post-circle, we share how the agreed upon actions are serving the individuals involved and the community. This phase is to reconnect and reevaluate the practical effects of the agreements made in the circle meeting and to modify them as indicated.

In the post-circle, the facilitator holds space for open communication and heartfelt sharing. He or she may offer simple reminders to speak directly to one person, to speak using "I" statements rather than "you" or "they." And the facilitator invites what people share to be reflected by the person being spoken to. The post-circle tends to be abbreviated, as agreed upon actions are discussed in their relevance to restore dignity, repair the damage, and bring people back into a state of cohesion and harmony. Modifications of existing agreements or the inception of new agreements to fulfill these purposes can be made together in this phase.

The practice of restoring justice and dignity in the shape of circle meetings brings the rawness of our humanity into the room. When people speak directly to one another and are received with respect and understanding, power is restored to the community. This speaks to potent grassroots formation of healthy and vibrant local systems for social justice. It represents egalitarian justice in action for all members of our planet.

CHAPTER SIXTEEN
Compassionate Action

To be alive in this beautiful, self-organizing universe – to participate
in the dance of life with senses to perceive it, lungs that breathe it,
organs that draw nourishment from it – is a wonder beyond words.
----Joanna Macy

With freedom and expansiveness blooming inside, we are motivated to take empowered, compassionate action. The inward journey brings us back to ourselves and to the vulnerable yet potent state of being human. Ironically, it is from the fact of our vulnerability that we summon the strength of character to live courageously. Vulnerability instills in us the impetus to care and to steward our charges responsibly, whether ourselves, those we love, or a piece of the world at large. It reflects our need for one another and the simple truth that we are influenced by and affect each other. The inner world is our center, the point of light that moves our souls with meaning and purpose. It is clarity of purpose that we need now, drawn from the depths of connectivity with ourselves, to one other and our planet, Earth. As Joanna Macy reminds us, "Here connected consciousness stems from a widening of our self-interest, where we are guided by the intention to act for the well-being of all life."[69]

Wise Reasoning

Wisdom comes from our connections with others, relates a new study shared in *Science Magazine.* According to researcher Igor Grossmann, it isn't raw intelligence

---

[69]   Joanna Macy and Chris Johnstone, Active Hope--How to Face the Mess We're in without Going Crazy. (Novato, CA: New World Library, 2012) p 100.

that determines our ability to get along with others. It is wisdom, or the ability to employ "wise reasoning."[70] Grossman notes that it is our perceived need for support from others that indicates our ability to work things out together. And it is our ability to work through difficulties with others that determines a person's level of wise reasoning. Grossman's University of Canada at Waterloo experiment showed that people in lower socioeconomic classes—people with less income, less education, and more worries about money—scored twice as high on the wise reasoning scale than did their more socially affluent counterparts. Wise reasoning in this experiment simply means to have a greater ability to work through conflicts together—in other words, to problem solve creatively so that all those involved are taken into consideration. Collaboration, then, sprouts organically out of need. Helping one another is our default mode, our intrinsic means of successfully living and working together.

Necessity is the mother of invention, as the saying goes. As a species, we are in critical need of collective, wise reasoning. Those of us who still have abundant food and clean air and water at our disposal can fairly easily ignore the signs. The distractions of our busy lives and high daily doses of screen time serve to keep our heads down and our vision myopic. Many of us are in the privileged position to pretend that we don't need others for our survival. But it takes very little reflection to realize the numbers of people and amount of resources that went into having our morning cup of coffee alone. At the same time, it is those of us with means to see and hear about the signs and symptoms of our disrupted ecosystems and social inequities that are in a position to take wise action. It is those of us who willingly step into our compassionate observer who can see and feel the hardships of those less fortunate, while at the same time maintain our equilibrium.

Indeed, the global climate is in dire straits socially and ecologically. And yet, to be filled with anxiety, fear, and helplessness in response undermines our internal resources and, thus, our ability to take action. We need deep self-connection and our inner authority in tact to be productive in our lives and follow through with our intentions. When our actions are meaningful to us, when they feed our unique way of being and our passion for what we do, we make the world a better place. When we know what truly matters to us, what inspires and enlivens us, we are guided to share our unique gifts with the world. Each of us has an opportunity to shine. Not only that; we can also live fulfilled, love life, and give back out of joy. To give from joy, we need to

---

70 Michael Price, *Science Magazine. The Lower Your Social Status, the 'Wiser' You Are,* Dec 20, 2017. https://www.sciencemag.org/news/2017/12/lower-your-social-class-wiser-you-are-suggests-new-study.

be full and to replenish ourselves regularly. To care for others, we must also prioritize taking care of ourselves.

Heart of the Earth

A simple and beautiful way to replenish ourselves and to find joy as well as peace, is to connect with nature. The words may sound hollow until you know firsthand the delight of walking through the woods on a clear October day or hiking in the desert after a rain or snorkeling over colorful, fish-filled reefs in the turquoise-blue ocean. To know such beauty is deeply nourishing. It invites our appreciation and sense of belonging to the Earth, the stuff of which we are made. The wisdom of John Muir comes through in his admonition, "Keep close to Nature's heart and break away once in awhile, and climb a mountain, or spend a week in the woods. Wash your spirit clean." Indeed, clarity arrives unbidden when we connect deeply with nature. The natural world instills us with gratitude for life and all that we have been given. Nature bring us back to our physical being and to the crux of what really matters. This is a crucially important practice for us now.

There is wisdom in our bodies. And our bodies are the portal to the wisdom of the Earth. Buddhist practitioner and author Amelia Williams tells us that, "To encounter our human body is to encounter the natural world. . . The closer we come to the body, the closer we draw to the truth of our own wildness. This connects us to the planetary wildness that we aspire to protect. While the mind is tugged into the past and future, the body is fully present."[71] Awakening to our earthly connections reminds us that we are here, now. Our presence is a potent resource that brings our hearts into play and engages care. Author Robin Kimmer, a member of the North American Potawatomi tribe, realizes that, ". . . when we fall in love with the living world, we cannot be bystanders to its destruction. Attention becomes intention, which coalesces itself to action."[72] It is our open heartedness then, our love and care, that translate into taking compassionate, purposeful action. Such care comes into being when we know our belonging to ourselves and our mother planet.

To know our belonging to our bodies and the body of the Earth is the surest way to navigate the disorienting disruptions and upheavals occurring. Charles Eisenstein

---

[71] Amelia Williams, "Five Practices for Working with the Immense Challenge of Climate Change," Nov 6, 2017. One Earth Sangha. oneearthsangha.org

[72] Robin Kimmer, "Returning the Gift." *Minding Nature*: Spring 2014, Vol 7, #2.

tells us, "Climate change portends a revolution in the relationship between nature and civilization, but this is not a revolution in the more efficient allocation of global resources in the program of endless growth. It is a revolution of love. It is to know the forests as sacred again, and the mangroves and the rivers, the mountains and the reefs, each and every one. It is to love them for their own beingness, and not merely to protect them because of their climate benefits."[73] To appreciate nature's wildness and beauty summons our desire to care for the Earth. Compassionate action naturally follows.

Our successful evolution leads us to a new world wherein we care for the planet as well as each other. As Joanna Macy relates, "When our central organizing priority becomes the well-being of all life, then what happens through us is the recovery of the world."[74] As leaders of our lives, this is no less than our mandate. We are transformed by spending time sensing the heart of the Earth—her well-being becomes paramount. Pioneer conservationist, marine biologist and author, Rachel Carson, understood that, "The more clearly we can focus our attention on the wonders and realities of the universe about us, the less taste we shall have for destruction."[75]

Profound personal benefits result when you regularly give yourself the gift of being in nature. The smells, sights, and sounds of the natural world reorient our internal compass and reestablish equilibrium. The emotional and psychic chaos from the noise and bustle of city life is smoothed out, and our energies are realigned. We remember the ground of our being and the resonance of quietude.

Spending time connecting with nature renews and replenishes us. So nourished, we have greater internal resources to focus our energies and to give back. As Rachel Carson knew well, "Those who contemplate the beauty of the earth find reserves of strength that will endure as long as life lasts."[76] It is imperative now that we remember our intrinsic connections to the Earth and experience the natural world first hand so that we are strengthened by it and motivated to care.

It is connection that illuminates the path to our redemption. Connection with ourselves brings us peace and wholeness. Connection with nature and with others brings us the richness of belonging. We remember how much we care when we feel ourselves as part of the whole, complex web of life. What we appreciate matters to us,

---

[73] Charles Eisenstein, *Climate—A New Story* (Berkeley: North Atlantic Books, 2018).

[74] Joanna Macy and Chris Johnstone, *Active Hope--How to Face the Mess We're in without Going Crazy* (Novato, CA: New World Library, 2012) p 100.

[75] Rachel Carson, *Silent Spring* (Boston, New York: Houghton Mifflin, 1962).

[76] Carson.

and thus has meaning and gives us a sense of purpose. To care is a primary purpose: it is the language of the heart in action. Charles Eisenstein says, "If we honor our inner nature lover and speak from that place, others will hear us. Perhaps we have been speaking the wrong language, seeking a change of mind when really what we need is a change of heart."[77] When we engage our hearts, we inevitably live with purpose. We are motivated by compassion, and love giving back to the world.

Know Your Purpose

To bring the conceptual into form, let's explore what brings you the most joy and where your greatest passions lie. This process will reveal what really matters to you. And you may be living the life you most desire right now. Or you may live the "chop wood, carry water" lifestyle. This is a Zen Buddhist term that speaks to living a very simple life infused with the spirit of mindfulness. It is akin to the Hindu "karma yoga." Karma yoga is a path that invites us to be fully present in all that we do. We bring our intentionality to live embodied and in a coherent state of awareness to our words and actions, no matter how simple or mundane our work and activities themselves. In this case, it isn't so much what we do to make our living but the attitude with which we approach it. Whether we live the karma yoga lifestyle or do work that has more personal meaning, what we bring to the world will be enhanced by our full, embodied presence. Mindfulness is always a welcome medium for living and invites compassionate action.

The following practice can help you gain clarity on what your purpose is if it isn't clear to you. It can help to shed light on what you love and what you have to share with the world.

Explore this Practice: Gaining Clarity of Purpose

Sit quietly and follow your breath for a few minutes. When you feel yourself drop into presence via your compassionate observer:

1. Look inside and scan for the most significant and meaningful moments in your life. What was happening? What were you doing? Describe each experience as

---

[77] Charles Eisenstein, *Climate—A New Story.* (Berkeley: North Atlantic Books, 2018).

you remember it. Then name each one with the particular quality of life that captures it.

2. Allow the experiences that have brought you great fulfillment to come to mind. Reflect on what experiences bring you the most joy. What was happening? What were you doing? Again, describe each one and then name it with a quality of life.

3. Note whether there is another category of living and experiencing yourself and life that you want to reflect on, such as where you feel most alive, most creative, and most inspired. As in 1 and 2 above, distill each of your experiences into a quality of life that describes the state you most enjoy and most long for.

4. Look at your list of experiences and their defining qualities. Choose three to five or more that had the greatest impact on your life in some way—that stand out to you in this moment. Write each quality of life at the top of its own separate sheet of paper. Then, one quality at a time, list the specific ways that you have previously fulfilled and can imagine fulfilling the experience described by that quality of life. There may be infinite ways to fulfill the quality of life as the experience you want to have. Allow your imagination to run free as you come up with varying avenues to fulfill your desired longing. Right now, this is open-ended, waking dreamtime. It isn't about figuring out *how* these desired experiences might come to pass. It's simply about expanding the possibilities and engaging with potential options in a freely creative manner. If you find yourself holding back on something because you hear a thought that tells you, *That can't (or won't) ever happen!* or something like it, notice it and let it go. Stay in creative dreamtime and allow any and all possibilities to bubble up and out. Write them all down.

5. Now distill the dreamtime experiences down to the one, two, or three that you feel most deeply drawn to and/or inspired by. Sometimes tears come unexpectedly when imagining a scenario that has truth and meaning for us. Use your strong feelings as a guide to your heart's deepest desires. Make choices from there.

6. Sit with each scenario separately. Dwell in the experience of it in your imagination. Make a note of what you feel inside your body, your emotions, and your heart as you embody as fully as possible the experience as it is fulfilled through each different strategy you noted in step 5.

7. If one clearly pops out as the most significant, note that and allow the other options to drop away. If not, continue to let them percolate in you for twenty-four

> **Until one is committed,** there is hesitancy, the chance to draw back, always ineffectiveness. Concerning all acts of initiative (and creation), there is one elementary truth, the ignorance of which kills countless ideas and splendid plans—that the moment one definitely commits oneself, then providence moves too. All sorts of things occur to help one that would never otherwise have occurred. A whole stream of events issues from the decision, raising in one's favor all manner of unforeseen incidents and meetings and material assistance, which no man could have dreamt would have come his way. I have learned a deep respect for one of Goethe's couplets:
> **Whatever you can do, or dream you can, begin it.**
> **Boldness has genius, power, and magic in it!**
>
> --- William Hutchison Murray[78]

hours and come back to step 6. Once you get clarity on the experience that inspires the sense of meaning, purpose, and fulfillment in you, sit with this awareness in the back of your mind for twenty-four to seventy-two hours.

8. When you come back to it, take time to drop in and dwell fully in the experience of fulfillment through the strategy you experienced in your imagination. Ask yourself, Does it still ignite my passion? Does it still feel true and right and good? Does it inspire me with a sense of purpose? If so, you do not need to know how it will come to pass right now. If not, go back to your strategies for fulfillment of quality of life experiences you want, your responses to step 4, and continue through to the end.

9. Without the pressure of trying to figure out how it will come about, make a commitment to yourself to follow through on your choice for intelligent action—that is, your purpose as you've recognized it. Dwell in the reality of it as a quality of life in the embodied state daily for twenty-one days. Allow your meditative state to soften your thinking mind. Let images and insights arise freely in your awareness. Write them down if you feel moved to. In your daily doings, pay close attention to situations and people who may hold a key to the "how" of your intention. Collect information and ideas in your journal when they come to you. With full commitment to your vision, the how will oftentimes unfold effortlessly before you. If you are clear about how it will happen, then start your path to manifesting it. Know in your heart that it is your goal and purpose and commit yourself to its unfolding.

10. As you sit with your intended purpose over the next three weeks, notice what happens. The idea for manifesting it may morph. The whole picture of what

---

[78] William Hutchison Murray, *The Scottish Himalayan Expedition* (London: J. M. Dent & Co., 1951, p 6).

your purpose is may change. Your life may reveal opportunities to live your purpose seemingly out of nowhere. Or your life may take unexpected twists and turns as your old life unwinds and your new one foments. Pay attention to who comes into your life and what opportunities show up. When you are drawn to something with your goal or purpose in mind, walk toward it.

11. When clarity comes, write out the steps to achieve your goal, the intelligent action applied to manifesting your purpose. Solicit the help, guidance, and support you need to carry it out. Acknowledge yourself for stepping into clarity and empowered action.

When you know what really matters to you, finding where to put your energy can be simple. Search on Google for organizations already working with your passions and interests. Jump in and volunteer where you are drawn and when it fits into your daily life. In time, you may find that your efforts are sorely needed and contribute greatly to the organization's vision and mission. Eventually, the organization may have a paid position for you. Or volunteering can lead to greater clarification about where you want to put your time and energy. It is your passion and commitment that will serve you and the world. Let them catalyze and bring forward your efforts where it matters the most—to you. A simple rule of thumb for getting started is: What can you do? Do what you can.

Collaboration Happens

You don't hear much about it on the news. You have to look beneath the surface of mainstream media to find it. Publications like *Yes!* magazine, *Orion* magazine, *Kosmos* journal, and *The Intelligent Optimist* write about the many people and organizations all over the world that work to benefit the planet and the people on it. In addition, there are visionaries who connect organizations working to solve similar issues so that more far-reaching effects can occur.

In Nevada County, California, for example, a number of organizations collaborate to protect and restore river watersheds (the South Yuba River Citizens League, or SYRCL); to build sustainable, local food production, to educate children about healthy food and teach farmers how to farm, as well as to connect farmers with land to farm (Sierra Harvest); and to protect and preserve wildlands for future generations (Bear Yuba Land Trust). Other nongovernment organizations, such as The Sierra Fund and the Sierra Nevada Conservancy, work collaboratively to restore and protect the environment in and around the northern Sierra Nevada Mountains.

Clean water and wildlands matter a lot to me, so I get involved. I live in what is known as, "the Gold Country." The colorful gold-mining history of the gold rush era is proudly displayed in local museums and city parks. And the waterways and soil continue to reflect the deleterious effects of gold and silver mining in the Sierra Nevada Mountains. Many of our streams and waterways are contaminated with mercury and arsenic, for example. Dams and mining also altered and disrupted the wildlife habitat along the local river corridors.

As an example of restorative collaboration, SYRCL has been working with large mining companies (Western Aggregates, Teichart, and SRI) and other private landowners to implement large scale conservation and restoration efforts in the region. Currently, they are comprehensively addressing fifteen river miles impacted by mining from the gold rush era and since. Their efforts are intended to restore river floodplain habitat for endangered and threatened salmon species, create recreation and educational opportunities, and to protect and rehabilitate the river corridor. My husband and I have participated in two of SYRCL's salmon habitat restoration educational raft tours. The positive impact of their efforts over the two-year span between our first and second trips was impressive. The comprehensive approach is brilliant and inspired, and—it is working.

Here's how this project works: The mining companies own the land and use their equipment and facilities to remove many tons of gravel that was deposited during the gold rush. The gravel and sediment from that era is blocking fish habitat. They sell the gravel for use in roads and building projects, which decreases the total cost of the restoration project. This is a true win-win for the economy and the environment. Mining operations are no longer allowed within the active river floodplain, but restoration projects are. It is a very expensive prospect to remove such large amounts of gravel in order to restore the river to its natural state. SYRCL recognizes that it could not carry out its mission without all the other parts working collaboratively. It has taken the league over a decade to get where it is today with a solid, productive plan to restore river habitat and to keep industry in business. It is indeed an innovative and remarkably successful endeavor.

Specifically, SYRCL works in partnership with agencies such as the US Fish and Wildlife Service (USFWS), the California Department of Fish and Wildlife (CADFW), the Army Corps, the BLM (Bureau of Land Management), and TRILIA (Three Rivers Levee Improvement Agency). They also collaborate with local consulting firms, such as CBC, ESA, and Cramer Fish Sciences. The USFWS and CADFW provide expertise and funding, along with foundations, like the Bella Vista and Long Foundation. The consulting firms manage projects, provide habitat and fish monitoring expertise and create ecologically based engineered designs. SYRCL also manages projects, brings habitat and fish monitoring expertise, has worked on upholding long-term relationships with landowners, does fundraising, and engages with stakeholders and the local community.

There are many moving parts to such a comprehensive vision. It is successfully facilitated by passionate, committed individuals and focused groups. It's awe-inspiring to be a part of the vision to restore habitat and repair ecosystems and see tangible results. The encompassing project highlights SYRCL's commitment and clarity of intention. This is an example of a small group of impassioned people who have successfully turned their vision into empowered, collaborative action.

Rights of Personhood for Nature

To increase our success, we look to the tried and true methods of nature. Cooperation and collaboration are intrinsic to the multitudinous strands of species interwoven within every ecosystem. Their interdependent lives exist in harmony. Each individual life-form feeds and supports the whole in some way, such that, if one species is added, extracted, or goes extinct, the system loses its dynamic equilibrium. Nature functions as one complex, interdependent whole, and so we are obliged to view the world and lead with the same understanding. Said succinctly by Miki Kashtan, "Collaborating for change points to a vision of leaders as stewards of the whole." One significant factor in our approach to building a new world is to hold the whole in mind as we make decisions. To protect the environment and the people affected by corporate activities, for example, is absolutely necessary.

It may take laws changing such that nature has the "rights of personhood" in order to bring the level of respect and care necessary to protect our natural resources and the Earth herself. Rights of personhood means that an individual or entity (corporations now have rights of personhood) has legal rights. The Yurok Tribe has declared rights of person hood for the Klamath River, the first to do so for a river in North America.[79] Ecuador is

---

[79]   Anna V. Smith, The Klamath River now has the legal rights of a person. *High Country News,* Sept. 24, 2019. https://www.hcn.org/articles/tribal-affairs-the-klamath-river-now-has-the-legal-rights-of-a-person

the first country to recognize Rights of Nature in its Constitution. Articles 73 – 74 of Ecuador's Constitution reads, "The Ecuadorian government promises to: motivate natural and juridical persons as well as collectives to protect nature; it will promote respect towards all the elements that form an ecosystem."[80] I feel such a sigh of relief and renewed hope when I think of nature having equal rights to the rest of us. I sense relaxation deep inside my body that stems from trust that the Earth has support and protection.

I am heartened by Ecuador's commitment to restore environments already impacted by exploitation, too. Article 72 of their Constitution reads, "In the cases of severe or permanent environmental impact, including the ones caused by the exploitation of non-renewable natural resources, the State will establish the most efficient mechanisms for the restoration, and will adopt the adequate measures to eliminate or mitigate the harmful environmental consequences." I celebrate Ecuador's initiatives and look forward to the rest of us following in their footsteps. Stewardship of our planet is intrinsic to being leaders in a new world.

Twelve Principles of Collaboration

As we live into a new way of being on the planet and in the world, our collaborative efforts emphasize how much we need each other. Jacob Morgan, who explores and writes about the future of work, explains the twelve principles of highly collaborative organizations. Published in *Forbes* magazine,[81] the principles he details are:

1. Individual benefit is just as important as the overall corporate benefit, if not more so.
2. Strategy comes before technology.
3. Listen to the voice of the employee.
4. Learn to get out of the way.
5. Lead by example.
6. Integrate into the flow of work.
7. Create a supportive environment.
8. Measure what matters.

[80] "Ecuador Adopts Rights of Nature in Constitution," GARN-Global Alliance for the Rights of Nature. https://therightsofnature.org/ecuador-rights/ Accessed Oct. 2019
[81] Jacob Morgan, *Forbes Magazine,* July 30, 2013. https://www.forbes.com/sites/jacobmorgan/2013/07/30/the-12-habits-of-highly-collaborative-organizations/#480df39e3683.

9. Persistence brings results.
10. Adapt and evolve.
11. Employee collaboration also benefits the customer.
12. Collaboration can make the world a better place.

Some of the points may sound familiar. They mirror some of what has been addressed in the handbook. The most obvious is number 5, "Lead by example." This emphasizes the significance of living the values or embodying the qualities of life that you want to experience. When you bring them into your relationships, whether at work or at home, you make the world a better place.

You may find ways to apply these principles to your work environment or in your family. To be the leader of your life can simply mean to live your truth and, thus, to model to others the values that matter to you. To lead by example is to live aligned with your authentic or higher self. It is an act of integrity and generosity.

The Doorway of the Heart

The heart is the doorway to expansion because love is inclusive. Love has the capacity to hold each separate life and to transcend our individual lives, holding it all tenderly at once. As we nurture the heart's role in navigating our lives, apparent opposites have much less of a polarizing impact on us. We find the juice in diversity and can enjoy the adventure of understanding our differences. The heart connects us to our higher mind, to the cosmos, as well as to our physical being. This then becomes our calling---to practice being embodied and fully present in ourselves, while at the same time to engage a compassionate, openhearted witness to life as it unfolds through and around us. To stretch our internal capacity to hold both of us at once is key to being the change we seek. When we include others and our differences, we make the shift from competition to cooperation. When we embrace the spaciousness inside that holds all of it at once and let it spread out around us, that is expanded embodiment. It is evolution in action, invoking our awareness of the whole from our individual standpoint. Your heart's calling is your gift to the world, your compassionate action, and fulfills evolution's purpose—for the benefit of all.

PART FOUR
Divine Intimacy

It is only through letting our heart break that we discover something unexpected: the heart cannot actually break, it can only break open ... To live with a broken-open heart is to experience life full strength ... When the heart breaks open, it marks the beginning of a real love affair with this world. It is a broken-hearted love affair, rather than the conventional kind based on hope and expectation. Only in this fearless love that can respond to life's pain as well as its beauty can we be of real help to ourselves or anyone else in this difficult age. The broken-hearted warrior is an essential archetype for our time.

—John Welwood

CHAPTER SEVENTEEN
Inspired Relationship

In truth, everyone alive struggles with how to stay awake. While there are no answers except to stay concerned, there are small clues. One comes from Goethe who says, "every object well contemplated creates an organ within us." What a startling shift. He suggests what sages and lovers have known forever; that beholding anything with ultimate care makes it come alive within us. Put simply, embracing the world animates our being.
—Mark Nepo

I was sitting in a relationship workshop in front of an interesting and attractive man whom I'd just met the day before at the workshop venue. As it turned out, he would become my husband four years in the future. Sitting on the floor facing one another in anticipation of the next experiential exercise, he looked me in the eyes and said with a deadpan face, "I'm glad I'm not the only one in the room without an upper lip." My first reaction was shock at the audacity of it. My eyes dropped to his mouth and immediately saw that he, too, had a very thin upper lip. I looked up at his eyes, saw the amusement there, and burst into laughter. We both laughed heartily at the absurdity of the whole situation, his off-the-wall comment, and the freedom that we could laugh at ourselves, even though we'd just met.

Lightness of Being

The ability to laugh at ourselves is wonderfully freeing. Personal evolution requires diligence and tenacity beyond many aspects of life. Although elevating overall, it can get heavy at times. We need to rise up to the surface and breathe and remember the joy, humor, and beauty of life's little moments. We are the accumulation of these time bytes. To notice and appreciate them brings fulfillment and, with it, gratitude. It is a way to remember ourselves as part of it all. To look honestly at ourselves takes a certain lightness of being, like a wry smile held internally as we notice our own antics with amusement. The essence of life holds a great reverberating laugh at itself—what I think of as the cosmic joke.

Descending into Divinity and the Cosmic Joke

One Thursday night, while chanting in *zikr*, the Sufi circle-prayer of remembrance, I was desperately yearning to *really know* my connection to God. I yearned with all my being to experience it firsthand. I was fed up with the decades of spiritual study and practices I'd done with few tangible results. With tears in my eyes, I was silently imploring that I be given a glimpse of what I'd been longing to understand for so long. As I held my heightened desire with single-minded fervor, the floor suddenly disappeared beneath me. The whole circle of devotees was sitting in empty space, lighted up and floating like a ring of flower petals on ... *nothing.* Stunned by the sparkling beauty and emptiness, I felt myself both as an observer and as an integral part of everything. There was no separation; I was being breathed by the pulsating light.

When the chanting ended and the circle dispersed, I remained in a state of awe. As if in a different world, I got into my car and drove home, still in an amplified state of awareness. On the way, I noticed that everything was alive. The asphalt beneath the car, the sidewalks lining the streets—everything breathed and vibrated with life. As I turned into my neighborhood, I heard a great resounding laugh come from the space all around. I knew that the laugh was about how seriously we take ourselves, blindly trudging along with our heads down, not noticing what's *really* going on. The cosmic joke was on us, on me, to think that we are separate from everything and that inanimate things are not alive. In that moment, I knew that everything is thrumming with life, with consciousness, and with *humor*! I felt it in everything around me, scintillating and laughing with all-pervasive love and understanding.

I had an intimate encounter with the divine that evening. I descended into myself, through the density of my physicality, and came to an intimate awareness of the true lightness of being—of which I know we all are an integral part.

The Alchemy of Intimacy

Transcendence uplifts us with a lightness so welcoming that it feels like coming home. It touches us so deeply and opens us so fully that the usual sense of separation no longer exists. This is true intimacy. In intimacy, whether with another person or with the divine, we surrender into our hearts. The heart is the seed of our own transcendence, the center point that connects us both to the earth and to what is beyond. Although it is a physical organ, the energetic of the heart is like a universal joint. It functionally translates our earthly human nature into our transcendent, celestial nature. The heart moves our life energies along the horizontal plane, facilitating our connections with others and the natural world. The heart's energetics also travel from our ground of being into the heavens along the vertical axis through the crown of our heads. We know our connection with all that is through our hearts.

An intimate life is a transcendent life, one that invites our descent into our divinity through our physical being. Our body is the mooring we need to safely go beyond our physicality and venture into subtler realms. The body is our home base, our place of return. Our central nervous system is perfectly suited to be struck with simultaneous awareness of our autonomy and our inherence within all that is. It is also evolution's trajectory—to know our self intimately as an individual and as inseparable from everything, all at once. The intimacy and awe of such an experience inspires us to a life of compassionate action.

Active Surrender

Intimacy is the path of the warrior of the heart. It draws on our courage and the acceptance of all of who we are. With it, we land in the heartland of our own being and are primed to explore further, to surrender through the limits of our known edges. Our accumulated self-awareness is the ground of being that stabilizes us as we drop through the veils of separation and into transcendent connection.

On the journey to connection, love is the cauldron that tenderizes us. Love is the only true agent of transformation. We come to it through surrender. To surrender into our hearts is to live fully at choice and to be fully empowered. Surrender is not synonymous with giving up. Rather, it is the active form of acceptance. (See the explanation of how to surrender through resistance in the section, *Surrender, Acceptance and Will*, pp 106-7). It is the catalyst of transformation and transcendence because, through surrender, the heart inevitably opens. With courage and the intention to surrender into our hearts, remnants of the small self alchemically transmute into our higher self. The dross of our lower self burns off in the alchemical fires of love.

Let's explore this alchemy in regard to intimacy itself. We can create intimacy within the context of a mate, lover, spouse, or partner relationship. We can also do it within ourselves as individuals, with the natural world, and with the divine. All avenues of intimacy deeply satisfy us because intimacy invites transcendence of our sense of separation. With it, we experience belonging at a profound level. The experience of nonduality is a deep human longing. The desire to transcend our own boundaries is like a beacon drawing us home, back into the deep connections we so crave.

Intimacy: What Is It Really?

References are often made to intimacy in personal growth circles and workshops to enhance our significant partnerships. But what is intimacy really? Many people use the word *intimacy* synonymously with sex. Intimacy certainly can be a significant part of sexuality, but it is also much more than that. Conversely, sex can happen without intimacy. *Intimate*, the root of intimacy, is defined in *Webster's Dictionary* as, "1. Inmost; most inward; essential: as, the *intimate* structure of an atom. 2. Most private or personal: as, one's *intimate* feelings. 3. closely acquainted or associated; very familiar: as, an *intimate* friend." From the definition, we can see that intimacy means a lot more than sexual relations. It is about our own inwardness that, when shared with another, invites deep connection between us.

Intimacy is one of those things that is frequently bantered about, but rarely achieved. A professional couple who skillfully facilitate insightful, yet practical relationship workshops break down intimacy as *in-to-me-you-see*.[82] If in-to-me-you-see describes intimacy, then we need to be honest with ourselves and transparent with our partners. Openheartedness increases with trust, which comes when we allow ourselves to be seen and known. In a relationship, this usually happens incrementally over time. When we are received for who we are, trust grows, our hearts blossom, and love is exalted.

Intimacy is born of trust and transparency between people no matter what the nature of their relationship. I think of the intimacy between people in desperate or

---

[82] For info on Sonika Tinker and Christian Pederson's offerings, go to: www.loveworksforyou.com.

traumatic circumstances, such as soldiers of war or survivors of disasters. They see one another in oftentimes horrific circumstances and know each other stripped to the core. When we see and accept the best and the worst in each other and remain closely connected emotionally, that is intimacy.

Intimacy with yourself facilitates intimacy with something or someone beyond yourself. The practices given in part one of the handbook are oriented to increase self-trust through self-connection and self-acceptance. This provides the opportunity for intimacy with yourself, by knowing yourself deeply. It is these same qualities that facilitate intimacy between you and other people. Trust in another comes over time with the experience of being seen and accepted for who we are. It is self-trust that lays the foundation to let our self be seen and known intimately by another person. And it takes more than trust alone to invite us to open to intimacy. It also takes courage, because intimacy necessarily takes us beyond the bounds of what we already know.

Intimacy and Inspired Relationships

In an inspired relationship, we use our significant partnership as fodder for our continued growth into greater self-realization. This means that, when we come up against encumbrances that keep us small or closed and that magnify our sense of separation, we are willing *to surrender our attachment to the known and familiar.* When we let go of attachment to our familiar responses, the patterns that keep us stuck are metabolized. This is alchemy in action. Self-compassion, or love, is the catalyst.

Subtler and subtler versions of our old self are revealed when we willingly walk openheartedly toward another person. Intimacy is nurtured with transparency and the intention to open our hearts further. At times, ugly parts will rear their heads unannounced. Grounded in self-awareness, we learn to take it all in stride, to not take affronts personally, and to let a lightness of being spread in us. This is a stretch point, a place to find room inside for all of it. To make space for both of us, we avoid the tendency to defend ourselves, which only compounds the obstacles rising up. We can sidestep blaming others or castigating ourselves for not being farther along or whatever we expect to be different than it is. Acceptance is key to letting go of what no longer serves us. With it, the energetic patterns unravel, are composted, and effortlessly serve the next version of ourselves.

On the path of the warrior of the heart, we soften and become more openhearted and, at the same time, more empowered. In the alchemical process of surrendering into love, we are honed and refined, allowing intimacy to flower. What no longer serves our growing evolution melts away in the process. Soon, our budding intimate connection will start to have a life and direction of its own, designing a path heretofore unimagined, and yet impeccably suited to both people's personal evolution. Perseverance and trust in the process will bring many unforeseen benefits, both individually and together.

Relationship as Spiritual Path

As grand as the ideas of transcendence and intimacy are, the fact remains that we are all human. Our foibles, fallibilities, and flat spots will undoubtedly show up in an intimate partnership, no matter how much personal growth and spiritual practice we have done. This is the gift of relationship. Close relationships mirror and reflect to us every nuance we have not healed and made whole, and thus holy, within ourselves. If an expansive, open heart is the goal, intimacy is a direct path.

Have you ever noticed that the same annoying patterns of past relationships tend to show up in your new relationship? We unconsciously choose that person who inevitably brings out our remaining psycho-emotional wounds. If we have not made the connection that our triggers are *inside* of ourselves and that our discomfort is *stimulated but not caused* by the other person, then we do not yet understand the key to transformation. There is no *out there* out there. There is only the reflection of our own essence in the myriads of ways that it's shown to us. When we allow ourselves to be deeply seen by another person, we start to witness ourselves in a whole new light. It is about surrendering what keeps us separate—the notions of who we are as defined by our own mental constructs and past experiences.

Mental constructs, the source of our habitual patterning, are synonymous with our personal stories and thereby define our personalities. They are patterns of thought and feeling in the form of beliefs that give us the sense of solidity and continuity through time. We are comprised of patterns, because in essence, the material world is energetic patterns of vibrating light. Repeating patterns serve life by making physical form possible. Because their nature is to repeat, habitual patterns can be challenging to change. Since life at its essence is energy, change occurs most readily at the energetic or quantum level. Fortunately, we have direct access to this potential through embodying coherent states.

Intimate partnership facilitates the shedding of our worn-out skins. Layers no longer beneficial to us are pushed to the surface and fall away as new impulses quicken within, inviting us to explore new horizons both inside and outside of us.

Transformation in the Holographic Universe

In the holographic model of the universe, all parts also contain the whole. As mentioned in chapter 4, this is a relatively new model of the universe and our place in it, developed in the 1970s. In his groundbreaking work, quantum physicist David Bohm proposes, "Everything in the universe is part of a continuum. Despite the apparent separateness of things at the explicate level, everything is a seamless extension of everything else ... "[83] In his fascinating book *The Holographic Universe*, Michael Talbot explains the intricacies of cutting-edge science and why it matters to us. At the subatomic level, interconnectedness is a given and, thus, explains the effect of *nonlocality*. Nonlocality, also referred to as *entanglement*, simply means that even when we are in different locations, we still affect one another. At the quantum level, everything is connected, an invisible web of interdependence.

David Bohm takes the interconnectedness theory a giant step further and includes consciousness in it. "Even a rock is in some way alive, says Bohm, for life and intelligence are present not only in all of matter, but in 'energy,' 'space,' 'time,' 'the fabric of the entire universe,' and everything else we abstract out of the holomovement and mistakenly view as separate things."[84]

This explains how we can "see and know" information about other people or other circumstances when we let our mental constructs dissolve and open to new ways of experiencing the world. When we choose to embody a coherent state like gratitude or compassion, for example, we have transcended our familiar habitual thinking as it informs our perceptions. We have gone directly to the energetics of the holographic universe, the *holomovement*, as Bohm terms it, and have invited ourselves to vibrate with a subtler, more cohesive state of being. These coherent states vibrate in resonance with the consciousness of the universe itself. Over time, the cumulative effect of embodying coherent states changes our whole way of being and experiencing ourselves. We tune ourselves to higher vibratory frequencies and thereby raise our consciousness in the process.

---

[83]   Michael Talbot, *The Holographic Universe* (HarperCollins Publishers, Inc., 1970).
[84]   Talbot.

Relationship as spiritual path will necessarily bring forth stories from our past, often remnants of childhood wounds not fully reconciled that keep us fettered in some way. Our partner is our mirror. As trust and love deepen, more of our historical patterns surface, often showing up as challenging relationship dynamics. When we can see difficult interactions as gateways to our own healing, the rough spots become prepared soil for growth opportunities. By looking inward first, we can see our part in difficult dynamics. This is how to use relationship as path, the path to self-knowledge, as well as to freedom and intimacy. We look inside first, to see what is being reflected to us by our outer circumstances.

When we surrender our familiar habits of relating with their constrictions and judgments, we transform our mental and emotional constructs of separation. This process can be uncomfortable, like crawling out of a rigid, tight-fitting skin. Emerging parts can feel raw and awkward. We can feel uncertain about how to be or do or say what used to seem so easy and natural. But by shedding our old ways, we take responsibility for ourselves and our part in the relationship's dynamics. Then the relationship is free to morph, just as we are morphing, into new ways of being.

The practice of embodying coherent states as universal qualities of life is a streamlined way to tap into the energy field of the holographic universe. In an instant, we can become the experience we most want to have, painlessly. In that same moment, alchemy does its work, and the old habit fades as new options come into play. In this way, the past is transmuted, and we are free to live in the present. In the process, we naturally gain access to the voluminous heart beating inside our chest. We see beyond our personalities and into the heart of love. Freedom and bliss reside here. We transcend separation and come into connection with something within and, simultaneously, beyond ourselves. We experience being integral to each other and to the whole holographic universe.

And oftentimes, we need to simply function on the day-to-day activities plane. In partnerships of all kinds, we have choices to make about critical and mundane topics alike. To do so, we can use the spectrum of love and the embodiment practice to support decision making together, as a team.

The following practice is a modified form of embodying qualities of life from the spectrum of love. Here we apply it to enhance our partner relationships. We join our ability to embody the experience we most want with our partner in that intention. This practice can offer clarity and guidance for couples or groups to look at options and to make choices from the same vantage point. This helps alleviate the potential for discord and conflict, while facilitating creativity and collaboration. It can also serve as a foundation for greater intimacy.

Explore this Practice: Converging Circles

There are three parts to this practice. The first part is done separately, as individuals, and the second and third parts are done together with your partner.

1. *Personal list of qualities*: Have paper and pen handy to write on. Sit quietly for a few minutes, breathing and coming into self-connection. When your mind is clear and your body relaxed, ask yourself, "If everything in my life and my relationship were exactly as I would most love it to be, what are the words that would describe that state?" This is a direct way to drop into the essence of what matters most to you and what qualities you most desire to activate and experience. These are the values, named as qualities of life, that motivate your choices and actions. This exercise might seem familiar. It is a modification of earlier practices using the spectrum of love to guide our intentions. Allow yourself to fully explore the qualities of life that speak to you and write them down. Take the amount of time you need. If you want help, go to Appendix A "Universal Qualities of Life" and see if there are more that resonate to fill out your list.

2. *Overlapping qualities*: Sit down with your partner and both of your personal lists of qualities. Go through your lists and mark the ones you share. At this point, you can also explore more qualities of life that you both share in your core values for the relationship. On a new sheet of paper, write down the qualities that you share and any new ones you agree are important to both of you. This is your relationship's converging circle. These are the shared values in terms of the qualities of life that matter to both of you and that feed the relationship. It shows where the most natural ease and flow will be in the partnership and where you can most readily agree and make choices from the same perspective.

   The visual image is that of two overlapping or converging circles. One circle is you and your list, and the other is your partner and his or her list. Where the lists overlap is where both of your qualities intersect. This is your converging circle. These shared qualities help you and your partner to consciously choose together what qualities you want to embody and be motivated by in interactions and for making decisions together.

3. *A working acronym*: The list also can be narrowed down and simplified into an acronym. Look more closely at your convergent qualities. Think of a succinct word that you both enjoy the meaning of and see which of your shared qualities of life start with the letters of that word. Then use the acronym you come up with to filter and prioritize joint decisions and choices that affect both of you and the relationship. This practice will go a long way to creating harmony, ease, and flow, as well as consistency and trust as you navigate resolving conflicts and making decisions together.

For example, my husband and I frequently use the acronym LIFE when sorting and prioritizing options. We ask ourselves, does this choice fill our priorities for LIFE? It stands for love, integrity, freedom, and ease. LIFE can also stand for love, integrity, fun, and expansion. I also like the acronym LAUGH. It stands for love, adventure, understanding, gratitude, and humor. Each of these qualities is very important to both my husband and me. If we're facing something tough or have conflicting ideas on how to proceed, we bring in the acronym for clarity of perspective. This ensures that we are looking at the issue from the same vantage point and that what we decide is aligned with our core values and intentions for the relationship and our lives.

You may or may not find an acronym that fits your most cherished qualities. In any case, see what happens when you distill your converging circle list into those that resonate most strongly with both of you. Choose four to six or so that speak to both of you and utilize them to support making harmonious agreements.

When we have consistent access to our hearts, which means to choose to live from and to be motivated by the qualities of life we resonate with, then we have much greater balance, ease, flow, and harmony in our lives and relationships. To choose to live in an embodied state, infused with the living energetics of our chosen qualities, is a transcendent state of being. It is an intimate connection with the coherent consciousness of life itself. We are living in the playing field of life, our hearts primed and ready to meet our partners in daily life.

By this point in the handbook, you have learned the skills needed to navigate difficulties with yourself and with others. The practices in each chapter have offered practical ways to increase your personal sovereignty, to develop compassionate self-connection, to embody qualities you desire to experience, and to hone the ability to empathize with yourself and others. You have also learned ways to work through conflicts and disagreements, to cooperate and to move into collaboration. The next practice integrates many of those skills. It's included here specifically as it supports transparency and connection in close relationships.

Explore this Practice: Working through a Painful Dynamic

This is the format I use when working with couples to specifically find their way through a painful, repeating dynamic or debilitating pattern. It facilitates them to come back to their hearts. This process is to be used by each person individually to sort through his or her part in a pattern, to take responsibility for his or her experience, and to discover what he or she can choose to do differently. Using it will leave blame and judgment out of your interactions.

Another option is to do it together as a couple. In this case, have one person facilitate the other's process and then switch. This would take both people's ability to remain dispassionate and not to take things personally if the pattern is between the two who are facilitating one another's process. It is much easier to facilitate one another if the issue does not involve both of you directly or after the charge has dissipated. Please make wise, considered choices as to whether you facilitate each other through the process. The wisest option might be to each do your own process; write it down in a journal; and, once the charge has dissipated, come back together and decide how you both want to proceed. Refer to your converging circle list to support your decision making when you come back together.

This is a wonderful process to illuminate the interstices of any conflict, judgment, or painful dynamic. It can be very helpful to see it all written out in front of you. This will unravel the knots and open the possibilities to more constructive, resourceful options. Have a large sheet of paper and pen or whiteboard and markers available to write on. I was first shown this process by Robert Gonzales, NVC facilitator and mentor for many and for whose work I have immense gratitude.

To begin

1. *Name it*. In a simple, clear statement, name the issue.

For example, "She went out and bought a new couch without talking to me about it."

2. *Name the judgmental thoughts* about the issue and about the other person's role in it.

   This is called the "jackal show" in the NVC lexicon. Without editing, write down any and all stories, judgments, blame, and so on that you have about the issue. These thoughts often have the words "always or never" and "should or shouldn't" or a similar moralistic sentiment in them. Let it rip!

   For example, "She always makes unilateral decisions about things that affect both of us. There is no room for me and my ideas. She always does things first and tells me later. She always talks over me in conversations and never listens to what I have to say. It's like I don't even matter here. My opinions should matter too. She should take my ideas into consideration before doing things that affect both of us."

3. *Name the feelings* about the jackal show stories. List any and all emotions you feel about the jackal stories and thoughts.

   For example, "I feel angry, frustrated, sad, disappointed, hurt."

   Be on the lookout for thoughts masquerading as feelings, such as, "I feel that she should talk with me before buying furniture." The phrase, "I feel that ..." is not an emotion. It is a thought—a jackal thought. Write it down and add it to the jackal stories. It may look something like this: "She should talk with me before buying furniture," or, "I think that she should talk to me first," or, "I wish that she would talk to me first."

   Go back and name more judgments or jackal stories that arise as you list the emotions, if they come up.

   If more stories come up at any point, jot them down with the others.

   For example, more jackal statements might be: "She never listens to me. She always interrupts. She doesn't understand me. She always wants to have things her way. I can't get a word in edgewise. I'd like to have a say in how things go down around here."

4. *Name the universal qualities of life alive for you.* List any and all qualities that you are wanting to experience in this situation. The jackal statements, stories, and judgments have the qualities couched inside of them. Look at the jackal statements to find them. Sense what is really mattering to you within the statements and inside the judgments. Look at your personal list of qualities for help as needed.

For example, the universal qualities from the spectrum of love couched in the above jackal statements could include:

To be heard
To be understood
To be included
Mutuality
To matter
Empathy
Choice
Consideration

5. *Narrow the qualities to the most relevant one or two. Embody them.*

For example, *to be understood* and *to matter* might be the most relevant.

As you focus on embodying the qualities, feel the precious longing you have for them—your yearning to experience that in the relationship. Feelings may come up as you drop into embodiment. Allow them to arise and let yourself feel them.

6. *Surrender into the feelings that come up as you start to embody the qualities you long for.*

Surrender, in this instance, is a form of letting go of our attachments to being right or righteous, to making someone else wrong, or to being in control. Surrender into the pure desire to experience the qualities you chose—into what truly matters to you. Allow the process of feeling your emotions to open and lighten you, to take you more closely into connection with yourself, and to feel your heart's tender longings. Feel your emotions; let them wash through you, cleansing and opening your heart.

7. *Clarify the most important quality or qualities and embody them again.*

With greater clarity after having felt and released the emotions associated with the desired qualities, embody the clarified quality.

For example, let's take the quality *to matter*. Allow the energy of this quality to fill you from the inside out, to flow through and around you. Rest in the energetic aliveness of the quality for a few minutes or for as long as desired. Breathe it in, let it fill you up and expand around you. You are tapping into the holographic field via embodying the cohesive state *I matter*. All the qualities of life in the spectrum of love will stimulate a coherent state when embodied.

8. *As you remain in the state of embodiment, bring the original issue to mind and the image of your partner into view.*

Continue to embody the quality of life you chose and view the original scene objectively.

Notice and name what you see, how you feel, and what occurs in your mind's eye while in the holographic state of awareness.

For example, "I sense myself as mattering. I know that I matter. Even though I want to be included, I also see how much she cares about the aesthetics of the house and that she wants to be efficient. She cares more about how the furnishings look than I do, so I get why she didn't bother to ask me about it. But I do want to be connected with her and know that she thinks about me when she makes decisions about buying new things for the house."

9. *Make a request of yourself* that flows naturally from your internal experience and what you see in the realm of possibility.

What do you see as possible from this state of awareness?

For example, "Well, I see that she cares a lot more about interior decorating than I do. I see that I feel left out because we've both been so busy lately we haven't spent any quality time together. I see she makes time for her girlfriends, and I want us to make time together too. I want to ask her to sit down with me, to reconnect and decide what we want to do together for fun and connection. I will ask her to go on a date."

10. *Make the request of your partner clear, specific, and doable*; include what, when, how, and where.

Decide when, where, how, and what you will do or say.

For example, "Will you sit down with me this evening so we can talk about making time to do something fun together? I realize I miss hanging out with you and want to share what's going on with me and hear what's going on with you. Maybe we can decide tonight what we want to do and make a date for the weekend. Does that work for you?"

As the example responses show, internal clarity and equilibrium can come to us during this process. From the state of the embodied witness, personality foibles lose their significance and judgments seem to evaporate. We tap into the holographic field of awareness. From that viewpoint, we can "see" or sense the other person's needs and objectives at the same time as we see and sense our own. Our jackal stories and blind assumptions readily dissipate as we come into the holographic field, an expansive awareness beyond the notions of right and wrong.

The Final Frontier

To come into full self-knowledge can be a long, convoluted trip. To descend deeper into ourselves might seem antithetical to liberation. But to truly dissolve the psycho-emotional structures of separation and kindle our connection with spirit, coming into our core-self is necessary. It's a perfect example of life as paradox. We discover wholeness by being both inwardly autonomous and intimately connected with life. In the process, we become more clearly ourselves and go beyond the sense of separation, all at the same time.

The experience of intimacy is akin to the "spiritual death" of our separate self. The ego is transmuted when we surrender into our intrinsic connection with all of life and the cosmos beyond. Interpersonal intimacy derives from the release of unnecessary components of self, the structures of our personality that keep us removed from the expanded consciousness of our hearts. To the uninitiated, the prospect of transcendence can be disorienting or even frightening. The experience takes us into the void, the uncharted territory where our familiar mapping dissolves. To surrender these components is tantamount to a death of our sense of self as we have known it. A part of our ego is transmuted and released. In this sense, intimacy is the final frontier. It is an adventure of the highest order and brings fulfillment of the grandest kind.

CHAPTER EIGHTEEN
Into the Eye of Love

Lovers don't finally meet somewhere. They're in each other all along.
—Rumi

The eye of love is the still point at the center of our being. Like the eye of a tornado, the swirl of life goes on around us as we maintain our equilibrium. From there, our quiescent center spreads out into the jumble of life, inviting spaciousness and balance. This harmonious center is really a field of consciousness that bathes our cellular makeup with coherent energy. It can also fill the space around us. We might call it a field of empathy because the coherent matrix we shape in and around us includes the others in our vicinity. By doing so, it dismantles separation. Very simply put, this is a demonstrable method of living in the state of connection and wholeness. To embody a coherent quality of energy includes and transcends polarity, thereby freeing us to bring ourselves forward with creative dynamism.

Freedom from Polarity

When we think of freedom, we usually put it in the context of being free from something that limits or inhibits us. We also want to be free to choose what we want—from the people we love to the laws that govern us. To be free to choose consciously, we need to be fundamentally free from the conditioning that would keep us locked in a battle with ourselves and in conflicts with others. Contentious relationships are polarizing and function to tie up our attention and energy in non-resourceful endeavors. We crave freedom to choose, but when we come up against resistance to that freedom, we tend to push back. We react impulsively. We are no longer free to expend our energy creatively or collaboratively in the push-pull of opposing efforts.

In fact, the harder we push back, the stronger the resistance becomes. Martial arts philosophies tell us that force naturally follows from force. To fight against something often doesn't bring us freedom from it. In fact, it melds us to it, binding us in a tug-of-war dynamic that keeps us hobbled by resistance and defensiveness.

When we invoke a coherent field, however, struggle melts into collaboration. A coherent field is naturally connecting and invites empathy because it is inclusive and accepting of *what is*. Empathy is about accepting others just as they are, not about changing them. The fascinating thing is that, when we change *ourselves* into what we want to experience, the effect spreads through and beyond us. I call this *expanded embodiment*. The next practice is a dynamic experiment to explore the effects of your intention on the field and your relationships. It is a way to live from your center, at the eye of love, and to invite others to meet you there, in the field of all possibility.

The Field Possibility

It seems almost too simple to be so empowering, but we can, in fact, apply the seeming magic of the new physics to our everyday lives. To establish a coherent field in and around yourself is an extremely resourceful state, and the effects can be profound. Although others may not be consciously aware of it, your good intentions applied to the field will affect interactions. The following practice will be particularly helpful in partnerships of all kinds, in adult-child relationships, and in any conflictual dynamic. You can find out more about this practice as it is integrated with principles of Aikido from David Weinstock.[85]

Explore this Practice: Expanded Embodiment—How to Be the Change You Want

By now, you probably have the embodiment practice down. To be the change you want, you will simply expand the embodiment practice to include the space around you and the people in it. This practice preempts conflict. By holding the relaxed and expansively aware state of being that embodying a quality of life brings, you can

---

[85]   David and Judith Weinstock, www.liminalsomatics.com

harmonize conflictual energies before they happen. Beyond that, the established effect will invite acceptance, inclusion, and collaboration with the other people in your sphere. This is expanded embodiment.

To Begin

Sit quietly for a few minutes and come into presence with yourself. Breathe and relax into your body. Invite in your compassionate observer.

1. *Bring to mind a conflict you've had recently with someone.* Or imagine a future situation you think will be challenging to navigate.
2. *Notice any changes in your body, your breathing, and your emotions* when you think about that situation, whether in the past or the future. Those changes represent disorganized or chaotic energies running in you. They constrict and contract the flow of possibilities through you.
3. *Name the qualities of life you want to experience* in the situation you brought to mind. Breathe and come back to your compassionate observer. Notice and write down the qualities of life you desire to experience in the situation.
4. *Put yourself back into the situation in your mind* and imagine each quality of life, one at a time, being applied to the situation, using your breath to stay present and self-connected. Choose the one quality that brings the most relaxed fullness and harmony to you when you imagine it within the context of your situation.
5. *Breathe into yourself the quality you chose.* Now let go of the situation as you have remembered or imagined it. Focus on slowing your breath and sensing your heart. Inhale the quality of life you chose in step 4 into your heart center, and on each exhale, allow your breath to be like a golden cloud filling you up from the inside. Breathe the energetic quality as golden light into every part of your body, from heart to belly to feet to back to shoulders, neck, and head. As it fills you up more and more, let it start to billow out around you, emanating from your heart, front, and back. With each exhale, make the light cloud bigger. Let it expand to a few feet above you; below you; behind, in front, and beside you. Notice how your body-heart-mind feels now. Stay present and full, permeated by that quality of life and continue to let it fill the space inside and around you. Enjoy this expanded, coherent state of being for a few more minutes. Notice how your body-heart-mind feels.

6. *From the state of expanded embodiment*, bring the situation from step 1 back to mind. From the perspective of your expanded state of embodiment, what do you see happening? How do you see yourself responding to it? What do you hear yourself saying and to whom? Make a note of your insights. From them, choose what you want to do or say and to whom, if anything. You can use your insights as you approach the situation in real time, either as a do-over, or in the setting yet to come. The practice invites confidence to hold yourself and everyone involved with respect and consideration.

7. *Acknowledge yourself with gratitude* or appreciation for setting your intention to do this practice and for the results you had. Decide how and where you would like to apply this practice to situations in your life.

To more fully be the change you'd like to see in the world, I recommend making a shortened version of expanded embodiment into a daily practice. Choose the top one to three qualities on your personal list that you want to cultivate in your life. Spend three to five minutes a day in expanded embodiment with one of the qualities on your short list. Do this for one week to a month daily for each quality you want to embody. This practice will bring ready empathy and connection into your relationships and interactions with others.

The ego may stomp about in resistance when we first suggest to ourselves that our most immediate personal desire may not be the optimal option to pursue. The compassionate observer continues to play a role here, noticing and accepting what arises. Take time to address any disappointment or frustrations that come up. Remember to be with *what is*. Our internal lightness of being, along with our mental agility, are engaged, too, as we pop in and out of focused self-connection and expanded awareness within the field.

It is our heart and soul that we feed when we choose to embody and express our deeper calling. Whatever our endeavors are, when we live from the values that we profess matter to us, then we are being the change, which is synonymous with leading the change. We are transforming the paradigm both inwardly and outwardly. When we allow coherent embodiment to infuse our doing with our being, we transmute our small self's inclinations. In doing so, we naturally find love and joy in our daily activities. We tap into our clarity and creativity. This is the basis for real sovereignty. It empowers and primes us to be authentic, both in our private lives and in the world. Thus, we are the leaders of our lives. We live at choice and can access the abundance that is life.

The inward journey culminates in the inspired actions we take. Our decisions are informed by the clarity and compassion rising up from our center at the eye of love. Here, the wholeness of who we are comingles with the field of all possibility. Creative action is at our fingertips. We breathe it into the world effortlessly. Our effectiveness is potentiated, and we find our way is naturally collaborating with others.

Evolution in Intimate Partnership

Trust is the basis for intimacy in our close relationships and life partnerships. When we choose partnership as a spiritual path, then intimacy is both the process and the result. The practice of surrender inevitably leads to deeper trust in ourselves and our connection to the sacred—to that which is beyond our self and yet is simultaneously intrinsic to our self. The act of surrender, although it goes against the grain of the small self, opens us to a more comprehensive rendition of ourselves. This is evolution in action. Our personal evolution is served by the grist of surrendering into deeper intimacy. It transforms what keeps us separate and nourishes our authentic self.

The barrier of separation dissolves readily when we willingly stretch through our fears and allow the river that is our emotional life to run its natural course. It is the flowing of emotions that lubricates our heart and transforms calcified feelings into vibrancy. Emotions are the mediator between our physical and spiritual beings. They purify and transform what is lodged in our past and can catapult us into presence, as well as transcendent connection. As we surrender into deeper intimacy, feelings will naturally unfold, ushering us into the present moment. Like the black surface of a lake that blends into the night sky, surrender is seamless and profound. It provides an unexpected coming home to ourselves, and affords peace and gentleness in our expansion.

Sacred Sexuality

To follow our higher self's call to evolve, we make life sacred in that all we do. That simply means to approach situations with intention and to implement our energies purposefully, meaning aligned with our deeper values. We also consider the consequences of our actions, as well as our energetic imprint, by holding awareness of both of us at the same time.

If the earthly plane is considered the horizontal axis, then the transcendent or celestial plane can be viewed as the vertical axis. We are cultivating our access to the vertical plane, not by denying our earthly anchorage but by invoking spirit into our physical form. Because there is no real separation between the physical and spiritual realms, this can be accomplished gracefully. This is the purpose of ritual and ceremony. In sacred ceremony, we evoke the magnetism between the temporal and eternal or the physical and spiritual dualities of our nature. Human sexuality, too, mirrors these broader magnetic forces at play in us.

Author Thomas Moore speaks of Eros, the primeval god of love, as representing that irrevocable pull we feel toward sexual expression. "Eros is not the physical expression in sex alone but is rather the physical and the emotional combined. More accurately, it is the meaningful connection established by sex, felt and understood by the people making love."[86] This is the connection we feel when we open our hearts to our lover and let our souls entwine. It is a practice of surrender so deep that it can transport us into the light of our own divinity. The life force energy that resides within, called *kundalini* in Sanskrit, meaning "coiled snake," is catalyzed by love and comes to life. It rises like a living entity from the base of our spine, travels upward through the energy centers, or chakras, expands our heart and can even open our pineal gland, the seat of enlightenment. This transcendent effect is one aspect of living our intimate relationship as a spiritual path.

What we seek in our sexual relations is so much more than just physical satisfaction. We long for all that life offers us. We are inextricably drawn to experience our wholeness. The germination of our expansion occurs at the center of the horizontal and vertical axes, where the heart resides, and naturally, is facilitated by love. When we approach lovemaking as a sacred act, our transcendent natures are evoked. In lovemaking, we bring the expansive nature of our heart to bear while crossing the threshold into ecstatic states of union. Sexual magnetism and the reverberating pleasures it brings are another avenue for merging our dualistic natures through surrender, in the act of love.

When we touch upon the sacred in our love, we are truly aligned with our higher self, making our deepest values accessible in our thoughts and actions. The sacred is here, in each breath, every beat of the heart, every turn of the planet, and every tear cried, whether in joy or sorrow. When we transmute the dynamics that separate us and open our hearts in the face of the unknown, the sacred breathes us and takes us

---

[86] Thomas Moore, *The Soul of Sex* (Harper Perennial, 1998).

directly into the eye of love. Transparent communication and the desire to know and understand one another, to care for and to honor one another, naturally arise from the sacred space in the eye of love.

Explore this Practice: The Openhearted Observer

The openhearted observer is the part of us that is willing and able to see our own and others' humanity when to do so goes against the impetus of the wounded or survivor-self. As we allow for our own and others' idiosyncrasies and fallibilities to be as they are, we also grow our ability to see and understand our commonalities and deep connections. To do so, we learn to see with the eye of our heart.

Intention

To investigate the option to meet life with an open heart. To disentangle our stories from our *presence*; to live beyond judgment, fear, and blame.

Overview

The knee-jerk reaction to self-protect with defensiveness, blame, and judgment is a learned behavior. It is perpetuated by the surrounding culture and is not a natural inclination. When we realize that the underlying cultural values are not congruent with our own, we gain the leverage needed to make changes. It's simple to say but not necessarily easy to do. The values of care, respect, and inclusion reveal humanity's calling and become a practice in our relationships. Surrender into intimacy with our lover is a path to spiritual intimacy. We are calling ourselves to live a new vision, to take the journey to a new level of consciousness, through our hearts. Intimate partnership can facilitate this beautifully.

To begin

Sit quietly for five to ten minutes, following your breath. Become aware of your body relaxing into the chair, or wherever you are sitting. Let your breath wash through you, allowing any tension to dissolve and flow out through your legs and feet into the purifying fires at the Earth's core.

1. *Bring your attention to your heart center,* the area in the center of your chest slightly above the nipple line and at the center of the breastbone. Lay your hands over your heart and breathe into your palms. Bring to mind something you love and feel grateful for—a place in nature, a pet, a person or something you love to do. As you think of that specific person, place, or thing, bring your awareness to your heart. Let your heart relax and expand with the feeling of love, the natural state of your being. Dwell in this state and allow it to spread throughout your body. Take as much time as you wish. If your focus wanders, simply bring it back.

   For example: You may love sitting quietly in a secluded place in nature or sitting face to face with your lover, looking into his or her eyes without speaking. Embody that experience in your imagination.

2. *Once you've expanded into the state of love, recall a recent interaction in which your heart shut down.* This could be an argument, a judgment or blame you had about something or someone, or a moment of wishing harm to someone else. Notice what happens in your chest when you bring up that scenario. Make a note of what that feels like inside. What emotions do you feel? Notice the thoughts that readily show up to support your judgment, blame, or sense of righteousness. This is the story that perpetuates your closed heart, feeding the emotions that shore up the story. This makes it seem true; you can *feel it*. However, you have just created the experience you are having with your mind, by intentionally thinking about it.

   For example: You may have judged and blamed your partner for forgetting a request you made, or for responding to you with impatience or deriding you about something.

3. *Use your compassionate observer to notice the contraction of your heart that you just felt and come back to your expanded heart as described in step 1.*

   Ask yourself, What is it about this person or situation that stimulates me to close my heart? Make a mental note or jot down what comes to you. Notice what you wish to be different than it is. What you wish to be different holds the key to what you *do want* to experience. This also points to your *values*—the qualities of life you want to live. Jot them down when they come to you.

   For example: I want him to treat me with kindness. I wanted to be cared about, to know that I matter; I wanted to be understood and heard with empathy.

4. *Surrender into your heart. Ask yourself,* If I didn't close my heart, what would I feel? Let yourself sink into the emotions just below the surface. Allow them to flow through you and dissipate. Make a note of what you felt.

    For example: If I didn't close my heart, I would feel hurt, sadness, disappointment, and regret.

    Ask yourself, How would the situation appear to me if I viewed it with an open heart? Is it possible to see the situation from the other's perspective when I keep my heart open? Note what insights and feelings come as you reflect on these questions.

    For example: When I feel my feelings without blame and judgment, I feel centered and notice my partner is preoccupied with other concerns. He is focused on work and the people he needs to communicate with to support the project going well.

5. *Now return to the openhearted state* you first embodied in this practice. Dwell in the state of openheartedness for a few more minutes before completing the practice in the next step.

    For example: In an openhearted state, I have no constriction and no hurt feelings. I simply notice *what is*. I can sense my partner's focus on other things and remember how much I love him.

6. *While embodying the state of openheartedness*, bring in the scenario in which you closed your heart. Continue to embody your openhearted state, and at the same time, view the scene of contraction. Feel the internal stretch, like expanding inside, as you remain in the state of love while observing the scene with compassion. Allow yourself to stretch and expand into the experience. Notice how you feel. Journal the experience. This stretch is the moment in which transformation happens.

7. *What request do you have of yourself from your openhearted place?*

    For example: When embodying openheartedness and seeing where and why I closed my heart, I no longer have a reaction. I see him from his perspective and me from mine. I want to approach him with care and support. I will request we take time together to connect. Or I could see where I wasn't attended to as I would have liked, but I have no judgment or blame. I will ask to sit down with him and talk about how it was for me. I want to know if it matters to him and what was happening for him at the time.

    Follow through with your request of yourself.

Gently bring the practice to a close, remembering to stay with your openhearted embodiment.

Takeaway

Make a practice of noticing when your heart closes throughout the day. Hold yourself with compassion and acceptance when you notice it and decide if you'd prefer to breathe into and open your heart or not. It is up to you to decide and to choose what state of being you wish to live into and embody. Remember, there is no external "right or wrong." There is only your preference to live as you choose. Every choice has its specific consequences. Choose the consequences you most want to live with and experience.

Cumulative effect

It is the apparent dichotomy between our sovereignty and our undeniable interdependence that we are faced with in the swirl of life. All that we long for—connection, confidence, ecstasy, transcendence—takes shape in us as a result of the cumulative effect of embodying coherent states over time. The refined skill of connecting our hearts with our brains allows us to navigate all of our challenges more gracefully. This ability originates with our hearts, there, at the most inward place we inhabit. Our intention to go inward, to know ourselves deeply, and to live in love bring our inner authority and wisdom forward. The deeper we drop inside, the more intimately aware of our belonging we also become.

The cumulative effect of practicing embodied states of coherence, engaging the heart and brain connection, becomes the ballast of a life well lived. This anchors us to our belonging, the place deep inside that weaves us together with everything and everyone else. Your personal sovereignty is your gift, the package that delivers your purpose to the world while at the same time fulfilling you with the significance of being alive—as *you*. This is the living story of your evolution and being the leader of your life, of coming home, to the heart of yourself. Distilled and refined, you have garnered greater freedom to take back in to the world, with living compassion and clarity of action. If not before, now you are empowered to assume leadership for yourself and give your gifts to a world waiting to receive them.

APPENDIX A
Universal Qualities of Life

(Referred to in Formal Nonviolent Communication as, Universal Human Needs)

Note: This list is provided only as a tool for study. No list is any substitute for each one of us finding our own truth using our own words that fit our experience and recognition of qualities of life that matter and resonate with us. List provided by Miki, Inbal, and Arnina Kashtan.

Subsistence and Security

Physical sustenance
air, food, water
health
movement
physical safety
rest/sleep
shelter
touch

Security
consistency
order/structure
peace (external)
peace of mind
protection
trust
stability

Freedom

Autonomy
choice
self-reliance
power
self-responsibility
space
spontaneity

Leisure/Relaxation
humor
play
pleasure
rejuvenation
ease

Connection

Affection
appreciation
attention
closeness
companionship
harmony
intimacy
love
nurturing
sexual expression
support
tenderness
warmth

Connection, cont.

To Matter
acceptance
care
compassion
consideration
empathy
kindness
mutuality
respect
to be heard
to be known
to be seen
to be trusted
to be understood
understanding others
respect

Belonging

Community
communication
cooperation
inclusion
mutuality
participation
partnership
self-expression
sharing
support

Meaning

Sense of self
authenticity
competence
creativity
dignity
growth
healing
honesty
integrity
self-acceptance
self-care
self-connection
self-knowledge
self-realization
mattering to myself

Understanding
awareness
clarity
curiosity
discovery
learning
making sense of life
stimulation

Meaning
aliveness
challenge
consciousness
contribution
creativity
effectiveness
exploration
adventure
integration
purpose

Transcendence
peace (internal)
unity
joy
beauty
presence
hope
inspiration
faith
flow
communion
mourning
celebration
love
awe

APPENDIX B
Components of Connected Communication and the Container of Care

This is a synthesis of the explorations described throughout the handbook. When we put all the pieces together, we can then hold a container of care for meetings, conversations, and dialogues. This is a method to further develop and utilize the heart as our organ of navigation by embodying and implementing the values of respect, inclusion, curiosity, and consideration in discussions and group efforts. Read and use the explanations as needed to support your own understanding and implementation of the container of care practice as well as for heartfelt communication.

universal quality of life. The qualities of life offer a way to recognize, name, and embody specific aspects of the universal life force within the spectrum of love, which is always present, flowing, and accessible. They are words that describe a variety of qualities inherent to the zero point field, from which we are not separate. A useful metaphor is light; all the colors of the spectrum are contained within plain, clear light, which is ever present. We define the color spectrum by naming the distinct colors we see. Specific qualities within the spectrum of love function in a similar fashion, love being the all-pervasive "clear light" in which the others rest. The qualities of life within the spectrum of love allow us to name a specific known or desired experience that is universal to most people. Naming the qualities of life alive for us functions to establish the common ground of our shared humanity and, thus, is instrumental in verbalizing empathy and creating connection and mutual understanding.

To notice and name the quality of life is a tool to know ourselves specific to any time and place. It represents what core value is up, alive, or mattering to us or others and wanting to be activated. This offers self-connection through self-awareness of what is happening in us and facilitates empathy for ourselves and others. As a practice, we can then choose to embody that quality and enhance our insights and connection to ourselves, other people, and the world around us, as related in chapter 4.

In this way, we also have access to the field, as every quality of life is a current that flows through the field, or the universal life force. When we tap into the field through the embodiment practice, we engender a coherent state. In this way we can also access a transcendent perspective that we ourselves have generated from our heart-mind and that extends beyond the boundaries of our self. When tapped into the field, we have easy access to empathetic presence with self and others, as well as heightened clarity, intuition, and insight.

Because the qualities of life are universal aspects of the field, we can both know ourselves, as well as guess where another person is in the same universal spectrum. This offers the possibility of mutual connection and understanding with oneself and another simultaneously. To hold empathetic presence coupled with the intention to hold both of us with equal care simultaneously is a transcendent function of the heart. It demonstrates in practical terms how to shift the paradigm from me versus you to both of us.

empathetic presence. Empathetic presence is like surround sound. You can't pinpoint where it's coming from, but you know it's there. It's palpable. It's the firm yet fluid martial arts stance with an open, activated heart. Empathetic presence allows a flexible spaciousness inside to hold all of us with care and curiosity at the same time. We are primed to share ourselves transparently and to listen openheartedly to others. The bottom line is that *when we trust our intention* to hold others with care and curiosity in a conversation, *a great ease and spaciousness* pervades the dialogue. It is a true gift to the setting that supports connection and understanding.

dance in the gap of uncertainty. In dialogue with others, the outcome is uncertain. We acknowledge this uncertainty and play with the concept by calling it a dance. The dance is between the two or more participants in the conversation, who give voice to their thoughts, needs, and feelings and receive one another with empathy to further develop connection and mutual understanding. We take turns leading and following, by way of honoring the space between us as alive with creative potential. In this shared reality, seeming magic happens. Ideas, insights, openings, and downloads that neither of us would or could have arrived at independently often flood in. The compatibility that arises can bring restoration, healing, and collaboration in unforeseen ways.

clear requests. When we speak, we are inadvertently asking for something, even if just to know that we were heard. Because a request is often experienced as a risk, we can be hesitant to ask for what we need or want. If we feel vulnerable, it may take courage to make a clear request. In the asking, we transparently reveal our needs and wants to others. While this opens us up to possible rejection or disappointment, it also makes us more human and invites connection. And the fact remains that we have a much greater chance to get what we need when we ask for it than when we don't. It's a matter of making a simple request after speaking and to being willing to hear a no. A no is simply an invitation to dialogue, to find out what is important to the other person in that moment.

Whether consciously aware of it or not, we want to be heard and understood. When we make a request after we speak, it lets us know how we have been heard and understood. It also makes room for much greater clarity between speaker and listener. Clarity brings understanding, and together they preempt conflict. To avoid conflict and disagreement all together is not realistic, but we can approach them with an attitude of adventure. Our own internal resources and attitude can facilitate even greater connection through resolving conflict.

APPENDIX C
Restorative Circle Reference Guides

Integrating Restorative Justice with Nonviolent Communication, there is much to learn from the practice of restorative circles. The following sites offer insights about how to implement them.

Building Community with Restorative Circles (Edutopia)
https://www.edutopia.org/article/building-community-restorative-circles
Teaching Restorative Practices with Classroom Circles (Healthiersf.org)
https://www.healthiersf.org/RestorativePractices/ ... /Teaching%20Restorative%20 Practi ...

Restorative Circles
https://www.restorativecircles.org/

Connection Circles: How to Establish a Restorative Circle Practice
https://knowlesteachers.org/ ... /connection-circles-establish-restorative-circle-practice

Circles, Defining Restorative, and Restorative Practices
https://www.iirp.edu › Defining Restorative

Talking Circles: For Restorative Justice and Beyond (Teaching)
https://www.tolerance.org/magazine/talking-circles-for-restorative-justice-and-beyond

Teaching Restorative Practices with Classroom Circles *www.centerforrestorative process.com/teaching-restorative-practices-with-classroom-ci ...*
Circles | Restorative Schools Toolkit
https://restorativeschoolstoolkit.org/practices/circles

APPENDIX D
Message from Hopi Elders

TO MY FELLOW SWIMMERS

We have been telling the people that this is the Eleventh Hour
Now you must go back and tell the people that this is the Hour
And there are things to be considered

Where are you living?
What are you doing?
What are your relationships?
Are you in the right relation?
Where is your water?
Know your garden.

It is time to speak your truth.
Create your community.
Be good to each other.
And do not look outside yourself for the leader.

There is a river flowing now very fast.
It is so great and swift that there are those who will be afraid.
They will try to hold onto the shore.
They will feel they are being torn apart and they will suffer greatly.
Know the river has its destination.

The elders say we must let go of the shore, and push off and into the river, keep our eyes open, and our head above the water.

See who is in there with you and Celebrate.

At this time in history, we are to take nothing personally.
Least of all ourselves.
For the moment that we do, our spiritual growth and journey comes to a halt.

The time of the lone wolf is over,
Gather yourselves!

Banish the word struggle from your attitude and your vocabulary.
All that you do now must be done in a sacred manner
And in celebration.

WE ARE THE ONES WE'VE BEEN WAITING FOR...

Hopi Nation, Oraibi Arizona, September, 2001
http://www.angelfire.com/moon/fae/hopi.html

APPENDIX E
Further Resources

A short list of resources for further exploration of topics broached in the handbook.

Climate Action

American Rivers / Rivers Connect Us, https://www.american rivers.org
American Rivers protects wild rivers, restores damaged rivers and conserves clean water for people and nature. American Rivers combines national advocacy with field work in key river basins to deliver the greatest impact.

The Foundation for Conscious Living, https://foundationforconscioiusliving.com
The Big Leap Home Online Programs support individuals, organizations, and communities in generating agency, connection and creativity on our shared planet.

One Earth, One Sangha
Eco-sattva training: https://oneearthsangha.org/programs/ecosattva-training/
The course will begin at the level of experience, a good place to start given our pervasive stress. Climate psychologists are demonstrating that the way we experience climate crisis and losses in the rest of nature is at some level traumatizing, with the attendant adaptions to trauma showing up in both our individual and collective defenses. We will spend time in this course understanding that dynamic and then bring in specific Dharma and trauma-informed practices can soothe our eco-stressed bodies, hearts and minds.

Stockholm Resiliency Centre, https://www.stockholmresilience.org/
A reference point for research on global sustainability.

South Yuba River Citizens League, United for the Yuba. https://syrcl.org
As a member of the Waterkeeper Alliance, SYRCL is the first Waterkeeper established in the Sierra Nevada and serves as the official Yuba River Waterkeeper. SYRCL established the Yuba River Waterkeeper as a new program dedicated to fostering regional and statewide coalitions to address complex issues related to water quality and watershed health including the restoration of wild salmon. Yuba River Waterkeeper's aim is to combine SYRCL's 35-year record of strong local, grassroots advocacy with the power of the Waterkeeper Alliance, an international coalition of river advocates.

Work That Reconnects Network, https://workthatreconnects.org
"The central purpose of the Work that Reconnects is to help people uncover and experience their innate connections with each other and with the systemic, self-healing powers of the web of life, so that they may be enlivened and motivated to play their part in creating a sustainable civilization." –Joanna Macy

Community Building

Bill Kauth and **Zoe Alowan Kauth**, timefortribe.org
Online program; Time for Tribe, timefortribeonline\course
Books:
We Need Each Other

Bill Kauth, co-creator of the New Warrior Training Adventure/ co-founder of the ManKind Project, https://mankindproject,org
Books:
A Circle of Men

Miki Kashtan
The Fearless Heart, thefearlessheart.org
Inspiration and tools for creating the future we want. Courage to live it now.
Convergent Facilitation Primer available here: http://thefearlessheart.org/product/convergent-facilitation-primer-packet/.
Books:
The Little Book of Courageous Living
Spinning Threads of Radical Aliveness: Transcending the Legacy of Separation ion our Individual Lives

Reweaving Our Human Fabric: Working Together to Create a nonviolent Future

Byron Katie, The Work. https://thework.com

Francis Weller, francisweller.net
He offers, The alchemy of initiation: Soul work and the art of ripening, and more.
Books:
The Threshold Between Loss and Revelation;
The Wild Edge of Sorrow—Rituals of Renewal and the Sacred Work of Grief. "It is a comprehensive manual for conscious grieving and opening to the unprecedented joy and passion that result from embracing our sorrow."

Nonviolent Communication Networks:
> The Center for Nonviolent Communication, https://www.cnvc.org
> Bay Area Nonviolent Communication, https:www.baynvc.org
> NVC Academy, https://www.nvctraining.com
> Center for Living Compassion, https://www.living-compassion.org
> Robert Gonzales' Awakening to Life Intensives at www.living-compassion.org

Bill Kauth and Zoe Alowan; timefortribe.com
Books:
We Need each Other—Building Gift Community

It's Time to Revoke the Doctrine of Discovery, Indigenous rights activist Steve Newcomb discusses how the Doctrine of Discovery has enabled the subjugation of Native peoples for hundreds of years. 5 min
https://www.lakotalaw.org/resources/revoke-the-doctrine?emdi=3251e103-4be5-e911-b5e9-2818784d6d68&emci=c3fa8c28-a4e3-e911-b5e9-2818784d6d68&ceid=2464111&fn=Holly&ln=Thomas&em=holsthomas%40gmail.com&add1=872+30th+Ave+&ci=Santa+Cruz&st=CA&pc=95062&utm_source=ea&utm_medium=email&utm_content=piclink&sourceid=1037511

Conscious Evolution

Gregg Braden, https://www.greggbraden.com
Books:
The Science of Self-Empowerment; Human By Design; The Divine Matrix; Resilience from the Heart; The Spontaneous Healing of Belief; The God Code
Video Series:
Missing Links; Human By Design; both can be found on Gaia TV at www.gaia.com

Bruce Lipton, brucelipton.com
Books:
The Biology of Belief; Spontaneous Evolution: Our Positive Future (and how to get there from here); The Honeymoon Effect: The Science of Creating Heaven on Earth

Joe Dispenza, drjoedispenza.com
Books:
Becoming Supernatural

Joanna Macy, joannamacy.net
Books:
Coming Back to Life: The Updated Guide to the Work that Reconnects; Active Hope: How to Face the Mess We're In Without Going Crazy
An Interview with Joanna Macy https://emergencemagazine.org/story/widening-circles/

Lynne McTaggart, https://www.lynnemctaggart.com
The Field; The Bond; The Power of Eight; Living the Field

Barbara Marx-Hubbard, barbaramarxhubbard.com
The Foundation for Conscious Evolution. The ultimate goal of the Foundation for Conscious Evolution is the awakening of the spiritual, social, and scientific potential of humanity, in harmony with nature for the highest good of all life.

Miguel Angel Vergara, "http://www.casakin.org"www.casakin.org
PORTAL TO MAYA SACRED WISDOM
Sharing the spiritual knowledge of the ancient Maya as found in their ceremonies, temples, pyramids, elders, shamans, priests and priestesses, healers, ancient books, stele, pottery and oral traditions.
Miguel Angel has made the study of the Maya Sacred Wisdom his life's work and shares his vast knowledge through online teachings and journeys to Maya sacred sites.

Economics

Charles Eisenstein, https://www.charleseisenstein.org
Books:
Sacred Economics: Money, Gift and Society in the Age of Transition
Climate: A New Story
Videos:
Sacred Economics with Charles Eisenstein – A Short Film, https://www.youtube.com/watch?v=EEZkQv25uEs
A New Story of the People: Charles Eisenstein at TEDxWhitechapel https://www.youtube.com/watch?v=Mjoxh4c2Dj0

David Korten, davidkorten.org – Seeking a pathway to a future that works for all. "We will prosper in the pursuit of life or we will perish in the pursuit of money. The choice is ours." David Korten
Books:
Change the Story Change the Future—A Living Economy for a Living Earth
Agenda for a New Economy---from Phantom Wealth to Real Wealth
The Great Turning---from Empire to Earth Community
The Post-Corporate World

Publications

Emergence Magazine, https://emergencemagazine.org
It has always been a radical act to share stories during dark times. They are a regenerative space of creation and renewal. As we experience the desecration of our lands and waters, the extinguishing of species, and a loss of sacred connection to the earth, we look to emerging stories. In them we find the timeless connections between ecology, culture, and spirituality.

Orion Magazine, https://.orionmagazine.org
Orion brings ideas, writers, photographers, and artists together, focused on nature, the environment, and culture, addressing environmental and societal issues.

Kosmos Journal—Journal for Global Transformation, https://www.kosmosjournal.org

The Optimist daily, https://www.optimistdaily.com
Creating a shift in global consciousness; a new model for news; a movement; an independent, reader-funded project.

The Intelligent Optimist, https://www.magzter.com
The Intelligent Optimist (formerly Ode magazine) is a print and online publication about positive news, about the people and ideas that are changing our world for the better.

Yes! Magazine, https://www.yesmagazine.org
Journalism for people building a better world.

Huffington Post, https://www.huffpost.com

Sound Healing and Music

Tom Kenyon, tomkenyon.com
Tom Kenyon's work in brain/mind re-education is a scientifically based art form that transforms consciousness in rapid and elegant ways.

Karina Schelde, soulvoice.net
The Soul Voice Method: Liberate the voice to experience your ultimate potential.

Michael Franti, michaelfranti.com
A messenger of love, connection and hope in these difficult times.
    Film: Stay Human
    Music: Michael Franti and Spearhead, Stay Human, volumes I and I

Videos

Heart Brain Coherence
https://**www.youtube.com**/watch?v=RwSw0ppwQZ8 When the heart and the brain are in optimal sync with one another, the frequency measured is **0.1 hertz**. This is called heart brain coherence.
Heart Brain Coherence Music (7min) 0.1 Hertz Synchronization

Living in the Future's Past, directed by Susan Kucera and produced by Jeff Bridges "In this beautifully photographed, tour de force of original thinking on who we are and the life challenges we face, Academy Award winner Jeff Bridges shares the screen with scientists, profound thinkers and a dazzling array of Earth's living creatures to reveal eye-opening concepts."
1 hr. 40 min

Stepping Into A New Paradigm with Bruce Lipton, Gaia TV, www.gaia.com "Gregg Braden and Bruce Lipton join forces in this special multi-part season finale as they share their experience in meeting with the United Nations."—Gaia TV

Missing Links with Gregg Braden, Gaia TV, www.gaia.com "Explore the deep truths of our origin, history, destiny and fate, with celebrated author and luminary Gregg Braden."—Gaia TV
3 Seasons, 42, approx. 30 min Episodes

Human by Design with Gregg Braden, Gaia TV, www.gaia.com "Unleashing the Power of the New Human Story presents evidence that rewrites human history and rethinks the role of evolution in our lives. The emerging science of neuro-cardiology — the bridge between the brain and the heart — has overturned 150 years of thinking about human potential. Your heart is more than an organ; its neural connections can transform your views of money, health, relationships, and success."—Gaia TV
10, 90 min Episodes

Healing Matrix with Dr. Sue Morter, Gaia TV, www.gaia.com "Gain the tools you need to help heal yourself, physically, emotionally and spiritually. Dr. Sue Morter connects you with top researchers and visionaries exploring alternative healing modalities and emerging sciences to bring you information that can help you make better informed choices concerning your health and wellbeing."—Gaia TV
64 Episodes

ABOUT THE AUTHOR

Loren has spent a lifetime searching for practical strategies to realize her divine self and overcome the personal trauma and addictions of her past. Her history as a horsewoman and massage therapist informed her work as a licensed psychotherapist and Certified Nonviolent Communication Trainer. She knows intimately the value of hard physical labor and tough inner work. Along her own journey toward greater self-acceptance and interpersonal connection, she has collected many tools and resources to help others. It's with an increasing sense of inspiration and clarity that she is now sharing her accumulated wisdom and experience with a broader audience. She lives in Nevada City, California with her husband and has a daughter in college in Santa Cruz, CA.

Printed in the United States
By Bookmasters